Ethical and Methodological Issues in Researching Young Language Learners in School Contexts

EARLY LANGUAGE LEARNING IN SCHOOL CONTEXTS

Series Editor: Janet Enever, *Umeå University, Sweden*

The early learning of languages in instructed contexts has become an increasingly common global phenomenon during the past 30 years, yet there remains much work to be done to establish the field as a distinctive area for interdisciplinary investigation. This international research series covers children learning second, foreign and additional languages in educational contexts between the ages of approximately 3 and 12 years. The series will take a global perspective and encourage the sharing of theoretical discussion and empirical evidence on transnational issues. It will provide a platform to address questions raised by teachers, teacher educators, and policymakers who are seeking understanding of theoretical issues and empirical evidence with which to underpin policy development, implementation and classroom procedures for this young age group. Themes of particular interest for the series include: teacher models and teacher development, models of early language learning, policy implementation, motivation, approaches to teaching and learning, language progress and outcomes, assessment, intercultural learning, sustainability in provision, comparative and transnational perspectives, cross-phase transfer issues, curriculum integration – additional suggestions for themes are also most welcome.

All books in this series are externally peer-reviewed.

Full details of all the books in this series and of all our other publications can be found on http://www.multilingual-matters.com, or by writing to Multilingual Matters, St Nicholas House, 31–34 High Street, Bristol BS1 2AW, UK.

EARLY LANGUAGE LEARNING IN SCHOOL CONTEXTS: 6

Ethical and Methodological Issues in Researching Young Language Learners in School Contexts

Edited by
**Annamaria Pinter and
Kuchah Kuchah**

MULTILINGUAL MATTERS
Bristol • Blue Ridge Summit

DOI https://doi.org/10.21832/PINTER1425

Library of Congress Cataloging in Publication Data

A catalog record for this book is available from the Library of Congress.

Names: Pinter, Annamaria, editor. | Kuchah, Kuchah, editor.

Title: Ethical and Methodological Issues in Researching Young Language Learners in School Contexts/Edited by Annamaria Pinter, Kuchah Kuchah.

Description: Bristol, UK; Blue Ridge Summit: Multilingual Matters, 2021. | Includes bibliographical references and index. | Summary: "This book focuses on ethical and methodological issues encountered by researchers working with young language learners in school contexts. The chapters are written by researchers working with children in different classroom contexts around the world and highlight how ethical dilemmas and tensions take on a complex form in child-focused research"— Provided by publisher.

Identifiers: LCCN 2020052318 (print) | LCCN 2020052319 (ebook) | ISBN 9781800411418 (paperback) | ISBN 9781800411425 (hardback) | ISBN 9781800411432 (pdf) | ISBN 9781800411449 (epub) | ISBN 9781800411456 (kindle edition) Subjects: LCSH: Language and languages—Study and teaching (Elementary)—Moral and ethical aspects. | Language and languages—Research—Methodology. | Language teachers—Training of—Moral and ethical aspects.

Classification: LCC LB1578.E84 2021 (print) | LCC LB1578 (ebook) | DDC 372.65/044—dc23 LC record available at https://lccn.loc.gov/2020052318

LC ebook record available at https://lccn.loc.gov/2020052319

British Library Cataloguing in Publication Data

A catalogue entry for this book is available from the British Library.

ISBN-13: 978-1-80041-142-5 (hbk)
ISBN-13: 978-1-80041-141-8 (pbk)

Multilingual Matters
UK: St Nicholas House, 31–34 High Street, Bristol BS1 2AW, UK.
USA: NBN, Blue Ridge Summit, PA, USA.

Website: www.multilingual-matters.com
Twitter: Multi_Ling_Mat
Facebook: https://www.facebook.com/multilingualmatters
Blog: www.channelviewpublications.wordpress.com

The policy of Multilingual Matters/Channel View Publications is to use papers that are natural, renewable and recyclable products, made from wood grown in sustainable forests. In the manufacturing process of our books, and to further support our policy, preference is given to printers that have FSC and PEFC Chain of Custody certification. The FSC and/or PEFC logos will appear on those books where full certification has been granted to the printer concerned.

Typeset by Nova Techset Private Limited, Bengaluru and Chennai, India.
Printed and bound in the UK by Short Run Press Ltd.
Printed and bound in the US by NBN.

Contents

Contributors

Jane Andrews works in the Department of Education & Childhood as an Associate Professor of Education and has research and teaching interests in languages and education and in particular children developing English as an Additional Language. A recent research project involved exploring how creative arts approaches can be integrated into teaching and learning for children developing EAL, which was funded by the Arts and Humanities Research Council. Jane is co-programme leader of the Professional Doctorate in Education (EdD) and contributes to teaching on the BA (Hons) Early Childhood.

Yuko Goto Butler is Professor of Educational Linguistics at the Graduate School of Education at the University of Pennsylvania. She is also the director of Teaching English to Speakers of Other Languages (TESOL) program at Penn. Her research interests are primarily focused on the improvement of second/foreign language education among young learners in the US and Asia in response to the diverse needs of an increasingly globalizing world. Her work has also focused on identifying effective second/foreign teaching and learning strategies and assessment methods that take into account the relevant linguistic and cultural contexts in which instruction takes place.

Gail Ellis is a teacher, teacher educator and author based in Paris. She was awarded an MBE in 2004 for her services to the teaching of English to young learners. She is a co-founder of Picturebooks in European Primary English Teaching (PEPELT) – a finalist in the ELTons Awards 2020. Her publications include *Tell it Again!* (with Jean Brewster, British Council, 3rd edn, 2014), *Teaching Children How to Learn* (with Nayr Ibrahim, Delta Publishing, 2015) and *Teaching English to Pre-Primary Children* (with Sandie Mourão, Delta Publishing, 2020). Gail's interests include children's rights, picturebooks in primary ELT, young learner ELT management and inclusive practices.

María del Pilar García Mayo is Professor of English Language and Linguistics at the University of the Basque Country (Spain). She has published widely on the L2/L3 acquisition of English morphosyntax and the study of conversational interaction in EFL. Her most recent edited volume is *Learning Foreign Languages in Primary School: Research Insights* (Multilingual Matters, 2017). García Mayo is the director of the Language and Speech (www.laslab.org) research group, highlighted by the Basque Government for excellence in research in the field, and the director of the MA program Language Acquisition in Multilingual Settings. She is also the editor of *Language Teaching Research*.

Nayr Ibrahim (PhD, University of Reading) is Associate Professor of English Subject Pedagogy at Nord University, Norway, and holds a PhD in trilingualism, triliteracy and identity. She has participated in various EU projects on multilingualism, including reviewing the EU's *Key Competencies for Lifelong Learning* (2018). Nayr is a member of the Research Group for Children's Literature in ELT (CLELT) and associate reviewer for the CLELE Journal. Her publications include *Teaching Children How to Learn* (Delta Publishing, with Gail Ellis) and her research interests are in early language learning, bi/multilingualism, multiple literacies, language and identity, learning to learn, children's literature and children's rights.

Kuchah Kuchah is a Lecturer in Language Education at the University of Leeds, UK. Previously he worked in EYL as a teacher, teacher trainer and policymaker in Cameroon. He has also served as a Consultant on language policy and practice with the British Council, the Council of Europe, and Windle Trust International and is currently President IATEFL and Member of the British Council English Language Advisory Group. Kuchah's research interests include teaching English to young learners, English-medium education, context-appropriate methodology and language teacher education. He is co-editor of *International Perspectives on Teaching English in Difficult Circumstances* (2018).

Rama Mathew is an ELT consultant and retired as Professor of Education from the University of Delhi in 2016. She was involved in ELT and teacher education at the EFL University (Hyderabad) for over two decades. She was also Head of the Research, Monitoring and Evaluation Unit of *English in Action* project in Bangladesh. She has been involved in several teacher development and assessment projects, and published articles and books in the area. Working with teachers on continuing professional development initiatives helps her to keep growing and developing. She is currently helping teachers in Sierra Leone to do classroom-based research.

Lizzi O. Milligan is a Reader in the Department of Education at the University of Bath, UK. Her research and teaching interests focus on educational inequalities and social justice in low-income countries, particularly in relation to English as a Medium of Instruction. She currently leads two UK Economic and Social Research Council funded projects which explore girls' education in EMI schools in Rwanda and the relationship between epistemic, environmental and transitional justice in secondary education in Nepal, Peru and Uganda.

Sandie Mourão (PhD) is a Research Fellow at Nova University Lisbon, with over 30 years of experience in ELT as a teacher, teacher educator and educational consultant. She is presently investigating children's literature for intercultural citizenship education in primary English education. Her main research interests focus on early years language learning, picture-books in language learning, intercultural awareness, assessment practices and classroom-based research. Her recent publications include, *Teaching English to Pre-primary Children* (DELTA Publishing, 2020), *Fractures and Disruptions in Children's Literature* (Cambridge Scholars Press, 2017) and *Early Years Second Language Education: International Perspectives on Theory and Practice* (Routledge, 2015).

Victoria A. Murphy is Professor of Applied Linguistics and Deputy Director of the Department of Education, University of Oxford. She convenes the Applied Linguistics, and the R.E.A.L. (Research in English as an Additional Language) research groups. Victoria's research focuses on understanding the inter-relationships between child L2/FL learning, vocabulary and literacy development. Her work focuses on examining cross-linguistic relationships across linguistic systems in the emergent bilingual child and how foreign language learning in primary school can influence developing first language literacy. She has published in a wide range of Applied Linguistics journals in the area of young language learners.

Annamaria Pinter is a Reader at the Department of Applied Linguistics, the University of Warwick, UK. Her research interests focus on all aspects of second/ foreign language education for children, task-based second language teaching and learning and engaging children actively in research. She has published widely in the area of teaching English to children and has a strong international reputation in TEYL and second language teacher education. She is the author of *Teaching Young Language Learners* (Oxford University Press, 2nd edn, 2017) and *Children Learning Second Languages* (Palgrave Macmillan, 2011).

Gail Prasad is an Assistant Professor in the Faculty of Education at York University. Her research focuses on critical multilingual language awareness, children and youth's social representations of plurilingualism, and teacher preparation for multilingual school contexts. Through creative and critical classroom-based research in Canada, France, the United States and Burkina Faso, she has engaged children as co-researchers to investigate their plurilingual and multimodal communicative practices.

Her work has been published in English and in French in *TESOL Quarterly*, the *International Journal of Bilingualism and Bilingual Education* and *Glottopol*.

Samaneh Zandian is a Senior Teaching Fellow in Language Education at Moray House School of Education and Sport, University of Edinburgh, UK. Originally she comes from Iran where she worked as an English language teacher of young learners for eight years. Her research interest lies in the processes of adaptation in relation to child sojourners and raising intercultural awareness in language classrooms. She is also interested in exploring the advantages and limitations of using innovative participatory research methodologies with children.

1 Researching Young Language Learners in School Contexts: Setting the Scene

Kuchah Kuchah and Annamaria Pinter

Introduction

This book is about research in second/foreign language education in formal schooling contexts. It focuses on the ethical and methodological complexities in research involving children as second/foreign language learners in classroom contexts and discusses a range of issues, dilemmas and experiences that have emerged from empirical work in young learner classrooms. The chapters are written by researchers working with children in different classroom contexts around the world, and their main focus is on the interconnected complexities between research methodology and research ethics. Many of the issues and dilemmas discussed in this volume are left implicit or even ignored when child-focused research is written up. In fact, the often neatly presented accounts of published research tend to veil methodological and ethical complexities, giving the impression that research involving children is straightforward and predictable. The different chapters in this collection aim to highlight how ethical dilemmas and tensions take on a complex form in child-focused research, requiring researchers to pay particular attention to the social and cultural norms of the different communities within which children are educated as well as their school-based experiences.

In this introductory chapter, we set the scene by discussing the historical developments to date in international legislation, policy and practice regarding children in research and present an overview of child research ethics particularly in relation to English for Young Learners (EYL) research. We examine some of the key debates around issues such as the conflict between child protection and child participation, showing how conceptions of children and childhood are at the centre of the research processes adopted by researchers and how these processes each raise a set of ethical issues which may affect the research outcomes. The chapter concludes with a brief summary of the contributions to this volume and makes a case for research ethics with children to take on a more critical perspective that recognizes specific cultural affordances and limitations and addresses them in ways that protect children's rights to participation in decision making about their language education.

Research in Second/Foreign Language Education for Young Learners

The teaching of second/foreign languages to young learners has been described as the cornerstone of the language teaching profession (Copland & Garton, 2014), yet, until recently, it has not constituted the central focus of language education research. As Brumfit (1991) explains, developments around communicative language teaching in the 1980s saw a concentration on adults and secondary school pedagogy and research, with relatively little concern for primary level activity. In the last two decades, however, owing to the increasing policy trend of including second/foreign languages into the early years of formal schooling (Cameron, 2003; Enever, 2011; Johnstone, 2009; Rixon, 2013), a significant number of publications have focused on young learner language education in different contexts. However, emphasis has often been on the pedagogical challenges and possibilities of implementing early English language education (e.g. Garton *et al.*, 2011; Kuchah, 2019; López-Gopar, 2014). More recently, growing global trends in migration (UN, 2017) and the consequent linguistic and intercultural complexities for young children attending school in contexts where languages other than their home language are taught or used in school, have further led to a renewed interest in how children navigate different linguistic and cultural spaces. As a result of these policies and demographic realities, the field of second/foreign language education is now witnessing an ever-growing volume of research studies involving younger and younger language learners (e.g. Bland, 2016; Blom & Bosma, 2016; Enever & Lindgren, 2017; García Mayo, 2017; Garton & Copland, 2019; Mourão & Lourenço, 2015; Muñoz, 2014; Nikolov, 2016; Pfenninger & Singleton, 2016; Pinter *et al.*, 2016; Rich, 2014).

While this body of research suggests that the language learning experiences of children are being taken seriously, it also calls for a critical examination of the methodological complexities and the ethical nature of research that informs our understanding of children's language learning experiences and the pedagogic practices that are meant to enhance their second/foreign language learning in school contexts. As Pinter (2011) has argued, there are inextricable links between methodological and ethical issues in child research. This is mainly due to the diverse nature of cultural conceptualizations of children and childhood around the world. As the chapters in this volume show, whatever conceptualization we have of children, research involving them is predominantly based on adult agendas, and this requires a careful consideration of the nature of interactions between adults and children. In all societies, there are significant physical, social, political and cognitive distances between adults and children which influence the relationship between these groups. Even if adults attempt to build rapport and close relationships with child research participants, as Graue and Walsh (1998) explain, in doing research with children, an adult never becomes a child but remains a very definite and readily identifiable *other* who exerts some form of power on children. As a result, while methodological processes might be rigorously developed and implemented, their validity, reliability and trustworthiness depends, to a large extent, on the ethical values and actions underlying them. Rose and McKinley (2017: xvii) have suggested that 'in the presentation of published research as the "ideal", the reader is often made oblivious to the methodological journey of the project and of the compromises made along the way.' This is even more so with research involving young learners where matters of research ethics may sometimes be overlooked or treated as simply akin to adult-focused research.

Pinter (2019) points out that most books covering research methods in applied linguistics have been written with adult learners in mind and devote very little or no space to children. What is more, an overview of child-focused research in second/foreign language education suggests that on the one hand, researchers have not attended explicitly to the wide range of ethical dilemmas and complexities arising from school-based research with various age groups involving various types of interventions facilitated by adults such as teachers, teacher researchers or outsider researchers. On the other hand, children's own understanding of research and their roles and status in research involving them has been rather neglected in the field of second/foreign language education even though general discussions about research ethics in English language teaching (ELT) (such as Copland & Creese, 2016; De Costa, 2015; Kubanyiova, 2008) have been rife. These studies are beginning to highlight challenging issues in ethical practice such as the ever-present tension between macro and micro perspectives of ethics or the various cultural interpretations of ethical practice. While the above ethical issues apply to all researchers and participants, irrespective of their age, the contributions in this volume demonstrate that in addition to general issues, special ethical considerations arise when working with children and therefore it is timely and necessary to shed light on ethical practices, dilemmas and challenges in classroom research involving child second/foreign language learners. The chapters in this volume draw from standard ethical principles and reflect on the complexities of research processes when involving children in a variety of school contexts around the world. They highlight a number of dilemmas and considerations for researching children, showing the different extents to which these may be navigated by researchers interested in working with children.

Why Research Young Learners in Second/Foreign Language Education?

Children's education has been formally recognized as a basic human right embedded in Article 26 of the United Nations Declaration of Human Rights (UNDHR, 1948). This provision entitles all children to free and compulsory education at least at elementary school level. Other subsequent treaties such as the UNESCO Convention against Discrimination in Education (1960), the Convention on the Elimination of All Forms of Discrimination against Women (1981), the United Nations Convention on the Rights of the Child (UNCRC, 1989) and the World Declaration on Education for All (UNESCO, 1990) have further strengthened global perspectives on children's rights to education.

The UNCRC (1989), for example, broadens the concept of children's right by outlining four main core principles: non-discrimination (art. 2); the best interests of the child (art. 3); the right to life, survival and development of the child to the maximum extent possible (art. 6); and the right of children to express their views in all matters affecting them (art. 12). There is a difficult tension in the document between the principle of 'the best interest of the child' as defined by adults, and children's own rights and views. Another key debate emanating from the rights-based perspective in research involving children revolves around two main priorities. On the one hand priorities are given to political and emancipatory perspectives related to children's rights as citizens and their rights to participation (UNCRC, 1989). On the other hand, an alternative priority focuses on more pedagogic perspectives regarding children's rights to exercise their agency *in learning*. As Bucknall (2014: 70) comments 'it is intended that... [children's rights] should be exercised in all areas of children's lives' and this must then include school contexts and research projects where they participate alongside either teachers or outsider researchers. This is because rights are fundamental in achieving social justice particularly for children whose voices are often not considered in decisions about their education. The social justice perspective argues that promoting social justice entails breaking down institutionalized barriers to equitable social interaction and that dismantling injustices, is premised on, among other things, parity of participation (Fraser, 2013). In the context of second/ foreign language education, *participation* refers to the right of children to fair participation in decisions about their linguistic and educational rights.

Unfortunately, as we have observed above, children's voices are not often sought in decisions about matters relating to their education and as a result, their learning needs are often imagined, or made up by adults. In fact, underlying the international policy treaties cited above is the institutional provision of the UNDHR (1948) entrusting the prior right of choosing the kind of education that shall be given to children firmly in the hands of parents alone. As a result, children's educational choices are determined by parents, based on their own aspirations. In the field of language education, studies that have examined the global spread of English and English Medium Instruction (EMI) (e.g. Dearden, 2014; Tembe & Norton, 2011), have pointed to a dramatic rise in the number of children exposed to English language, both as a subject in the curriculum and as a medium of instruction, as part of a dominant view held by policymakers and parents who perceive early exposure to English as essential for success in the global labour market. This view is promoted despite compelling evidence that children's exposure to foreign language education is not necessarily beneficial to their cognitive development and might in fact be a hindrance to their educational prospects (Kuchah, 2016; Pinnock, 2009; Sawamura & Sifuna, 2008; Williams & Cooke, 2002). There is a danger therefore that the real language needs and experiences of children may be ignored if research that takes their views into account is not conducted.

Language is fundamental in children's social, emotional and cognitive development and in fact underlies children's right to quality education (UNESCO, 2007). Researching young learners in language education therefore enables us to find out about their real life; to engage them in exploring their language learning experiences and to understand their realities in order to better serve their language learning needs. Involving them in research ensures their right to participation and promotes social justice and helps researchers gain insights that can inform or even challenge policy and practice. As Graue and Walsh (1998) affirm, researching children helps us to find out about what we need to know about them,

> ...and to keep finding it out, because if we do not find it out, someone will make it up. In fact, someone probably has already made it up and what they make up affects children's lives; it affects how children are viewed and what decisions are made about them. Finding it out challenges dominant images. Making it up maintains them. (Graue & Walsh, 1998: xvi)

In other words, finding out about children's language learning needs and realities is a moral and ethical imperative.

What are Research Ethics?

The history of research ethics or human ethics originates from biomedical and medical sciences, following unethical practices in World War II. The original principles were developed to counteract the potential risks that all researchers and research projects potentially pose due to their elevated status and special authority over participants. Traditionally, research ethics consists of a framework which protects participants' human rights, including the right to decide whether or not to participate or withdraw without fear of prejudice, as well as safeguards their physical, mental and emotional well-being throughout and beyond a research project. Ethical procedures are also important for guaranteeing that the real or perceived power differential between researcher and participant does not influence the nature of the data collected in a pervasive manner. In order to protect participants, research ethics guidelines require researchers to ensure that the following four moral obligations summarized by Beauchamp and Childress (1979) are respected.

- *Autonomy:* participants must be able to consent through free choice; without fear or worry or any negative consequences if they decline.
- *Non-maleficence:* participants must not suffer any harm in the research process.
- *Beneficence*: the overall benefits to the participants should outweigh the potential risks in the research study.
- *Justice*: all participants must be treated fairly and equally.

However, the key questions that attract most attention centre around the concepts of 'informed consent', 'confidentiality' and 'anonymity'. O'Reilly *et al.* (2013) argue that these questions must be carefully and clearly addressed no matter who the participants are (adults or children) but as we shall see below, if the participants are children, immediate further complications arise.

Developments and Core Principles of Child-Focused Research Ethics

The first important document that mentioned the special status of children as research participants was the *Declaration of Helsinki* (1964) stating that if the child/ the minor is able, informed consent should be sought from the child as well as from the parent/guardian. Gaining consent from both parents and children is of course far from unproblematic but still this was an important step towards recognizing children's rights to have a say about research targeting them. In addition, specifically in the UK, in 1985 the 'Gillick' criteria of competence were accepted and became law following a legal case about children's rights to make decisions about their own health and medical treatment. This law essentially states that if children (under 18) have sufficient maturity to understand the nature, purposes and likely outcome of the proposed medical treatment, their consent is sufficient and there is no need to approach parents. While this ruling came about as a result of a court case focused on medical issues, its influence on researchers and practitioners working with children in various fields of study has been wide-ranging, raising awareness about the need to listen to children and take their views seriously.

Etic and emic perspectives

Various guidelines and criteria for ethical research with children (such as those by AARE, 1993; AERA, 2011; BAAL, 2016; BERA, 2011) all differ slightly in their advice and focus but they do share a firm common ground in suggesting that children must be considered as 'at risk'/ 'vulnerable' participants in research. As a result, in addition to ensuring the core principles of informed consent, confidentiality and anonymity, research must ensure that all children involved in research are protected from harm and indeed, if possible, benefit from the research (Felzmann, 2009). It is the adult researcher's responsibility to make sure that child research participants are safe, comfortable, fully aware of the research purposes, happy with what is going on and understand what exactly their participation entails. This includes the understanding that they can opt out of the research any time without any negative consequences. However, these researcher responsibilities are not always straightforward to achieve given the nature of the power dynamics within schools. As Robinson and Kellet (2004: 91) explain, the balance of power in schools is 'heavily skewed towards adults, and children are least able to exercise participation rights. Adults control children's use of time, occupation of space, choice of clothing, times of eating – even their mode of social interaction.' Besides, relationship building can be inevitably harder for outsiders since their lack of familiarity with the children and their everyday lives, their discourse or their usual patterns of behaviours can restrict or impact on the type of data these researchers can elicit and the types of roles they can encourage children to take. As a consequence, as Murphy and Macaro (2017: 106) observe, if and when some children feel shy or uncomfortable in the company of these outsider researchers they are unlikely to perform to the best of their abilities and thus the reliability and the validity of the collected data may suffer.

Further dilemmas apply to the fast emerging field of practitioner research which, despite being perceived as part and parcel of everyday teaching, still has significant complexities which render child participant choices sometimes meaningless. For example, questions in relation to children's consent to participate, their rights to withdraw from being involved and the potential consequences of missing out on the benefits of the teacher's pedagogic/research activities are still not fully resolved (Bryan & Burstow, 2018). When teacher researchers undertake action research studies (Burns, 2011) or Exploratory Practice (EP) studies (Hanks, 2017) with their own learners, from an ethical point of view, this situation raises various questions about good practice. Does action research that a teacher decides to pursue in her/his everyday teaching fall under the same category as research undertaken by an outsider? Does classroom action research, especially if it is ongoing, still require the signing of formal consent by parents? This is a grey area and no doubt, ethical responses will depend on the actual circumstances of each situation, such as for example, how the teacher is planning to use and disseminate the findings from his or her action research.

Many other issues arise from the unique position of the adult researcher as an insider with an emic perspective and an intimate knowledge of the children as opposed to an outsider who lacks local knowledge and will spend only a short period of time in the research context. Some of these include the extent to which children can fully express their opinions especially when these are in conflict with the teacher's perspective and whether or not children's voices can be heard and considered in all aspects of the research or how their right to withdraw from participating in a study would be dealt with. However, as we shall show below, there are also ethical benefits of insider research which cannot be overlooked.

Access and consent

Key to research with children are a number of core principles which illustrate and extend the moral obligations put forward by Beauchamp and Childress (1979) above. At the outset of a research activity, researchers need to consider how and through whom they gain access to child participants. This can be complicated by the fact that in many contexts, children (under the age of 16 or 18) are not in a position to consent to their own participation in research even if they are considered fully able because it is a legal requirement that their parents/guardians must decide for them. Such legislation is in place to protect children but in cases where children are invited to contribute to the research in more active roles, total adult control can become problematic. Parents might not share the same ethical principles as the adult researcher in charge and/or they may not agree with their children's decision to participate or not to participate. In school based research, there is a further complexity emanating from the need to obtain consent from other 'legally recognised surrogate decision-maker[s]' (Felzmann, 2009) such as school management boards, head teachers, class teachers and even other children who might form part of the friendship network of any participating child. Finding one's way through these different gatekeepers requires different ways of presenting information about the research which reflect the responsibility of each gatekeeper over the child but also the age of the child participant and their network of friends where necessary.

Scholars who strongly believe in securing children's consent (or assent) for their study have been forthcoming with innovative tools and ideas (Kellett, 2010; Parsons *et al.*, 2016) to encourage children to think about their research participation and explicitly express their willingness about participation, in addition to the required adult consent. When children sign consent forms or otherwise agree to participate, it is essential that the adult researcher makes sure that the children understand that they have a choice about participating; they know that they have the right to with-draw at any time and they know what their roles are in the research study. This is all the more important in research with children because they may be susceptible to the adult researcher's social status and as a result, be dishonest about their real feeling about their participation (Ceci, 1991). As Gallagher *et al.* (2010: 471) argue consent is always more 'complicated and ambivalent' in practice than it looks on paper. The 'researcher may explain what a research project is about, and the participants might seem to understand and perhaps genuinely believe that they do - but none of this guarantees that they both share the same conception of the project' (Gallagher *et al.*, 2010: 474).

To ensure that children have full understanding of their involvement and rights in research, consent needs to be treated as a social process rather than as an isolated decision; one way of doing this is to incorporate an ongoing dialogue about consent and revisit it during the study at regu-lar intervals (e.g. Kuchah & Pinter, 2012). Doing so minimizes the risk of children not voicing their doubts just because they do not want to 'upset' the adult researcher or they do not want the researcher to dislike them, and therefore do not voice their doubt at all (Tinson, 2009). Although such goals and intentions are clear and uncontroversial, the chapters in this volume show that putting these principles into practice might be very challenging indeed because of the influence of coercive adults, peer pres-sure and other factors that might influence children's decisions.

Confidentiality and anonymity

Linked to gaining and maintaining informed consent in child-focused research is the principle of confidentiality. In all research, confidentiality is important in protecting participants and is generally achieved through anonymity in reporting research but the concept of confidentiality is ambiguous in child-focused research and anonymity itself can be elusive particularly in school/classroom-based research which includes multiple participants. Recent research with children tends to promote participa-tory practices involving (friendship) groups (Lewis, 1992; Mayall, 2008) because these are assumed to ensure that adult–child research encounters are non-threatening. However, this is not conducive to disclosing ideas that can be perceived as private. There is always the risk that such approaches to research with children render confidentiality issues more complex than in most forms of adult focused research. Felzmann (2009) argues that the promise of confidentiality is a standard requirement for the researcher and yet this does not take into account that by the very nature of the research as school/classroom-based, confidentiality might be broken by other participants especially where focus group or participatory approaches are used to generate research information. He explains that 'if information is shared in the group context the number of those in possession of this information multiplies, while their commitment to confidentiality is doubtful' (Felzmann, 2009: 106). This means that as part of the process of obtaining informed consent, researchers would need to ensure that participating children are aware that confidentiality cannot always be fully guaranteed. What is more, questions arise in child-focused research as to whether confidentiality and anonymity can ever be promised and guaranteed to children without caveats. In fact research (e.g. Bryan & Burstow, 2018) has also shown that in school-based research, confidentiality rules might inhibit teachers and other stakeholders from acting promptly upon sensitive information. While upholding confidentiality remains a key principle of research ethics, where children disclose issues such as abuse or bullying, for example, it is common to see the breach of confidentiality as a necessary ethical step to protect that child and prevent further harm happening. However, the children may interpret this as betrayal of their trust. Overall, privacy concerns arise around who can access the information that emerges from a study or what the children have said. Sometimes, parents or teachers may feel they have the right to know and they simply ignore children's rights to privacy.

Power and reflexivity

Another core principle of research, which is significantly more applicable to child-focused research because of cultural perceptions of children as vulnerable research participants, is the avoidance of harm. While social research does not pose the same kinds of physical risks as medical research, it has the potential, because of its interactional nature, to exploit vulnerable participants. The normal social order, as we have seen earlier in this chapter, dictates that children are positioned as subordinate to adults in society, which means that they lack power and authority in most areas of their lives, both at school and outside school contexts. Since research is often linked to power, and in children's eyes adults are associated with power and authority already, it follows that adult researchers working with children are potentially perceived as doubly powerful and this natural advantage puts them in a position to be able to exploit children consciously or unconsciously. Power and hierarchy are evident in both child–adult and child–child relationships and the specific power dynamics in children's groups and classrooms must also be taken into account as they too have potential to cause psychological and social harm to children (Felzmann, 2009; Thompson, 1990). Besides, the challenges of maintaining confidentiality in social contexts, such as the one we have described in the previous paragraph, make it equally difficult to manage the avoidance of harm beyond the research encounter and thus researchers within the social constructivist paradigm are constantly faced with the dilemma of ensuring that the benefits of social research outweigh the potential risks. Further questions arise whether it is ethical to invite children to contribute in active roles to studies where the outcome of the study will not directly benefit them, or how much time is ethical for the children to devote to the research study. Scholars argue that it is essential for the adult working with children to exercise critical reflexivity (Fraser *et al.*, 2014: 24) or dual reflexivity (Christensen & James, 2008: 6) to be able to come up with an ethical /methodological solution and participation patterns that seem most appropriate or even least problematic in any given situation. Alderson and Morrow (2004) add that adult researchers need to reflect on their own assumptions and status in this power relationship and ask themselves specific questions about ethical consequences at every stage of their study.

Language skills and embedding tools in familiar contexts

One of the commonly discussed issues in child-focused research is related to the limited linguistic capacities of children. This is an issue that may influence both the process of giving consent and the whole process of data collection. Child-focused researchers (e.g. Lewis, 1992) have recommended the use of the child's L1 in research encounters as a matter of principle. However, this is not always a straightforward solution particularly with younger learners who might still be developing their L1 competence. Child-focused researchers therefore often use creative, participatory or other innovative tools which do not rely on exclusively verbal data (Clark & Moss, 2005; O'Kane, 2008; Prasad, 2015). Other criteria for developing participatory data collection tools, apart from their appropriateness to the specific design of each study, are their ecological and pedagogical authenticity. Turek (2013: 35) suggests that participatory research tools should be designed to resemble the activities children routinely perform in real life (ecological authenticity) such as games, drawing and, to resemble types of tasks that children are familiar with, such as discussions, simple writing tasks or using smiley faces as responses to particular questions. While these recommendations are meant to ensure that children's voices are heard, it is important to bear in mind that participatory approaches often entail social interaction which will ultimately lead to verbal representation. However, non-vocalized forms and interpretations of children's lived experiences and reality have been identified as needing further exploration in social science and language education research in particular. It has also been suggested that with any research, conscious and unconscious biases come into play, and Sargeant and Harcourt (2012: 73) warn that children are particularly attuned to non-verbal communication and behaviour patterns that adults are often unaware of and therefore adults working with children will have to develop skills to pick up on subtle signs of discomfort, boredom or stress. Lewis (2010) argues that in some cases, children's silence may be more informative than their voice as it may be a statement of some reality. Listening to children's voices in research also involves 'hearing' their silence and being attentive to other non-verbal forms of expressions and understanding that these are never neutral or meaningless.

From Research 'on' Children to Research 'with' Children: A Historical Overview

The policies, principles, issues and dilemmas discussed above take on different dimensions and different levels of complexity depending on the nature and design of research being conducted with children. Naturally in large-scale quantitative studies different ethical dilemmas take centre stage as compared to more exploratory studies where adult researchers work with smaller groups of children, using largely qualitative tools and spending longer periods of time interacting with the children. What is more, in any study, the adult researcher's background, experience, implicit and explicit conceptions of childhood, and their knowledge about ethics will collectively have an impact on how they decide to conduct their research and how they navigate and mitigate some of the issues we have discussed above.

Historically, child-focused research has been dominated by the field of psychology where children mainly play the role of objects of adult research (e.g. Piaget, 1963). Woodhead and Faulkner (2008) explain that such research not only depersonalizes children but the data collected from such research is interpreted and presented through adult discourses entirely. While such research has been instrumental in shaping the field of education more broadly, there is concern that its 'rather measurement orientation [ignores] aspects of children and childhood that cannot be quantified' (Graue & Walsh, 1998: xv). For example, the work of Donaldson (1978) has shown that Piaget's apparently rigorous research on children failed to consider the familiarity of the situation in which the child participants engaged with tasks. In large-scale experimental studies, children are often unknowing objects who are not always fully aware why some research might be going on, and/ or the instruments or tasks they are asked to work with may be unfamiliar to them, causing them to potentially underperform.

Experimental studies where children are passive objects of the research are of course necessary to answer certain research questions, and they continue to be immensely useful in terms of contributing to our understanding of children's language learning processes but we need more focus on ethical dilemmas in these studies as well rather than present them as neat and unproblematic. For example, how can adult researchers in these large-scale experimental studies make sure that the tasks and tests they are using work equally well for all their participants? If some children feel bored or confused while working with these tasks and thus do not do well enough, is this important when it comes to interpreting the resulting data?

Since the majority of empirical research in EYL has been conducted to date with children in object roles, we also need more balance in the literature with more emphasis on studies where children can take on different, more active and informed roles. This would help us develop a richer picture of children's language learning experiences and achievements.

Overall, following the political impetus of the UNCRC (1989) questions around how children's voices are elicited and whether they are actually heard and acted upon during the research process have led to a significant shift in the nature of children's involvement in research over the last decades. As Greig *et al.* (2013: 253) explain:

> ...there has been a gradual change over the past two decades and the majority view in most circles is that children and adolescents have a right to participate and to have their voices heard, just as they also have a right to refuse to participate, and that research about children and young people should be with children and adolescents and not something that is done to them.

Children's more active involvement in research is an idea associated with the 'New Sociology of Childhood' (James & Prout, 1990) often referred to as the 'emergent paradigm' that positions children as active social agents and experts of their own lives. In particular, Articles 12 and 13 of the UNCRC emphasize the importance of recognizing the *rights* and *capabilities* of children and young people (Greig *et al.*, 2013). Scholars working in this emergent paradigm suggest that children are capable of contributing to research by offering unique perspectives about their experiences and therefore the core mission of this paradigm is to give children voice, recognize their active and agentive role in all areas of social life, and explore children's experiences from their own perspectives. Scott (2008: 88) for example affirms that 'the best people to provide information on the child's perspective, actions and attitudes are children themselves. Children provide reliable responses if questioned about events that are meaningful to their lives.' This perspective implies that research that involves children can no longer be conceptualized exclusively as research '*on*' children but instead as research '*with*' children (Kellett, 2005). Rather than acting as data sources, children can be encouraged to contribute to adult initiated research in active ways such as by suggesting alternative questions to explore, by evaluating draft research tools, by collecting data from their peers, and in some cases by taking charge of the whole of the research process as research assistants and researchers in their own right.

In various studies in ELT, more recently, children have taken consultative roles, co-researcher roles and have in the process helped adult researchers gain rich insights into children's lived experiences and understandings of different aspects of young learner language education. (Kuchah & Pinter, 2012; Kuchah *et al.*, forthcoming; Pinter & Zandian, 2012; Turek, 2013; Zandian, 2015). For example, children acted as evaluators and advisors in designing research tools for adults (Kuchah *et al.*, forthcoming; Zandian, 2015) and in another study children were instrumental in changing the direction of a PhD study through their input in participatory interviews with the use of drawings as starting points for conversations (Kuchah & Pinter, 2012). In Pinter and Zandian (2012) children took spontaneous interest in the originally adult-initiated research and as the study progressed they wanted to take a more active role than was originally planned. Since the participatory nature of their involvement afforded a space for spontaneous, unsolicited insights and questions, which the adult facilitators responded to, layers of meaning in children's understanding about research were uncovered. In Pinter *et al.* (2016) children undertook classroom investigations alongside their teachers to explore their own English learning in Indian primary English classrooms while Prasad (2013, 2014) worked with children as co-researchers or co-ethnographers in an attempt to make sense of the children's multilingual identities using art based creative methods and identity texts. Lundy *et al.* (2011) show how contribution made by children to the development of research questions and choice of methods and their involvement in the interpretation of the data and dissemination of the findings benefits both adults and children. The roles children are invited to take on in research projects will depend on the adult researcher's personal conceptions of children and childhood, the specific design of each study as well as socio-political/institutional exigencies of the context in which each particular study is conducted.

Summary of Contributions and Conclusion

Given the speed at which English language education is being introduced into the early years of formal schooling around the world and with more and more research being undertaken in schools with children as language learners, we believe that there is a great urgency to uncover and discuss some of the complexities that are involved in working with children in particular (rather than older research participants) in our field. The contributions to this volume focus specifically on the kinds of ethical and methodological issues we have discussed in this introductory chapter and provide insights from current researchers in the field with the aim of promoting reflection on good practice in research first of all but also indirectly for policy and practice for young learner L2 education.

All contributions discuss some opportunities as well as challenges relating to working with children in research in their own contexts. Many of the opportunities stem from the adult researchers' attempt to give children a space to reflect on the research process and invite comments and contributions, which are then taken seriously. At the same time, these chapters also illustrate the many challenges, such as the difficulty of getting the children to appreciate what research is all about, achieving a balance between facilitating children's contributions versus influencing them too much, or accessing children's creative insights in highly hierarchical contexts in schools where their views are usually ignored.

The chapters have been organized into three main parts. Part 1 ('Encouraging Children to Play Active Roles') brings together three papers which discuss the authors' experiences in classroom research in primary schools in Japan, Iran and Spain. All three authors have intentionally explored opportunities for involving the children in their research in more active ways.

The first chapter in this part (Chapter 2) by Butler shares insights from a study in which Japanese children were involved in designing computer game tasks to help them learn English vocabulary with the aim of understanding the elements that, from the children's points of view, were both attractive and effective for foreign language learning. In discussing the pedagogic merits of involving children in task design, Butler highlights a number of ethical and methodological dilemmas including how to define the role of the children, particularly at the study design and data analysis stages; how to resolve the power imbalances between adults and children and among the children themselves; and how to ensure that the elicited voices are a representation of the children's 'true' voices. She also highlights individual differences among children pointing out that not all children will take to participatory research of this kind. The second chapter by Zandian (Chapter 3) reports on the benefits of consulting with children about research tools prior to the main study and then the bulk of the chapter discusses the ethical issues related to children's right to be informed of the outcomes of research involving them. The author discusses ethical dilemmas around children's level of understanding of different aspects and components of research through the practice of reflexivity related to her PhD research project, which aimed to explore how 10–12 year old children understood intercultural issues. The children had an incomplete/partial understanding of the research that they had participated in earlier and many of them continued to associate research with assessment despite the adult researcher's great efforts to avoid this. The chapter illustrates how follow-up sessions present great opportunities to reflect collaboratively with the children about their experiences and nudge their understanding and appreciation of research forward. The key idea emerging from this chapter is that no matter how carefully we set up a research project, in situ dilemmas will always arise in everyday practice which need further reflexivity on the part of the adult researcher. García Mayo's chapter (Chapter 4) reflects on her experience in two large scale funded research projects in Spain focusing on English as a Foreign Language children's (ages 6–12) oral interaction elicited by means of interactive tasks. Ethical issues having to do with informed consent and practical challenges to do with experimental studies in general are problematized and discussed. Further, the author explores how some of the tasks used may have made the children feel with regard to their performance relative to other participants, and methodological issues such as creativity in task design and task engagement are considered and illustrated with data from her own research. The author also emphasizes that there is a great deal of variability in terms of children's interest and enthusiasm when it comes to research. The chapter ends with a reflection on how ethical and methodological challenges can be turned into opportunities to make all stakeholders (including researchers, children, teachers and parents) aware of the benefits of research.

The second part of the book ('Research with Children in Multilingual Contexts') is devoted to chapters that explore opportunities and challenges in multilingual contexts where adult researchers work with children who might be new arrivals in a country with varying abilities to communicate in the majority language of the new country or may be children who use a different language at home compared to the one used at school. Given that multilingual practices are becoming the norm in more and more contexts in the world, this section is the biggest one in the book. The contexts covered include the UK, Canada, France and Cameroon.

The chapters cover bilingual or multilingual learners and the particular challenges and affordances when it comes to research with children and their families. Issues around children in research not sharing the adult researcher's language and culture are discussed as well as the need to appreciate, include and celebrate all their languages when it comes to making judgments about their linguistic competence. Research with children often relies on the use of artefacts and other creative visual methods to scaffold their participation on research as the chapters illustrate here.

The first chapter in this section (Chapter 5) by Murphy highlights ethical and methodological challenges that arise when accessing linguistically diverse children studying in the medium of English in the UK. The chapter examines key questions around how consent for child participation might be obtained from, for example, newly arrived refugee parents who do not speak or read the language of their host community to be able to give informed consent; how migrant children's full range of linguistic skills (in their first language) can be assessed, how schools can deal with the rising multilingual realities of children in a context where the educational system adopts monolingual norms which marginalize a significant growing proportion of the school population. In attempting to respond to these questions Murphy shares practical insights through a range of processes and considerations for achieving and maintaining the highest ethical standards in educational research to enable researchers to offer evidence-based guidance on effective ways to educate children from a diverse range of backgrounds.

The second chapter (Chapter 6) by Prasad, draws on collaborative classroom-based language inquiry with culturally and linguistically diverse children in Canada and France over the past decade and traces the author's journey from doing research about children's multiple literacies to doing research *with* children as co-investigators of their plurilingual practices and experiences. The chapter critically examines how this positioning of children as active co-researchers creates an opportunity to reframe children as 'experts' of their lived experience rather than minoritized language learners. Drawing on vignettes from classroom-based research with children, the author problematizes whether a commitment to conceptualizing children as co-researchers guarantees that children's voices, identities and experience are honoured throughout the process of data collection, analysis and dissemination. The author focuses on three instances where children provided interpretations and insights that challenged the adult's initial views and understandings. The chapter concludes with four researcher dispositions that the author has learned from children through her collaborative language inquiry: attention, curiosity, creativity and humility.

Ibrahim, in Chapter 7 presents an example of how non-verbal data collection tools, such as objects or artefacts, might help children construct their multilingual identities. The chapter explores in depth, the methodological and ethical implications of employing an artefactual perspective when researching children; it analyzes the challenges and benefits of this approach and shows how objects and the creation of multimodal artefactual texts constitute an appropriate vehicle for eliciting children's complex identity narratives. Ibrahim suggests that this approach to research with children allowed for the emergence of children's spontaneous interpretations of their own identities rather than relying on the adult's interpretations alone. This material approach, she argues, advances our understanding of children's experiences of living and learning in multilingual contexts and meets ethical requirements in working with children.

Next, Andrews (Chapter 8) reflects on instances of ethical and methodological practice which occurred in a research study focusing on primary school children's perspectives on being multilingual in a UK school context. The chapter explores some selected aspects of the research process and practice, such as children's informed consent, continuous willingness to participate, trustworthiness in children's data and issues with task fulfilment in order to shed light on the detailed study-specific ethical and methodological planning, which researchers of children's experiences need to undertake. The chapter concludes with the author's reflections on what she learned during the research process and how it has influenced her subsequent practice of researching with children and also with adults.

The last chapter of part 2 (Chapter 9) by Kuchah and Milligan extends the discussions around the ethical complexities of research with children in a sub-Saharan African context showing how linguistic, cultural and sociopolitical forces within the broader environment and the school might be an obstacle to participatory approaches to research especially where the pedagogic practices children are used to are often teacher centred, allowing very little opportunity for child agency. The central theme in this chapter is the need for outsider researchers using participatory approaches in research with children to understand the sociopolitical and cultural dynamics of the context in their research design, methodology and interpretation of data from children.

The final part of this book ('Teacher Education and Research with Children') includes three chapters which share a focus and emphasis on issues relating to researching with children as relevant to teacher educators and teacher education.

The first chapter in Part 3 (Chapter 10) by Ellis and Ibrahim investigates teachers' conceptions of children and childhood based on existing conceptualizations of the children as *beings* rather than as *becomings* as well as categorizations of the children as objects, subjects, social actors and co-researchers. Data from early years and primary teachers from 38 countries reveal that the majority of respondents see the child as an adult in the making or a future citizen, rather than an individual with their own rights and valid views. Such a view of children and childhood certainly has implications for the level of control that teachers might be able to, or are willing to, hand over to children in learning environments. As Cox *et al.* (2010: 1) affirm, 'at the heart of questions over what decisions children should make and how and when, is how we conceptualise children, their abilities and their rights.' The findings from Ellis and Ibrahim's study suggest a need for teacher education to help teachers understand the implications of the UNCRC in order to develop a greater awareness of children's rights and abilities. In Chapter 11 Mathew and Pinter report on a study that involved outsider researchers, working together with teachers and children in Indian primary schools. The authors describe a British Council funded action research project in which they trained teachers on how the provisions of Article 12 and 13 of the UNCRC (1989) as well as the emerging ideas about children's roles in research from the 'New Childhood Studies' movement related to classroom research and practice, challenging them to view children as 'knowers' and 'experts' and giving them an elevated status of partners. The chapter then goes on to show how this shift in perspective was enacted through the action research projects in which teachers and children were co-researchers. Ethical issues related to the everyday 'in-situ' dilemmas of the local context are discussed and the authors conclude that the most important principles of local ethics, which are honesty/integrity, professional commitment and listening to one's conscience can only be resolved where there is school support for co-research between teachers and children. In Chapter 12 Mourão describes a small-scale study which investigated the practices of a group of MA students in Portugal engaging in action research projects in primary schools. Using data from interviews and examples of child consent sheets, Mourão outlines the challenges these teachers faced as they went through the process of obtaining informed consent from the children in their studies. She discusses the issues related to this stage of the research plan, especially when such professional development programmes are short-term, and concludes that this is an area of research which needs rather more attention and suggests a set of guidelines for researching children in such pre-service training contexts.

Overall, the chapters in this volume reflect critically on researchers' understandings of the notion and extent of children's rights and show how they might inform the methodological and ethical dimensions of finding out about children's views and lived experiences. Each chapter showcases how the researchers have mediated the range of ethical dilemmas that might arise in child-focused research in different contexts around the world; this is important in building up a holistic understanding of child-related research principles in our field. We hope that readers will find the contributions to this volume a useful basis for reflecting further and consequently refining future research involving children in the field of language education.

References

AARE (1993) *Code of Ethics*. Australian Association for Research in Education.

AERA (2011) *Code of Ethics*. American Educational Research Association.

Alderson, P. and Morrow, V. (2004) *Ethics, Social Research and Consulting with Children and Young People*. Ilford: Barnardos.

BAAL (2016) *Recommendations on Good Practice in Applied Linguistics*. British Association of Applied Linguistics.

Beauchamp, T. and Childress, J. (1979) *Principles of Biomedical Ethics*. Oxford: Oxford University Press.

BERA (2011) *Ethical Guidelines for Educational Research*. British Educational Research Association.

Bland, J. (ed.) (2016) *Teaching English to Young Learners: Critical Issues in Language Teaching with 3–12 Year Olds*. London: Bloomsbury.

Blom, E. and Bosma, E. (2016) 'The sooner the better? An investigation into the role of age of onset and its relation with transfer and exposure in bilingual Frisian–Dutch children'. *Journal of Child Language* 43, 581–607.

Brumfit, C. (1991) Introduction: Teaching English to children. In C. Brumfit, J. Moon and R. Tongue (eds) *Teaching English to Children: From Practice to Principle* (pp. iv–viii). London: Harper Collins Publishers.

Bryan, H. and Burstow, B. (2018) Understanding ethics in school-based research. *Professional Development in Education* 44 (1), 107–119.

Bucknall, S. (2014) Doing qualitative research with children and young people. In A. Clark et al. (eds) *Understanding Research with Children and Young People* (pp. 69–84). London: Sage.

Burns, A. (2011) Embedding teacher research into a national language programme *Research Notes* 44, 3–6.

Cameron, L. (2003) Challenges for ELT from the expansion of in teaching children. *ELT Journal* 57 (2), 105–112.

Ceci, S.J. (1991) How much does schooling influence general intelligence and its cognitive components? A reassessment of the evidence. *Development Psychology* 27 (5), 703–722.

Christensen, P. and James, A. (2008)Introduction: Researching children and childhood cultures of communication In P. Christensen and A. James (eds) *Research with Children: Perspectives and Practices* (pp. 1–9). London: Routledge.

Clark, A. and Moss, P. (2005) *Listening to Children: The Mosaic Approach*. London: National Children's Bureau Enterprises.

Copland, F. and Creese, A. (2016) Ethical issues in linguistic ethnography: Balancing the micro and the macro In P.I. De Costa (ed.) *Ethics in Applied Linguistics Research: Language Researcher Narratives* (pp. 161–178). New York: Routledge.

Copland, F. and Garton, S. (2014) Key themes and future directions in teaching English to young learners: Introduction to the Special Issue. *ELT Journal* 68 (3), 223–230.

Cox, S., Dyer, C., Robinson-Pant, A. and Schweisfurth, M. (eds) (2010) *Children as Decision Makers in Education: Sharing Experiences across Cultures*. London: Continuum International Publishing Group.

Dearden, J. (2014) *English as a Medium of Instruction: A Growing Global Phenomenon: Phase 1. Interim Report*. Oxford: University of Oxford and the British Council.

De Costa, P. (2015) Ethics and applied linguistics research. In B. Paltridge and A. Phakiti (eds) *Research Methods in Applied Linguistics* (pp. 245–257). London: Bloomsbury.

Donaldson, M. (1978) *Children's Minds*. Glasgow: Fontana.

Enever, J. (ed.) (2011) *ELLiE, Early Language Learning in Europe*. London: The British Council.

Enever, J. and Lindgren, E. (2017) (eds) *Early Language Learning: Complexity and Mixed Methods*. Bristol: Multilingual Matters.

Felzmann, H. (2009) Ethical issues in school-based research. *Research Ethics Review 5* (3), 104–109

Fraser, N. (2013) *Scales of Justice*. Cambridge: Polity.

Fraser, S., Flewitt, R. and Hammersley, M. (2014) What is research with children and young people? In A. Clark, R. Flewitt, M. Hammersely and M. Robb (eds) *Understanding Research with Children and Young People* (pp. 34–50). Milton Keynes: The Open University Press.

Gallagher, M., Haywood, S.L., Jones, M.W. and Milne, S. (2010) Negotiating informed consent with children in school-based research: A critical overview. *Children and Society* 24, 471–482.

García Mayo, M.P. (ed.) (2017) *Learning Foreign Languages in Primary School: Research Insights*. Bristol: Multilingual Matters.

Garton, S. and Copland, F. (eds) (2019) *The Routledge Handbook of Teaching English to Young Learners*. London: Routledge.

Garton, S., Copland, F. and Burns, A. (2011) *Investigating Global Practices in Teaching English to Young Learners*. London: British Council.

Graue, M.E. and Walsh, D.J. (1998) *Studying Children in Context: Theories, Methods and Ethics*. London: Sage.

Greig, A., Taylor J. and MacKay, T. (2013) *Doing Research with Children*. London: Sage.

Hanks, J. (2017) *Exploratory Practice in Language Teaching*. Palgrave Macmillan.

James, A. and Prout, A. (eds) (1990) *Constructing and Re-constructing Childhood*. Basingstoke: Falmer Press.

Johnstone, R. (2009) An early start: What are the key conditions for generalised success? In J. Enever, J. Moon and U. Raman (eds) *Young Learner English Language Policy and Implementation: International Perspectives* (pp. 31–41). Reading: Garnet Education.

Kellett, M. (2005) *How to Develop Children as Researchers: A Step-by-step Guide to Teaching the Research Process*. London: Sage.

Kellett, M. (2010) *Rethinking Children and Research: Attitudes in Contemporary Society*. London: Continuum.

Kubanyiova, M. (2008) Rethinking research ethics in contemporary applied linguistics: The tension between macroethical and microethical perspectives in situated research. *The Modern Language Journal* 92 (4), 502–518.

Kuchah, K. (2016) English medium instruction in an English-French bilingual setting: Issues of quality and equity in Cameroon. *Comparative Education* 52 (3), 311–327.

Kuchah, K. (2019) Teaching English to young learners in difficult circumstances In S. Garton and F. Copland (eds) *The Routledge Handbook of Teaching English to Young Learners* (pp. 73–92). New York: Routledge.

Kuchah, K., Milligan, L.O., Ubanako, V.N and Njika, J. (forthcoming) *English Medium Instruction (EMI) in a Multilingual Francophone Context: An Investigation of the Learning Resources and Strategies of Primary School Children in Cameroon.* London: British Council.

Kuchah K. and Pinter, A. (2012) Was this an interview? Breaking the power barrier in adult–child interviews in an African context. *Issues in Educational Research* 22 (3), 283–297.

Lewis, A. (1992) Group interviews as a research tool. *British Education Research Journal* 18 (4), 413–421.

Lewis, A. (2010) Silence in the context of child voice. *Children and Society* 24 (1), 14–23.

López-Gopar, M.E. (2014) Teaching English critically to Mexican children. *ELT Journal* 68 (3), 310–321.

Lundy, L., McEvoy, L. and Byrne, B. (2011) Working with young children as co-researchers: An approach informed by the United Nations Convention on the Rights of the Child. *Early Education and Development* 22 (5), 714–736.

Mayall, B. (2008) Conversations with children: Working with generational issues In P. Christensen and A. James (eds) *Research with Children: Perspectives and Practices* (pp. 109–22). London: Routledge.

Mourão, S. and Lourenço, M. (eds) (2015) *Early Years Second Language Education.* London: Routledge.

Muñoz, C. (2014) Starting age and other influential factors: Insights from learner interviews. *Studies in Second Language Learning and Teaching* 4, 465–484.

Murphy, V. and Macaro, E. (2017) It isn't child's play: Conducting research with children as participants. In J. McKinley and H. Rose (eds) *Doing Research in Applied Linguistics: Realities, Dilemmas, and Solutions* (pp. 103–113). London: Routledge.

Nikolov, M. (ed.) (2016) *Assessing Young Learners of English: Global and Local Perspectives.* Switzerland: Springer International.

O'Kane, C. (2008) The development of participatory techniques: Facilitating children's views about decisions which affect them. In P. Christensen and A. James (eds) *Research with Children: Perspectives and Practices* (pp. 125–155). London: Routledge.

O'Reilly, M., Ronzoni, P. and Dogra, N. (2013) *Research with Children: Theory and Practice.* London: Sage.

Parsons, S., Sherwood, G. and Abbott, C. (2016) Informed consent with children and young people in social research: Is there scope for innovation? *Children and Society* 30 (2), 132–145.

Pfenninger, S.E. and Singleton, D. (2016) Affect trumps age: A person-in-context relational view of age and motivation in SLA. *Second Language Research* 32, 311–345.

Piaget, J. (1963) *The Language and the Thought of the Child.* London: Routledge and Kegan Paul.

Pinnock, H. (2009) *Language and Education: The Missing Link.* Reading: CfBT Education Trust and Save the Children.

Pinter A. (2011) *Children Learning Second Languages.* London: Palgrave Macmillan.

Pinter A. (2019) Research issues with young learners In S. Garton and F. Copland (eds) *The Routledge Handbook of Teaching English to Young Learners* (pp. 411–424). London: Routledge.

Pinter, A., Mathew, R. and Smith, R. (2016) *Children and Teachers as Co-researchers in Indian Primary English Classrooms. ELT Research Papers 16.03.* London: British Council.

Pinter, A. and Zandian, S. (2012) 'I thought it would be tiny little one phrase that we said, in a huge big pile of papers': Children's reflections on their involvement in participatory research. *Qualitative Research* 15 (2), 235–250.

Prasad, G. (2013) Children as co-ethnographers of their plurilingual literacy practices: An exploratory case study. *Language and Literacy* 15 (3), 4–30.

Prasad, G. (2014) Portraits of plurilingualism in a French international school in Toronto: Exploring the role of visual methods to access students' representations of their linguistically diverse identities. *Canadian Journal of Applied Linguistics* 17 (1), 51–77.

Prasad, G. (2015) Beyond the mirror towards a plurilingual prism: Exploring the creation of plurilingual 'identity texts' in English and French classrooms in Toronto and Montpellier. *Intercultural Education* 26 (6), 497–514.

Rich, S. (ed.) (2014) *International Perspectives on Teaching English to Young Learners*. Basingstoke: Palgrave Macmillan.

Rixon, S. (2013) *British Council Survey of Policy and Practice in Primary English Language Teaching Worldwide*. London: British Council.

Robinson, C. and Kellett, M. (2004) Power. In S. Fraser, V. Lewis, S. Ding, M. Kellett and C. Robinson (eds) *Doing Research with Children and Young People* (pp. 81–96). London: Sage.

Rose, H. and McKinley, J. (2017) Realities of doing research in applied linguistics. In J. McKinley and H. Rose (eds) *Doing Research in Applied Linguistics: Realities, Dilemmas, and Solutions* (pp. 3–14). London: Routledge.

Sargeant, J. and Harcourt, D. (2012) *Doing Ethical Research with Children*. Maidenhead: Open University Press.

Sawamura, N. and Sifuna, D.N. (2008) Universalising primary education in Kenya: Is it beneficial and sustainable? *Journal of International Cooperation in Education* 11 (3), 103–118.

Scott, J. (2008) Children as respondents: The challenge for quantitative methods. In P. Christensen and A. James (eds) *Research with Children: Perspectives and Practices* (pp. 98–119). London: Falmer Press.

Tembe, J. and Norton, B. (2011) English education, local languages and community perspectives in Uganda. In H. Coleman (ed.) *Dreams and Realities: Developing Countries and the English Language* (pp. 114–136). London: British Council.

Thompson, R.A. (1990) Behavioural research involving children: A developmental perspective on risk. *IRB: Ethics and Human Research* 12 (2), 1–6.

Tinson, J. (2009) *Conducting Research with Children and Adolescents: Design, Methods and Empirical Cases*. Oxford: Goodfellow Publishers.

Turek, A. (2013) Engaging young learners in L2 research In C. Ciarlo and D.S. Giannon (eds) *Language Studies Working Papers* (pp. 32–40). University of Reading.

United Nations (1989) *United Nations Conventions on the Rights of the Child*. New York: United Nations.

United Nations (1981) *United Nations Convention on the Elimination of All Forms of Discrimination against Women*. New York: United Nations.

United Nations (1948) *United Nations Declaration of Humans Rights*. New York: United Nations.

UNESCO (1960) *Convention against Discrimination in Education*. Paris: UNESCO.

United Nations (1990) *The World Declaration on Education for All*. Thailand.

United Nations Migration Agency (2017) *World Migration Report 2018*. Geneva: International Organisation for Migration.

UNICEF (2007) *A Human Rights-based Approach to Education for All*. New York: UNICEF.

Williams, E. and Cooke, J. (2002) Pathways and labyrinths: Language and education in development. *TESOL Quarterly* 26 (3), 297–322.

World Medical Association WMA History: Declaration of Helsinki (1964) Available online: http:www.wma.net/e/history/helsinki.htm.

Woodhead, M. and Faulkner, D. (2008) Subjects, objects or participants: Dilemmas of psychological research with children In A. James and P. Christensen (eds) *Research with Children: Perspectives and Practices* (pp. 10–39). London: Routledge.

Zandian, S. (2015) Children's perceptions of intercultural issues: An exploration into an Iranian context. Unpublished PhD dissertation, University of Warwick.

Part 1

Encouraging Children to Play Active Roles

2 Researching with Children as an Opportunity for Active and Interactive Learning: Lessons from a Digital Game Design Project

Yuko Goto Butler

Introduction

There has been growing interest in *research with children* in child studies in the last couple of decades. Instead of treating children merely as research objects (e.g. giving children measurements in controlled experiments) or research subjects (e.g. observing and interpreting children from adult perspectives), researchers have been challenged to view children as social actors or even co-researchers. Under such an approach, children's agency – in both their learning and their experiences – is treated as central (Christensen & Prout, 2002). Inviting children to take an active role in research also aligns well with the spirit of autonomous learning and active learning, which have been given a great deal of emphasis in the school curricula in many countries in recent years.

Compared with other disciplines, second language acquisition (SLA) has yet to sufficiently address a number of methodological and ethical concerns surrounding *research with children* (Pinter, 2014). In SLA research, particularly instructed SLA research, one can generally expect that the findings will have useful implications for language learning and teaching, but it is often the case that participants do not directly benefit from their participation in research. Children, in particular, usually do not even have the means to reach out to the researcher or to access the findings of the research project that they were involved in (see Zandian's chapter in this volume for a notable exception). Thus, it is important for SLA researchers to design and conduct studies that might directly benefit participants through fruitful learning experiences. When conducting research, such considerations are of course important for any context, but it is especially the case if the research is conducted in a formal school context where children (and their teachers) have various constraints, such as curriculum requirements. Under such circumstances, implementing a research project outside of the curriculum requirement is often challenging. *Participatory research* is a collection of methods that aim to grant power to participants and allow them to engage in research processes so that they can benefit from the research results. Considering children's vulnerability to power imbalances (between children and adults) as well as their limited direct access to research results, participatory research is an attractive option both ethically and pedagogically, and is a promising approach to conducting research with children.

In this chapter, therefore, I approach participatory research with children as an opportunity for children's active and interactive learning in a formal school instructional setting. Of course, merely conducting participatory research itself does not guarantee that the participants will actually engage in the activities actively and learn from the experience (Horgan, 2016). Thus, this chapter aims to discuss both the opportunities and challenges in conducting participatory research with children in a school context as an effort to explore a more ethical approach to working with children in research.

Reflecting on a digital game design project that I completed with children and their teachers in Japan, where active and interactive learning is strongly emphasized in its national curriculum (Butler, 2015, 2017, 2019), I first offer some background information regarding two major issues associated with child participatory research (i.e. issues of power and contextualization) and Japanese educational policy. I then describe the Japanese children's digital game project, followed by issues that emerged from this case study. By addressing lessons learned from this project, I hope to help researchers better understand and promote *research with children* in SLA.

Background

Child participatory research

As a window to understand how children perceive and experience the world, a number of participatory research methods have been suggested, such as drama, drawing, group discussions, mapping, role play, storytelling (see Fargas-Malet *et al.*, 2010 for more examples), and more recently, the use of various kinds of visual and digital devices (Livingstone & Blum-Ross, 2017; Yamada-Rice, 2017). These methods are meant to be child-friendly techniques for helping children have active voices in research. Importantly, however, what makes the research 'participatory' is not the research methods per se but the social relations between the researcher and research participants that enable the co-production of new knowledge (Gallagher, 2008; Raffety, 2014). In addition, Christensen and James (2017: 4) argued that 'what is important is that the particular methods chosen for a piece of research should be appropriate for the people involved in the study, for its social and cultural context and for the kinds of research questions that are being posed'. Namely, to ensure meaningful participation by all parties, we must consider social/power relations among the actors (researchers and participants) and contextualize our methods.

In child studies, it is often noted that 'the biggest challenge for researchers working with children are [sic] the disparities in power and status between adults and children' (O'Kane, 2017: 190). While children's participation in data collection is increasingly popular, researchers often acknowledge difficulties in working with children in other phases of research, including planning, analysing, and reporting the results (Gallagher, 2008). But one can also argue that such 'difficulties' may in part stem from researchers' perception that treating children as research partners means that they should have the same research objectives as the researcher and be involved in at least some researcher roles. In reality, however, sharing research goals with children may be unrealistic or even impossible. More importantly, it might not even be necessary for researchers and children to share the same objectives in a participatory research project as long as all participants have an identified goal toward which they are working. Indeed, this is the argument that I make in this chapter through the presentation of a case study.

How researchers conceptualize children or childhood affects how they perceive the relationship between children and adults. Their perception, in turn, leads them to use different strategies to deal with power relations. Based on the premise that children are different from adults, some researchers take on the role of a participant observer, or what Mandell (1988) called 'the least adult' role, by transforming themselves to be more like children. Raffety (2014) criticized such approaches as 'minimizing *social difference* strategies' because they persist in viewing differences between children and adults as somewhat static and universal across contexts while at the same time viewing these social differences from the perspective of adults. She instead proposed a 'minimizing *social distance*' strategy in which researchers acknowledge social differences but suspend their own control by 'ceding control to informants' (Raffety, 2014: 414). By doing so, the strategy 'allows for the greater apprehension of the social rules of the community, enabling the researcher's relations to inform understanding of contextually specific social difference' (Raffety, 2014: 417). Gallagher (2008: 140) further questioned a prevailing assumption that power is something 'possessed' by a certain group or individuals (e.g. adults) and needs to be 'reduced, negated or worked around'. Instead, he proposed a revised model of power that 'must be able to acknowledge the existence of multiple shifting relations of power: between researchers and children, teachers and pupils, amongst peers, between children of different ages and genders, and so forth' (Gallagher, 2008: 143).

In line with Raffety (2014) and Gallagher (2008), I acknowledge social differences but believe that power resides in non-static and dynamic relations among all the participating parties (children, teachers and researchers); such relations are embedded in specific cultural and educational contexts. In the project described below, mutual learning among all participating parties is considered critical. In order to achieve mutual learning, it is important to acknowledge that everybody involved in the project has unique expertise that they can bring to the research project. The participants also identify each of their learning/research objectives that would facilitate their engagement and autonomy. All the participants are expected to negotiate power as it emerges in relations dynamically in order to make mutual learning possible.

Active and interactive learning in the Japanese school context

Active learning refers to any instructional methods where students are involved in activities and reflect on what they are doing; examples include problem solving, group discussions, case studies and oral presentations. Compared with more traditional, passive learning methods (e.g. listening to the teacher), active learning is considered to have better learning outcomes, including greater retention and transformation of information, stronger critical thinking and interpersonal skills and higher motivation for learning (Bonwell & Eison, 1991). Collaboration with peers in activities is found to be particularly effective, not only in terms of academic achievement but also in terms of affective and social-interpersonal development (e.g. fostering self-esteem) (Prince, 2004).

In Japan, as an alternative to teacher-centred and knowledge-transmitted approaches to education, a student-centred approach – more precisely, a focus on active and interactive learning – has gained substantial attention among educators and policymakers in recent years. An increase in globalization and an aging society, as well as technology innovations, require people to have flexible and creative abilities so that they can deal with unexpected and rapid change. Active learning and interactive learning – the latter often conceptualized as a promising form of active learning – are considered ways to develop such abilities.

In 2002, the Ministry of Education, Culture, Sports, Science and Technology (MEXT) introduced 'Integrated Study Periods' in the National Curriculum (referred to as *the Course of Study*) for primary and secondary schools, with the aim of fostering students' critical thinking and problem-solving skills through activities and projects going beyond academic subject boundaries. During Integrated Study Periods (2–3 hours per week), teachers are expected to choose topics, set goals, design lessons and take innovative instructional approaches that reflect their students' needs and school and community characteristics. The students are in turn expected to develop autonomy, diverse perspectives, cooperativeness, as well as greater thinking skills, decision-making skills and expressive skills through active and interactive learning (MEXT, 2017).

Integrated Study requires tremendous planning and preparation by teachers, which can be a heavy burden for teachers whose hands are already full. In Japan's highly centralized educational system, many teachers are used to transmitting the content of prescribed curricula and textbooks to their students. While some teachers see the Integrated Study Periods as an exciting opportunity for creativity and innovation, for others the new initiative has been a source of worry and stress. There has also been a great deal of confusion about what counts as student-centred pedagogy. Not too surprisingly, there is substantial variation in how Integrated Study Periods are implemented by teachers; the effectiveness of these periods also varies considerably. Moreover, there are some concerns that Integrated Study would be effective only after students have acquired a certain level of basic knowledge and skills; they may be effective for older students but not for primary school students (see MEXT, n. d., for a list of issues associated with the Integrated Study Periods). According to Mizuguchi (2015: 35), 'the development of creative lessons, which was originally intended to energize the educational scene, withered under pressure on teachers, along with lack of experience on the part of teaching staff.' Under this circumstance, there is a great need for teachers to rethink 'student-centred pedagogy' and 'students' autonomy' and to enhance their knowledge and skills for meaningfully implementing active and interactive learning. As described below, this is one of the learning goals for the participating teachers in this project.

Digital Game Design Project for English Vocabulary Learning

Project aims

As with many neighbouring countries, the Japanese government has introduced compulsory English education at the primary school level, first as an exploratory program in 2001 and then as an academic subject beginning in 2020 (although actual teaching of English as an academic subject has been already enacted in reality). This new policy has created tremendous challenges for the majority of in-service primary school teachers who were not originally trained to teach English. With a lack of sufficient professional training for teachers to improve their English proficiency and

English-teaching skills, the use of technology as an instructional tool is considered promising.

Among various technologies, this study focused on digital games as a potential learning tool because 'games can contribute to the implementation of pedagogic principles that are becoming increasingly mainstream, such as the use of tasks, authentic forms of interaction and collaboration, and community-based and situated learning' (Reinders, 2012: 2). In addition, a number of studies (from different parts of the world, including Japan) have repeatedly indicated that children tend to lose motivation to learn foreign languages by the end of their primary school years (e.g. Carreira, 2006). Because digital games are appealing to many children, using them may provide useful insights into how children are motivated to engage in tasks. Moreover, in task-based language teaching (TBLT) research and practice, learners' voices have not been sufficiently incorporated into task designs; instead, it has been a common practice for teachers or curriculum designers to develop tasks for learners and then for learners to merely execute them. Finally, it has been suggested that young learners growing up with digital games have cognitive processing and learning styles that may be different from earlier generations (Prensky, 2001). While this assumption needs to be empirically examined, it makes sense to listen to children and reflect on their preferred learning styles when designing tasks for digital games.

From a research perspective, the aim of this project was to understand what elements children identify as *motivating* and what elements they identify as supportive of *learning* in digital games for English vocabulary learning. By asking children to identify these elements, we, the research team, viewed them as consultants on the design of future tasks. Additionally, in order to make this a mutual learning project, as shown in Table 2.1, we defined objectives for the children as well as for their teachers. For the children, to participate in this research was meant to be an active- and interactive-learning experience. For the teachers, this project was designed to help them gain greater pedagogical knowledge and experience for active and interactive learning as well as for English teaching. Clearly identifying the unique expertise that each group brings to the project was important. And indeed, this way of formulating the research project turned out to make it easier for the school and teachers to collaborate with the researchers. We also deliberately reminded the children of their expertise at the beginning of the project. The project was implemented during sixth- and fifth-grade students' Integrated Study Periods in a local public school in the Tokyo Metropolitan Area. The sixth graders (ages 11–12, $n = 82$ from three intact classes) designed digital games for the fifth graders. After a game was developed (by a professional game designer) based on the students' designs, the fifth graders (ages 10–11, $n = 48$ from two intact classes) evaluated its effectiveness.

Table 2.1 Expertise and learning objectives of all the participating parties in the project

Participating parties	Expertise	Learning/research objectives
Researchers	• Knowledge about active and interactive learning • Content expertise (English language teaching and learning and curriculum designing) • Knowledge and experience with research	• To obtain and learn about children's perspectives about motivating and learning elements for digital game-based task designs for English vocabulary learning
Children	• Knowledge and experience about games and new technology-based learning • Learners' and/or users' perspectives	• To develop autonomy, multiple perspectives, cooperativeness, as well as greater thinking skills, decision-making skills, and expressive skills through active and interactive learning (targeted abilities and skills specified by MEXT)
Teachers	• Professional knowledge and experience of teaching in general • Knowledge about students and their needs	• To gain greater knowledge and experience of active and interactive learning • To gain content knowledge and experience (English teaching and learning)

Project planning and procedures

Prior to the project implementation, the teachers and the team of researchers (composed of the author, two curriculum development specialists and a professional game designer) held a series of discussions and planned the project. During this process, both the teachers and the researchers contributed their expertise to design the project to support meaningful active and interactive learning for the children while also matching well with their learning experiences and needs. In addition to considering the teachers' knowledge about their students based on their daily practice, we distributed a questionnaire to the children in order to better understand their game-playing experiences outside of school and their attitudes toward game-based learning. Admittedly, the children were not directly involved in this planning stage; however, the information gained through the survey was used for the planning.

After a couple of months of planning, we came up with a project consisting of five steps, as summarized in Table 2.2 (each step corresponded to a class period of the Integrated Study Period). Detailed lessons plans can be found in Butler (2015). The lessons were composed of a series of activities (indicated in italics), most of which were conducted in group-work formats. The first four steps were conducted among the sixth graders (in 4 weeks), and the final step was carried out by the fifth graders (in 2 weeks). All the activities except for English vocabulary learning were conducted in

Table 2.2 Project procedures

Steps	Teachers/researchers	Children
Step 1: Identifying game elements that engage learners (motivation elements)	*Introducing* the goals and procedures of the project to the students	
		Discussing and *identifying* game elements first as a small group (a group of 5–6)[a] and as a whole class, while *examining* some examples of existing serious games (games specifically designed for language learning purposes)
	Recording game elements identified by the students on the blackboard	
	Introducing 35 new English words[b] using flash cards, following the usual approach to teaching vocabulary in these classes (in order to motivate students to come up with a better way to learn, i.e. through digital games)	
		(As homework) *Learning* five words of their choice (out of the 35 words) while *paying attention* to strategies for learning them.
Step 2: Identifying learning elements that promote vocabulary learning		*Identifying* learning elements by *discussing* strategies that they used for the homework, first as a small group and then as the whole class.
	Recording learning elements identified by the students on the blackboard	
		Analyzing how the extracted learning elements are incorporated in serious games by *playing* some serious games
	Showing students (by the professional game designer) how to create story boards (graphic organizers used for game and animation designing and presentation)	*Understanding* how professionals use storyboards for designing and presenting games (so that they can create a simple storyboard in Steps 3 and 4)
Step 3: Designing a digital game task		*Developing* a digital game task plan in the small group while *using* an 'Idea Sheet' (which is meant to assist students brainstorm and organize ideas) and *incorporating* the motivating and learning elements they identified in previous steps.

(Continued)

Table 2.2 Project procedures (*Continued*)

Steps	Teachers/researchers	Children
	Listening to students' discussions in the designing process	*Creating* a storyboard for an oral presentation
	Making sure that students are on track	
Step 4: Presenting game task designs and conducting peer evaluation	*Listening* to students' presentation at the back of the classroom	*Presenting* their game task plan while *using* a storyboard and *answering* questions from their peers
	Clarifying the objectives and procedures for peer- and self-assessment	*Conducting* written peer- and self-assessment based on the criteria that they came up with (i.e. the extent to which their peers' or own designs incorporated motivation and learning elements that they identified) and making open-ended comments
		(After the class) *Writing* a short description *reflecting* their experience of participating in the project
	(After Step 4) Quantitatively and qualitatively *analyzing* students' interactions (videotaped), idea sheets, presented game-task plans, and peer- and self-evaluations.	
	(After Step 4) *Developing* a digital game, incorporating major elements identified by the students, their game plans and evaluation	
Step 5: Evaluating the game (by the fifth graders)		*Learning* English words through the game and *evaluating* its effectiveness
	Analyzing the students' evaluation survey and game-playing behaviours (log-in information)	

Notes:
(a) In Japanese primary schools, students engage in various group activities (both academic and non-academic), and they are often seated in groups of 5 to 6. We did not organize groups specifically for this project; we used the existing groups, assuming that the students had already established working relationship within the group.
(b) The 35 words were ambulance, aquarium, astronaut, caterpillar, comet, composer, conductor, cymbals, desert, dessert, dragonfly, firefly, floor, flour, jellyfish, librarian, lightning, owl, rectangle, refrigerator, rhinoceros, scale, sea lion, skyscraper, sleeping car, slide, sparrow, swallow, traffic light, triangle, tricycle, unicycle, vending machine, xylophone and wheelchair.

the students' first language, Japanese. The sixth-grade students were informed that a digital game would be developed based on their designs and their peer- and self-evaluation results. In the following discussion, I focus only on the first four steps in the project due to space constraints.

Project results

As summarized in Figure 2.1 below, the children identified 16 game elements (the research team treated these as proxies for motivational elements) and eight learning elements, most of which highly overlap with elements discussed among researchers of gamification (e.g. Garris *et al.*, 2002) and vocabulary-learning strategies (e.g. Gu, 2005). This result suggests that the children had very sophisticated understandings or 'theories' about what would motivate their engagement in tasks and what would work well for foreign-language vocabulary learning. Based on the elements identified by the children, the researchers coded and analysed the elements that appeared in the children's game-task designs and their peer and self-evaluations. In Figure 2.1, the first number in parentheses indicates the number of game plans that incorporated the given element (out of 15 game plans altogether), and the second number indicates the frequency that the element was mentioned as being valued by the peers in their evaluation (multiple responses

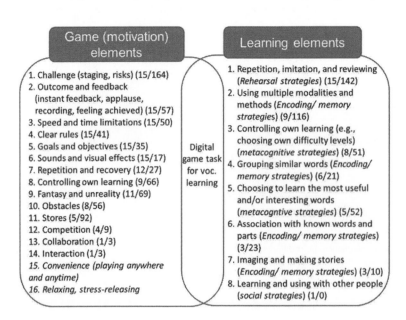

Figure 2.1 A digital game-task model based on motivation and learning elements identified by children

Note: With respect to the last two motivation elements in italics (#15 and 16), the research team was unable to judge whether they were incorporated into the students' game designs and evaluations. Adapted from Butler (2015: 97).

were allowed). Figure 2.1 shows that the children viewed challenges (e.g. staging by difficulty levels, and taking risks in order to complete tasks) and having control over their own learning (e.g. choosing the difficulty levels and types of targeted words for learning) as important.

In this participatory research project, the children contributed a number of insights that the researchers and teachers would not have otherwise taken note of. As I briefly describe below, their contributions provided us with opportunities to reflect on our own assumptions, which in turn can have great implications for curriculum development and teaching. (I describe only essential points here; please refer to Butler, 2015, 2017 and 2019, for more in-depth discussions.) First, while many adults may think that *repetition* is boring and tedious, the children tended to perceive it as enjoyable as long as it involved some variation and the children themselves were able to control it; specifically, they wanted to choose what to repeat, when to repeat it, and how to repeat it. This in fact corresponds well with the notion of *iteration* in complexity theory: a process in which 'the act of repeating results in a change to a procedure or system' (Larsen-Freeman, 2012: 202). Notably, however, the children's approach to repetition differed from a common form of repetition in language classrooms, where teachers ask their students to 'repeat after me.' In those cases, the students do not have much control over their repetition. Second, the children's designs revealed how important stories and fantasies are to children for their language learning. The children appeared to be motivated to learn foreign vocabulary in order to understand stories about topics of interest to them that are spoken or written in that language. Their curiosity about stories – accounts of characters with goals and actions – seemed to be their primary motivation rather than learning the language per se. This finding suggests that we should reconsider a frequent curricular task, in which curriculum designers or teachers identify words and grammatical forms in advance and create dialogues and texts that include pre-defined targeted words and forms. The children appeared to find this latter approach less exciting and less meaningful. Third, the children reminded us that people's motivation is indeed situated in social relations and cultural contexts. Their frequent discussions about how to allow learners to create cool-looking avatars as a reward for their learning illustrate this point well. Social perception and peer pressure seemed to be strong motivational elements – much stronger than the researchers and the teachers had anticipated. And finally, the children frequently incorporated 'unexpected' or 'accidental' elements in their designs – such as the players' vehicles suddenly breaking down – and placed a great deal of value on these elements. The unexpected elements were not identified initially, perhaps because the adult-made example games that the students played in Step 1 did not contain such elements. The children's discussions revealed that the reason for creating such nonlinear relationships between a player's learning of vocabulary and the game score was to motivate learners;

in other words, it would make the game more exciting and fun for everybody, including for students who may not be good at English, because they would still have a chance to win the game. From a teaching perspective, rewards should be used to motivate achievement in student learning. But the children's use of rewards in their designs tells us that such linearity would not be necessary to motivate learners intrinsically.

Next, the research team evaluated whether the research project supported active and interactive learning. The content of students' whole-class and group discussions, idea sheets, oral presentations, self- and peer-evaluations, and reflection notes collectively indicated that the participatory research project provided the students with experiences that were aligned well with the objectives of active and interactive learning as defined by the national curriculum in Japan, namely: (a) to think about and discuss their own language learning with their peers; (b) to work with peers to develop digital game tasks based on their knowledge and experience with computer games (i.e. their expertise); (c) to reflect on their learning; (d) to take different perspectives (developing game-task ideas while consider the perspectives of designers and younger learners [fifth graders']); (e) to present their ideas using multiple means (e.g. storyboards, oral presentations and discussions, reflection notes); and (f) to feel a sense of control and accomplishment. The students' reflection notes, which they prepared after completing the project, indicate their positive attitudes toward the experience. For example (see Butler, 2019: 86 for more examples):

> I think it was very important to discuss games using storyboards. By drawing storyboards, we could build up with better ideas. It was easier to exchange opinions because we had a chance to think about game elements in the first class.

> I felt a sense of accomplishment even though it was a small game and we designed it in a short period of time. I realize that it is important to design games that both designers and users can enjoy.

The students actively and seriously engaged in peer and self-evaluation (e.g. open-ended comments were completely filled out by every single child). This might be partially due to the fact that the children themselves came up with the evaluation criteria through discussions in advance. Moreover, the purpose of evaluation was clear to the students (i.e. to decide the best design).

Issues that Emerged

While the project achieved our original overall goal (i.e. eliciting the students' views on motivational and learning elements in digital game tasks through an active- and interactive-learning format), the research team members were left with a number of unresolved issues. Next, I discuss three major issues that we encountered at the intersection of research and practice: issues regarding (a) adults' assistance and facilitation, (b) reflection and evaluation and (c) individual differences.

Adults' assistance and facilitation

The first issue concerns the necessity of adult assistance in children's active learning in class (a pedagogical point) and how that assistance influences research outcomes (a research point) – and how these two issues converge in child participatory research. From the pedagogical point of view, because the format of group work itself does not guarantee effective learning (i.e. students may not necessarily engage in critical and analytical thinking in the group), teachers should consider acting as facilitators in active learning to assist students in deeper discussions (e.g. Rotgans & Schmidt, 2010). However, what the exact role of teachers as facilitators entails is unclear.

In our project, both the teachers and researchers walked around the classroom during group discussions and 'facilitated' the students' discussions. It turned out that the students were generally good at generating ideas, but they had a hard time analysing, organizing, and evaluating those ideas and developing them into a design as a group. Most of their ideas came from their daily experiences, commercial game-playing experiences in particular, and the students tended to have difficulty in thinking about applying them to a new purposeful context, namely, language learning. The idea sheet was designed to navigate students through the following steps: (a) generate various ideas for the content of the game; (b) compare the generated ideas and achieve consensus on the content of the game; and (c) decide which motivation and learning elements to incorporate into the game content and how to include them. The students needed particular help in the second and the third steps. These steps were very complicated processes because they required not only critical and analytical thinking but also social skills for dealing with various power relations associated with the decision-making process. We, the teachers and the researchers, struggled to identify the extent to which our involvement would 'facilitate' but not interfere with students' cognitive processes due to power dynamics. Even a teacher's brief affirmative comment on a student's idea, such as 'that sounds like a great idea,' has the potential to hinder the generation of other ideas and/or force other children to agree with the idea. Additionally, the children's group discussions often went 'off-track,' but it was not always easy to decide what should be considered 'off-track' and determine when and how to pull students back to 'on-track' discussions. Seemingly 'off-track' talks can potentially lead to a meaningful idea. Indeed, in this project, one group's seemingly off-track conversation about an expensive condominium that had recently been built near the school eventually served as the basis for the group's game design – specifically, a game involving city planning.

Power relations between children and adults and among children greatly influence the quality of interaction and, eventually, the outcome of the group work. This is a pedagogical concern as well. In the present project, for example, a group in which boys and girls could not agree on an idea ended up merging two game concepts into a single design, which they named 'Adventure or Cooking.' In addition to the various power relations that students bring with them into the classroom, power relations can be manifested or altered in a particular group-work context. Again, it appeared to be indispensable for teachers to make sure that power imbalances did not hinder students' interactive learning and to create contexts where the students could achieve what Cummins called 'collaborative creation of power' – namely, an environment where 'the more empowered one individual or group becomes, the more is generated for others to share' (2009: 263).

Teachers' roles as facilitators also posed a dilemma for the researchers. From the research point of view, this is potentially problematic because we wanted to elicit and understand the children's authentic views with as little adult involvement as possible. As mentioned, the adults' 'facilitation' could potentially alter the children's thinking. What makes the matter more complicated is that although developing autonomy is one of the primary goals for active and interactive learning as specified by MEXT, learner autonomy can be conceptualized differently depending on the context; as such, the concept of learner autonomy needs to be defined in particular contexts. Among SLA researchers, Holec's cognitive-based definition of learner autonomy – 'the ability to take charge of one's own learning' (1981: 3) – is widely accepted. However, researchers in East Asia have observed 'various manifestations of autonomy' (Murray, 2014: 242), suggesting a more socially oriented notion of autonomy than the conventional cognitive-based understanding. Indeed, Littlewood (1999), based on his long time teaching experience in East Asia, distinguished between *proactive autonomy* and *reactive autonomy*, the latter of which can be achieved through interdependency and collaboration, often through tasks and procedures initially set by the teachers. In other words, greater teacher involvement may be expected to achieve the goal of learner autonomy through active and interactive learning in Japan, and the research itself, if it is to be conducted as active and interactive learning, has to be situated in this specific context in order to meet local cultural and educational expectations. And this has to be achieved while negotiating various power relations among learners, teachers, and researchers. In our project, for example, the lesson plans and activities were prepared and presented initially by the adults (the teachers and researchers) because we believe this was expected in the Japanese context. However, one could argue that the elicited data might not reflect the children's 'authentic' voices or 'autonomous' behaviours because the activities were set up by these adults without any direct involvement by the children. Alternatively, as some researchers (e.g. Komulainen, 2007; Spyrou, 2011, 2016) argue, there may be no such thing as children's authentic voice in the first place; children's voice is socially constructed and, as a result, children speak with different voices depending on social contexts.

All of these issues make it clear that researchers need a theoretical framework for conceptualizing adults' involvements in children's participatory research. Depending on the epistemological traditions and kinds of questions that researchers formulate, it could be extremely difficult to theoretically consolidate various roles that both children and adults play in research. Moreover, pedagogically speaking, the research project should not merely be a one-shot event for children. Even if it is conducted over a short period of time, it needs to be meaningfully situated in the students' broader long-term learning. Researchers should reflect on how research participation contributes to children's successive learning and, when feasible, even follow up with the children to get their insights. Such pedagogical perspectives may need to be incorporated as part of the validity of research with children; research would not be sufficiently meaningful otherwise.

Reflection and evaluation

The second issue emerging from this project concerns the role of reflection in research with children. Reflection is considered critical for learning at school, which in turn promotes learners' autonomy (MEXT, 2017). Therefore, monitoring and fostering children's reflection was an important goal of our project, both in terms of pedagogy and research. In the process of figuring out how best to promote reflection, however, we encountered a number of difficulties.

With respect to pedagogy, similar to the first issue addressed above, the role of adults' involvement in the children's reflective processes was complicated. Developmental studies have observed some changes in children's self-reflective abilities sometime around their middle- to upper-primary school years, but 'the development of reflective abilities does not refer to the naturally occurring process' (Zuckerman, 2004: 10). In other words, social interaction and guidance are indispensable in order for children to develop self-reflective abilities, and education has to support these processes consistently and systematically. In our project, we provided the children with various opportunities to reflect on their actions and thoughts (e.g. thinking about their own game-playing behaviours in Step 1; discussing how they learned English words in Step 2; using an idea sheet to make their thinking process visible in Step 3; conducting self- and peer-assessments of their task designs in Step 4; and writing reflective notes at the end of the project). Nonetheless, we found it very challenging to systematically support the children's reflective abilities and monitor them in various steps, especially their reflections on the *process* of learning. Verbalizing one's own reflections is not always easy for adults much less children. Even though the participating children were occasionally asked to write reflective notes on various school activities (due to MEXT's curriculum requirement), it was hard to detect from their notes the extent to which meaningful reflection was indeed taking place. The children's reflection notes certainly gave us some information about their holistic reflections on the *outcome* of the project, as the preceding examples indicate, but not on the *process*. Similarly, children's discourse in interaction can provide only a partial picture of their reflective processes. Among primary school children, as Zuckerman observed, their seemingly unreflective discourse 'can considerably boost their reflective development and build up the capacity to look at the heart of their thoughts and actions' (2002: 13). Namely, researchers cannot fully access children's self-reflective processes through children's verbal discourse. As a result, it was even more challenging to guide the children's reflection so that it led to improved subsequent actions.

On the research side, we also found it challenging to conceptualize the role of reflection in our research. Since we wanted our project to be a mutual learning opportunity for all participants, reflection was considered important for the teachers and researchers as well as for the children. The role of researchers' reflection in research has been a heated topic in research literature. Those who value an 'objective stance' as central to research may not see a place for reflection or subjectivity in research. Burns (2011) stated that reflectivity or subjectivity is a problem for both positivist and interpretive research traditions and advocated action research that rejects the notion of researchers' objectivity.

My own view on this issue is that research with children – specifically, research viewing children as social actors or co-researchers – does not need to exclude positivist or interpretive research. It seems likely that any research with children has to create some space for reflection by all participants (children, researchers and teachers). Even the most controlled positivist research cannot be completely free of the researchers' reflections and subjectivity; after all, positivist researchers make various kinds of decisions in their studies. In this respect, there is always room for any type of research to create space for reflection. Of course, one's research tradition will influence how one conceptualizes reflection and theorizes its role. But no matter what shape that theorization of reflection ultimately takes, it appears to be indispensable for those who would like to conduct research with children.

Individual differences

The third issue concerns individual differences among participants. Active and interactive learning may not work best for everybody. The effectiveness of these approaches may depend on the content and the context of learning. Similarly, we cannot blindly assume that all children who grow up with technology are interested in learning through digital games or other digital approaches and devices. Participants may also respond to participatory research differently.

In our project, both teachers and children showed varying degrees of participation. Thus, determining how to respond to individual differences in preferred learning styles and interests was both a theoretical and pedagogical challenge. In SLA, researchers often naively assume that participants' responses (both quantitative and qualitative responses) are a reflection of their abilities. Missing responses in tasks and instruments, for example, are usually thought to be due to a lack of knowledge or ability rather than a lack of interest by the individual or even a mismatch between tasks and instruments. SLA researchers, including myself, have rarely investigated the reasons for individual participants' missing responses. In reality, however, various types of individual differences appear to greatly influence responses (including lack of response). This may be particularly important when it comes to researching with children, who may have greater variability in terms of coping well with the researchers' intention.

Despite the strong promotion of active and interactive learning by Japanese educational policies, the effectiveness of these approaches has been subject to heated debate – especially when the policies are used with primary school children who may not yet have acquired basic knowledge and skills to apply to active learning and interactive learning. Of particular concern among educators in Japan is the possibility of varying levels of effectiveness of active and interactive learning according to students' socio-economic status (SES), or more precisely their social and cultural capital. Examining the results of the nationwide academic achievement test released in 2017 by MEXT in Japan, Saito (2017) suggested a possible difference in the effect of active learning by students' SES. In schools that frequently implemented active learning, students' average scores were higher among high SES schools than low SES schools. SES level, however, did not appear to be a factor in academic achievement among students whose schools did not employ active learning. Saito speculated that students with higher SES backgrounds, due to their greater access to cultural capital (e.g. having more conversations about social issues at home, having more books at home), benefited more from active-learning methods. There are a number of potential factors responsible for the students' academic achievement, and Saito's analysis did not directly prove the differential effects of active learning by SES. However, if his observations prove to be true, additional consideration would be necessary to assist students who may not cope well with this type of learning. A contextualized needs analysis may be useful for researchers and teachers before planning a study.

Individual differences in content knowledge and experience, as well as in personality and communication style, also matter greatly in children's participatory research. In our project, we observed that the participating students differed in terms of their knowledge and experience as well as their interests in digital games, which in turn seemed to influence how they engaged in group work. However, we need to remind ourselves that seemingly less-engaged behaviours, such as being silent, do not necessarily indicate a lack of learning or motivation. The influence of the children's personality and communication styles appeared to be more complicated. For example, a student who hardly expressed her opinion turned out to be good at eliciting other people's opinions. The relationship between students' engagement styles and their actual learning is not yet well understood. To optimize positive learning experiences among children (a pedagogical concern) as well as to generate meaningful information from students (a research concern), the role of teachers who know their individual students' characteristics cannot be understated.

Not too surprisingly, individual differences were also observed among participating teachers. Since the present research was conducted as a school-wide project, all the teachers at the focus grade levels (grades 5 and 6) participated in the project. Some teachers more willingly engaged in project-related conversations with the students, sometimes even outside of class. The teachers differed in their attitudes toward participatory research and their perceptions of their own roles and the roles of the researchers. Some teachers made suggestions more openly at various stages of the research project, while others were more receptive to suggestions made by researchers. The teachers' initial notions of 'child-centred pedagogy' and the role of teachers in active learning appeared to be different as well. One could argue that these teachers' attitudes and beliefs about research and teaching, their understanding of the research content, and their knowledge about their students are all relevant to research validity concerns (even outside of the action research tradition). But we need more discussions about how to systematically incorporate such information into a theoretical framework for research validity.

Conclusions

Despite the growing interest in research with children, the field of SLA has not yet sufficiently addressed a series of methodological and ethical concerns associated with this area of study. While SLA research findings may be potentially beneficial for children in a general sense, participants often do not directly benefit from participating in research. In light of this situation, in this chapter I attempted to implement a more ethical approach to working with children in research, in that the children would directly benefit from their participation in the study. I discussed the possibility of conducting research in a formal school setting that can deliberately serve as an active- and interactive-learning opportunity for participating children. Reflecting on my own work on a children's digital game-design project that I recently conducted in Japan, I discussed a number of affordances as well as unresolved issues that emerged from the project.

As researchers, we tend to perceive power relations according to the socially defined roles of the participants (i.e. researchers, teachers and students) and treat those relations as static. In this project, however, we considered that the 'real' functions of researching, teaching, and learning should be subject to constant shifts and changes in response to dynamic and fluid power relations among researchers, teachers, and students; otherwise mutual learning among all the participants would not be possible. While we see this more dynamic approach as having great merit, it also poses a number of practical and theoretical challenges, as I outlined above. Our practical/pedagogical concerns – how to facilitate children's active and interactive learning, how to assist and monitor children's reflection, and how to deal with individual differences in their social, cognitive and interpersonal characteristics – indeed all turned into theoretical challenges in our participatory research with children; namely, we struggled with how to theorize the roles and influence of adults' facilitation, participants' reflections and individuals' differences. Fluidity and dynamicity of participants' roles make theorization extremely challenging.

We have just started our journey in search of better conceptualization and execution of research with children in SLA. In research with children in school contexts, pedagogical concerns cannot be separated from research concerns. Research for the sake of research is not only ethically problematic, but it also closes off opportunities to benefit from the unique knowledge and experiences that children and their teachers can bring to the research. There is no question that negotiating power relations with and among participants is complicated, but if we do not collaborate with participants, our research cannot be sufficiently and appropriately contextualized. And it is only when research is properly contextualized that it can be meaningful.

References

Bonwell, C.C. and Eison, J.A. (1991) *Active learning: Creating excitement in the classroom.* (ASHE-ERIC Higher Education Report No. 1.) Washington, DC: The George Washington University School of Education and Human Development.

Burns, A. (2011) Action research in the fields of second language teaching and learning. In E. Hinkel (ed.) *Handbook of Research in Second Language Teaching and Learning, Vol. II* (pp. 237–253). New York: Routledge.

Butler, Y.G. (2015) The use of computer games as foreign language learning tasks for digital natives. *System* 54, 91–102.

Butler, Y.G. (2017) Motivational elements of digital instructional games: A study of young L2 learners' game designs. *Language Teaching Research* 21 (6), 735–750.

Butler, Y.G. (2019) Inviting children's views for designing digital game tasks. In H. Reinders, S. Ryan and S. Nakamura (eds) *Innovation in Language Learning and Teaching: The Case of Japan* (pp. 71–96). New York: Palgrave Macmillan.

Carreira, J.M. (2006) Motivation for learning English as a foreign language in Japanese elementary schools. *JALT Journal* 28 (2), 135–158.

Christensen, P. and James, A. (2017) Introduction: Researching children and childhood: Cultures of communication. In P. Christensen and A. James (eds) *Research with Children: Perspectives and Practices* (3rd edn) (pp. 1–10). London: Routledge.

Christensen, P. and Prout, A. (2002) Working with ethical symmetry in social research with children. *Childhood* 9 (4), 477–497.

Cummins, J. (2009) Pedagogies of choice: Challenging coercive relations of power in classrooms and communities. *International Journal of Bilingual Education and Bilingualism* 12 (3), 261–271.

Fargas-Malet, M., McSherry, D., Larkin, E. and Robinson, C. (2010) Research with children: Methodological issues and innovative techniques. *Journal of Early Childhood Research* 8 (2), 175–192.

Gallagher, M. (2008) 'Power is not an evil': Rethinking power in participatory methods. *Children's Geographies* 6 (2), 137–150.

Garris, R., Ahlers, R. and Driskell, J.E. (2002) Games, motivation, and learning: A research and practice model. *Simulation and Gaming* 33, 441–467.

Gu, Y. (2005) *Vocabulary Learning Strategies in the Chinese EFL Context.* Singapore: Marshall Cavendish Academic.

Holec, H. (1981) *Autonomy in Foreign Language Learning.* Oxford: Pergamon.

Horgan, D. (2016) Child participatory research methods: Attempts to go 'deeper'. *Childhood* 24 (2), 245–259.

Komulainen, S. (2007) The ambiguity of the child's 'voice' in social research. *Childhood* 14 (1): 11–28.

Larsen-Freeman, D. (2012) On the roles of repetition in language teaching and learning. *Applied Linguistic Review* 3: 195–210.

Littlewood, W. (1999) Defining and developing autonomy in East Asian contexts. *Applied Linguistics* 20, 71–94.

Livingstone, S. and Blum-Ross, A. (2017) Researching children and childhood in the digital age. In P. Christensen and A. James (eds) *Research with Children: Perspectives and Practices* (pp. 54–70). New York: Routledge.

Mandell, N. (1988) The least-adult role in studying children. *Journal of Contemporary Ethnography* 16 (4), 433–467.

MEXT (2017) Shingakushu shidou yoryo [New Course of Study]. See http://www.mext.go.jp/a_menu/shotou/new-cs/1383986.htm (accessed 18 December 2018).

MEXT (n. d.) Sogotekina gakushu-no jikan-no seika-to kadai, omona iken [Positive outcomes and challenges of the Integrated Study Periods, major opinions]. See http://www.mext.go.jp/b_menu/shingi/chukyo/chukyo6/gijiroku/attach/1379547.htm (accessed 18 December 2018).

Mizuguchi, H. (2015) Sogoteki-na gakushu-no jikan-no yukue [The outcome of the period for integrated study]. *Kyoiku Kenkyu [Educational Studies]* 57, 35–45.

Murray, G. (ed.) (2014) *Social Dimensions of Autonomy in Language Learning.* London: Palgrave Macmillan.

O'Kane, C. (2017) Participatory research on kinship care in East Africa. In P. Christensen and A. James (eds) *Research with Children: Perspectives and Practices* (pp. 180–202). New York: Routledge.

Pinter, A. (2014) Child participant roles in applied linguistics research. *Applied Linguistics* 35 (2), 168–183.

Prensky, M. (2001) *Digital Game-based Learning.* New York: McGraw-Hill.

Prince, M. (2004) Does active learning work? A review of the research. *Journal of Engineering Education* 93 (3), 223–231.

Raffety, E.L. (2014) Minimizing social distance: Participatory research with children. *Childhood* 22 (3), 409–422.

Reinders, H. (ed.) (2012) *Digital Games in Language Learning and Teaching.* London: Palgrave Macmillan.

Rotgans, J.I. and Schmidt, H.G. (2010) The role of teachers in facilitating situational interest in an active-learning classroom. *Teaching and Teacher Education* 27 (1), 37–42.

Saito, T. (2017) *Active learning-wa gakuryoku-no keizaikakusa-o hirogeru?* [Does active-learning widen the economic achievement gaps]?. See http://benesse.jp/kyo-uiku/201710/20171023-1.html (accessed 20 December 2018).

Spyrou, S. (2011) The limits of children's voices: From authenticity to critical, reflective representation. *Childhood* 18 (2), 151–165.

Spyrou, S. (2016) Researching children's silences: Exploring the fullness of voice in childhood research. *Childhood* 23 (1), 7–21.

Yamada-Rice, D. (2017) Using visual and digital research methods with young children. In P. Christensen and A. James (eds) *Research with Children: Perspectives and Practices* (pp. 71–86). New York: Routledge.

Zuckerman, G. (2004) Development of reflection through learning activity. *European Journal of Psychology of Education* 19 (1), 9–18.

3 Constructing Joint Understandings of Research with Children

Samaneh Zandian

Introduction

The 1989 United Nations Convention on the Right of the Child highlighted children's rights to be considered as individuals whose voices needed to be heard. Consequently, researchers started seeing children as social actors who are able to talk about their experiences of, and perspectives on, the issues which concern them (Hood *et al.*, 1996; James *et al.*, 1998; Kustatscher, 2014; Pinter, 2014; Slepickova & Bartosova, 2014). This focus has also led to an increasing interest in developing appropriate methods to give voice to children (Greene & Hill, 2005; Matthews, 1998; Morrow, 1999; Pinter & Zandian, 2015). The particular social context of adult–child relationships, especially the unequal power dynamics that constitute these relationships require researchers' reflexivity and awareness (Davis *et al.*, 2000; James *et al.*, 1998). England (1994: 82) refers to reflexivity as 'the self-critical sympathetic introspection and the self-conscious analytical scrutiny of the self as researcher', which according to Barker and Weller (2003) can help in 'mapping the relationships between researcher and researched'. In this chapter, I draw on some ethical dilemmas concerning children's level of understanding of research through the practice of reflexivity. In particular, those related to my PhD research thesis, aimed at exploring how children aged 10–12 in Iran understood intercultural issues (see Zandian, 2015a). I first provide a brief overview of the project, and then focus on some of the methodological aspects and ethical issues which emerged from the follow-up sessions in-which I shared the initial findings of the study with the child participants. This latter approach was designed to explore the child participants post hoc interpretations of the research they participated in, and the discussions raised some ethical dilemmas which will be discussed in this chapter.

Overview of the Project

Recognizing the importance of fostering intercultural sensitivity and the need to introduce intercultural learning into the Iranian educational curricula, my PhD project aimed to explore how children, educated at primary level in Iran, make sense of/understand concepts such as intercultural interaction and adjustment. In this study, the child participants were asked to either reflect on their real intercultural experiences, or to imagine what it would be like to move to, and live, in another country. This project consisted of three phases: designing child-friendly research instruments, data collection, and sharing the data with the child participants.

Designing 'child-friendly' research instruments

Kellett (2010: 192) explains that 'children are party to the subculture of childhood which gives them a unique "insider" perspective critical to our understanding of their worlds'. At the beginning of my project three children (10 to 12 years of age) were invited to work with me separately and comment on my initial design of the research tools, and also to talk about the local children's needs, interests and preferred ways of engaging in research. This fitted with my belief that it is ethical to include children in the process of research design, and fulfilled the aim of making the research more inclusive. In these initial sessions, these child helpers commented on my proposed content and format of the research instruments (both the questionnaire and the group interviews which are describe later in this chapter). Their suggestions helped me modify the wording and layout of the questionnaire and the participatory activities. These sessions were ideal opportunities to obtain insider perspectives from the children. In their role as consultants, these child helpers also volunteered advice that I did not even request. For instance, one of the children was from the same school that the actual data collection was going to take place, and she advised me on the available and preferred spaces to conduct research and suggested whom from the staff to contact about this matter.

The children involved in this part were willing and enthusiastic to help and seemingly enjoyed the job of helping. Negotiating with children about the content and format of the research instruments was an attempt to reduce the adult's predictions/interpretations of children's preferences and needs, and facilitate the child research participants' engagement in the project. For more detail on this part of the research see Zandian (2015a).

Rapport building and reassuring participants' understanding of research

According to Morrow and Richards (1996: 98), 'the biggest ethical challenge for researchers working with children is the disparity in power and status between adults and children'. In order to redress the power imbalance, I visited all five schools several times before starting the data collection, to introduce myself, talk to the children during their breaks and establish a good relationship with them. In order not to resemble staff, I sat on the ground or a bench and had my own snacks during the breaks. During the second or third break, a couple of students approached me and asked: 'Miss, which grade's teacher are you?' I used this opportunity to explain that I was not a teacher and I was only a student who needed their help for my study. Following the advice of the child helpers, I introduced myself as a university student rather than a teacher so that students would trust me more readily. Some of the students offered me their snacks (which I believe was a good sign of friendship), some asked my name and gradually I could gain their trust. After a week, many of the students greeted me with a smile and sometimes gave me a hug; some even called me 'Miss university student'. Before starting the data collection, I took some time to explicitly discuss the participants' expectations of what was going to happen in my research sessions. I also encouraged spontaneous comments, questions, discussions and other child-initiated comments, and emphasized that there were no right and wrong answers, and any comment was appreciated. During the data collection, I reminded the children that their participation was voluntary and kept checking whether they were still willing to take part in the research.

Data collection

The data collection was conducted in the participants' mother tongue, Persian, and via the administration of 294 'child-friendly' questionnaires and conducting five group interviews with 27 students in five primary schools in Tehran (see Pinter & Zandian, 2017; Zandian, 2015a). The questionnaire was divided into two sections where the first part focused on children's perceptions of cross-cultural transitions and adjustment, and the second part investigated their understandings of intercultural interaction from the viewpoint of members of the host society.

Although the questionnaire was carefully designed to engage children and encourage them to express their feelings and opinions through activities like drawing, it was still difficult to gain comprehensive data about the participants' perspectives via the questionnaire alone. To obtain more in-depth data, I conducted semi-structured group interviews using participatory activities. The interview was in the format of two participatory activities, which addressed a set of specific questions, but in a more creative manner. In both activities children first worked in pairs, then the pairs were asked to compare their work with another pair and explain their decisions. In the first activity, I wanted to explore children's worries and excitement about the transition to a new context. Hence, I invited pairs to name their main concerns and excitement about moving to

Figure 3.1 Hopes-&-Worries activity: the overall format of the instrument

another country (see Figure 3.1). Then, groups observed each other's work and commented about it.

In the second activity, I wanted to explore children's views about the most helpful factors in managing the transition to a new sociocultural environment. To explore this, I gave one diamond shaped cardboard and sentences written on separate Post-Its to each pair. I invited the participants to place the Post-Its on the diamond, with 'the most helpful' at the top, the 'least helpful' at the bottom (see Figure 3.2). Then, I asked the two groups to compare their work and explain their decisions.

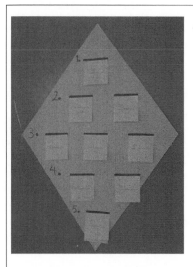

- *You are going to live in a country for a year, which one of these things could help you fit in more easily? Please Rank these ideas.*

Knowing the language
Having friendly neighbours and classmates
Knowing someone there
Being friendly and having a big smile
Having a pet
Being a good student
Being in contact with your friends in your home town
Knowing about the new place
Being good at games
Being with your family

Figure 3.2 Diamond ranking: the overall format of the instrument

There is no space here to discuss the results in detail, but in a nut-shell, children in this study expressed ambivalent feelings about experiencing intercultural encounters. Schooling, friendship and language were found to be the key influential elements in their understanding of intercultural interaction and adjustment. These three elements are related to one another. My findings contributed towards developing a model of cross-cultural adaptation which incorporates children's views about cross-cultural adjustment in a more comprehensive way. The findings also highlighted the importance of intercultural awareness in language education, which has far-reaching implications for English language teachers in Iran, such as a need to create opportunities for intercultural learning in language classrooms via introducing games and folk stories and immigrant literature from around the world (Zandian, 2015b), and establishing collaboration with international students who live in Iran.

Ethical Issues in School-based Participatory Research

Throughout the study I faced many ethical dilemmas, such as how to include children more actively in the research design, how to fulfil the expectations of the local schools and whom to include in the study, but for the purposes of this paper I am focusing on issues centred around the researcher's ethical responsibility to return to the children after data collection, which has been emphasised in the literature around research with children (Alderson, 2000; Grover, 2004; Kostenius & Öhrling, 2006; Lundy, 2007; Matthews & Tucker, 2000; Pinter & Zandian, 2015). Hence, in the following section, I focus on the third phase of the study, when I revisited some of the child participants of the data collection phase to share the initial findings of the study with them. I will also discuss the ethical and methodological issues which arose during this visit.

Sharing the findings with child participants

Having the ethical concern that it is the children's right to be informed about the findings of the study (Grover, 2004; Mann, 2016; Matthews & Tucker, 2000; Pinter & Zandian, 2015) and aiming to promote children's understanding of the research process, I carried out follow-up sessions with some of the child participants of the study, approximately four months after the data collection had been completed. In these sessions, the children and I reflected on the process of the research, focusing on their experiences as research participants.

When I visited the schools after four months, the children who took part in the data collection remembered me well and welcomed me back warmly. I intended to share parts of the transcribed interview data and explain to them how their contribution would shape my PhD thesis. I also wanted to explore how they remembered their role in my research. I started each session with a brief greeting and explaining the purpose of the session, reassuring them about their voluntary participation and reiterating the anonymity and confidentiality of the data. I also encouraged spontaneous comments, questions and discussions. Overall, children seemed relaxed and talkative from the very beginning of the sessions.

In total, I carried out four follow-up sessions in four schools. First, I invited participants to use drama activities to re-create the setting of the participatory interviews. One of the participants acted as the researcher (me), while the rest were playing their own roles as the child participants. By inviting children to do this task, I wanted to explore what exactly the participants could recall from their first experience of being part of a research project. This activity was also used as an ice-breaker to give the floor to the children and encourage them to express themselves. Rather than relying on verbal recall, drama, which is a creative medium of expression, was used to obtain rich data.

After the role-play, I displayed a poster in which the different phases of the research were listed (see Figure 3.3), and encouraged the participants to comment about the data collection phase (questionnaire and interview). I wanted the participants to reflect on what they remembered and what stood out, in order to get a better understanding of how they perceived the research.

Since my PhD thesis was not ready yet, I showed them my Master's dissertation, which presented findings from a small-scale research study with another group of child participants, so that they could see what the outcome of a project would look like. At the same time, anticipating that the dissertation may not be interesting for them, I made a large poster,

Figure 3.3 Poster of the research process

Figure 3.4 Poster showing the transcriptions

which illustrated how I matched the children's interview extracts to ideas in the wider literature about cross-cultural adaptation (see Figure 3.4).

Although children welcomed me back and asked for more questionnaires and interviews, despite my attempt at this time and previously (four months earlier) to refer to these as research activities and as such different from learning tasks and even tests, some children continued to talk about them as classroom teaching activities nonetheless. This might be due to the lack of research culture and practice in the Iranian education system or just the fact that the original research happened in the school, so children associated it with classroom activities. Moreover, most of the participants had never had the experience (before my project) of actively taking part in any research and this was still a new concept for them.

Overall, the follow-up sessions created a space where children asked me a series of spontaneous questions regarding the different aspects of research, and this initiated a discussion between me as the researcher and the participants. In the following section, I will present and discuss the findings of the discussion with the children about the purpose and procedure of the research.

Children's understanding of research

In preparation for the dramatization, the participants were encouraged to reflect on what they did four months earlier, and to describe anything they could recall from the session. In the extract below, Bloom, Sara and Nilou (all names in this study are pseudonyms chosen by the participants) together describe what they remember from the participatory interview. The words in brackets [ ] are not actually spoken by the participants, but added for clarification.

Extract 1

Bloom	I think first you came to us and had a chat with us … and we got excited, then we got into groups, and chose new names.
Researcher	Yeah, then you were divided into two groups, each group worked separately. Then, groups looked at each other's work. What happened next?
Bloom	Then, I commented about their … [work]
Sara	Then you said, let's look at each other's work together. Then you asked us why we have chosen these answers. anddddd
Nilou	You asked our opinions, then about our reasons for them, um then we started another activity.

These children remembered the research activities as being lots of fun, and they could recall that everyone was asked to choose pseudonyms. They also mentioned the activities they remembered and commented on being part of a group and sharing and explaining their opinions.

Children perceived research as a school task

Many of the participants assumed that the participatory activities in the interviews were mainly aimed at helping them to learn something new. The extract below is an example from the follow-up sessions to illustrate this.

Extract 2

Noura	I think the aim was that.. um we learn about our worries and excitements in another country. To learn about the differences between countries.. then to learn about the most.. the most and the least important things there.
Emilie	Um, the questions were really good, because others also learnt about our opinions. Now I think I am a complete girl who is ready for a journey.
Lavagirl	I think all these were to help us learn about our feelings. To compare our feelings with one another. For example or see that all the girls in this age prefer something rather another thing.

Again, this extract illustrates that according to the children the research project was about learning. This kind of assumption is linked to the main purpose of schools; that is, with learning and teaching. It is also possible that they are hinting at 'awareness raising' rather than learning but just have not got the right words for it. In fact, at the pedagogical level, one of the aims of this study was to raise awareness and curiosity among the participants about intercultural interaction; however, the central focus of the questionnaire and the interviews was to obtain children's viewpoints about intercultural issues. This brings to attention an important and interesting point about the pedagogical versus the research level aims of such projects, which can overlap, particularly in educational settings (see also Butler in this volume).

The methodological issue here is related to the challenge of collecting data from children in schools. How can we get the message across to the child participants that despite the fact that they are at school, they are being asked to be the 'experts', and they can be involved in a research project whereby an adult aims to learn from their views, rather than teach something to them? Or looking at it from a different angle, is it ethical to use the school time to conduct research, which although indirectly aims to contribute to the students education, does not purely focus on their immediate learning goals?

Evaluation

Despite the fact that I had explained throughout the project that there were no right or wrong answers (e.g. see Figure 3.5), in the follow-up session, it was revealed that many of the participants initially assumed that they were going to be assessed one way or another as part of my project/intervention.

> Remember, this is NOT a test. There is no right and wrong answer. Please read each question carefully and put an **X** in the box according to your own idea, you may have to choose which answer is closest to your feelings. If you have another idea, write your answer on the line next to the option 'Other'.
>
> Are you ready? Let's go!

Figure 3.5 Part of the first page of the questionnaire

The extract below is an example to illustrate that many of the participants assumed they were going to be assessed by the questionnaire.

Extract 3

Isabel	I didn't really think [it was a questionnaire].. I thought it was an exam, an English test.. I told my mom, I'm not sure if I want to do it. I was not sure.. Um, until I saw that it's like this.. then I found it very interesting.

During the administration of the questionnaire, I explained to the participants on several occasions that they did not need to write their names on the questionnaire and I would not be able to identify them as individuals. I also emphasised that the questionnaire was not designed for evaluative purposes. This information was also printed on the cover of the questionnaire which I designed in the format of a booklet to be different from exam papers. Interestingly, although I clearly stated that the questionnaire was in Persian, the participants' mother tongue, some students, like Isabel in Extract 3, assumed that it was still going to be an English language test. This could be because the information sheet and consent forms were given to the students during their English class. Similarly, Extract 4 illustrates that children's initial understanding of the group interviews was also entangled with a concern about being assessed or evaluated.

Extract 4

Sara	I thought you would do the similar activities with more children, like the questions you asked, and then you would compare them with ours and um like you would say they are better than us
	(...)
Isabel	Um.. I thought you were asking us to do these.. and if we do it well, like if we respond in a way.. like.. I thought there was a correct 'answer' in your mind
Researcher	There is no answer in my mind. Now you know that? What I want to know is what you think. Your opinion is very important to me.

In Extract 4, Sara explains that she assumed their input was going to be evaluated and compared with that of other participants, which is very similar to what happens in norm-referenced testing. Similar to Sara, Isabel also thought that I was looking for specific responses. In the classroom context, teachers generally do expect specific responses to the questions they ask. Since these children were socialized into certain discourse patterns; they were used to closed questions with correct answers.

The extracts above highlight an important ethical issue about research with young people. Since students are used to being assessed in different ways at school, it is not always easy to convince them that they would not be evaluated on their input in a research project. This raises questions about how much children understand about the research when they sign up for it. Can the adult ever be sure that the children understand what will happen in the project and why? This raises a methodological questions such as if children think they will be evaluated through participation in research, how might that influence their participation? These are important ethical and methodological issues which researchers have to be aware of and deal with when working with children. As Kuchah and Pinter point out in Chapter 1 of this volume, if we are doing research with children, it is important to consider their school experiences and local cultures in deciding about how to explain the research purpose and how to conduct the research itself.

Children's Perceived Role in Research

In the final part of the follow-up session, the participants flipped through my MA dissertation to get familiar with the representation of a research study. They also read some extracts from the transcription of their own group interview, which I put on display as a poster (Figure 3.6) to show them the link between the related literature and their own comments. These transcripts were in Persian.

Figure 3.6 Poster of interview transcript and related literature

Extract 5 is an example of the participants' comments after they have seen how their input would be represented at the final stage.

Extract 5

Julia	I thought you would put a summary of our comments, for example the outcome of it.
	(…)
Lavagirl	I thought you would put parts of it. For example you would cut the um ..um bits and only put the important parts.

It seems that children assumed that whatever their role was it was only a very small/ insignificant role. Children's comments in the extract above match well with the previous findings about children's perceptions of their contribution in research (Pinter & Zandian, 2015). Similar to the findings of the study of Pinter and Zandian (2015: 243) about children's understanding of research procedure, 'children assume that the researcher's interpretations of their own words would automatically override what they had to say and how they said it'. This shows that children might have this general assumption that they may not be adequately knowledgeable even when the topic is related to their own lives; therefore, their input to the project requires rephrasing and modification before being represented in the final product (Pinter & Zandian, 2015).

In Extract 6, children express their excitement and satisfaction after realizing how their contribution to the research would be presented in the thesis.

Their comments also indicate that they saw me as a student with homework to do rather than a teacher or a member of staff. I assume this is mainly because I presented myself as a university student who needs children's help in completing her university work. And yet they seemed to move back and forth between different identities for me, sometimes a teacher/ member of staff and sometimes a student, trying to grasp my hybrid identity.

Extract 6

Lucy	Did you see how many pages that book [MA dissertation] was?!
	(...)
Sabrina	I think um ..I thought that maybe... it was a homework for you, as we have homework. it was a homework to do the questionnaire, ask some questions and make those games.. but I *NEVER* thought it's going to make a book out of it.

How we present ourselves in the research, and the impact this can have on the way child participants perceive us is another important ethical issue, which requires further consideration. In this project, I was a PhD student who needed the children's help in completing my study; however, this can become more complicated in other situations; for instance, when teachers conduct action research. It is important to acknowledge the potential overlaps between teachers' and researchers' roles and the impact this may have on the research procedure and the way children perceive adults' identities.

Extract 7 is another example to illustrate the excitement of the participants after they realized how their input would be represented in this research. Children's quotes in this extract illustrate their pride, ownership and a sense of accomplishment, which is in line with similar research with a group of primary students in the UK (Pinter & Zandian, 2015).

Extract 7

Ahmad	It's really cool!
Mr Lee	You mean really all I said will go in this [thesis]?
	(...)
Leon	Will you bring your thesis for us?
Researcher	Yes, I will bring one copy of it to the school.
Ahmad	Then our Miss will make copies for us?
Mr Lee	Is it one of those black cover ones?
Researcher	Yeah.
Mr Lee	WOW!
	(...)
Mr Lee	It' sooo good! Everyone will find out that it's us [in the thesis]
Researcher	No, not everyone.. your names are different here, so only you find out.
Mr Lee	It's Ok, Even this way is fine
Ahmad	Miss, can we change our names there?

Mr Lee's statement, 'Is it one of those black cover ones?' shows his familiarity with the common format of the thesis and his excitement about being part of one. Leon's question, 'Will you bring your thesis for us?', highlights the ethical responsibilities to children, which is to share the outcome of the research with the young participants and try to explore children's own interests and assumptions about research.

Another participant, Holly, asked an interesting question: 'In how many years [will you finish your work and bring it to us]?' This question touches upon the concept of time for children as the research participants. Three or four years of completing a PhD project may seem much longer for the child participants than for me as the researcher. This raises the question that although sharing the outcome of the research with child participants is our ethical responsibility, isn't the time between children's participation and sharing the outcome with them too long? Is it more appropriate/feasible to revisit the child participants as soon as the initial findings of the study are available, rather than waiting for the final outcome?

Children's understanding of research terminology

The discussion in the follow-up session revealed that children's understanding of the research was mainly limited to the data collection phase. In the extract below, children talk about their initial reaction when I first came along, in response to my question: 'What did you think research was going to be all about?' The children understood that research meant data collection. This is possibly due to the fact that at the beginning of the data collection phase, I mainly talked about their role in the research and emphasized on the ethical issues such as the voluntary nature of their participation, anonymity and confidentiality of the data, and did not talk much about the later stages of research.

Extract 8

Mr Lee	I thought it would be just doing these activities, things like this [referring to one of the participatory activities].
Leon	I thought you would just prepare a report for your thesis and leave
Milad	That's it, very easy and simple
Ahmad	Just asking for the children's opinions. Just that!

In Extract 8, Leon's comment refers to preparing a report about the data collection phase, which is only part of the research process. This extract highlights that since children are rarely involved in all the stages of a research project other than the data collection, they may naturally assume that the entire project is just devoted to data collection. This again shows the importance of sharing findings with children and explaining the stages of research to them. A question arises about how much information is enough to be shared with the child participants about the research procedure when their consent is obtained for participation? It is rather difficult to know the answer. This is also linked to the previously mentioned concern about how much children understand about the research when they sign up for it.

Transcription

Following suggestions by Matthews and Tucker (2000) and Pinter and Zandian (2015), I showed children examples of the transcriptions of their quotes from their own interviews. This was in the form of a poster (see Figure 3.6). Extract 9 portrays the fascination of the participants when they identified their own, or each other's, statements printed on the poster with links to ideas and references in the related literature.

Extract 9

Lavagirl	I thought that the 'ums'[filler] won't go in.. I talk like that, and I really liked that you kept our own way of talking.

Extract 10 also shows that some children believed that they would become famous after the publication of the data.

Extract 10

Sabrina	Now that it's in the book I think it would be better if you - we like just say our own name, (...)then we are famous *(smile)*
	(...)
DonDon	Everyone would know our name and they come to our school, and they'll be like 'wow! It's you, you are in a book!'
Researcher	What about you Lucy? I see you are shaking your head
Lucy	OK! I am going to be in a book, so seriously I need to improve my.. like I am reading these things that I've said and it doesn't make any sense, so I have to improve my.. talking.

In the last line of Extract 10, Lucy expressed her discomfort with the way she speaks and the way it would be represented. Mann (2016) argues this kind of reaction could be due to participants' lack of familiarity with transcripts. According to Pinter and Zandian (2015: 242) by introducing children to the format of transcription,

[t]he children not only become acquainted with the natural features of their talk, but they acquire some technical research know-how, and perhaps even more importantly, realise that what was assumed to be messy and untidy can at the same time be positioned as technically 'correct'. This messiness can be redefined as valuable and authentic from the researcher's point of view.

Children who participated in this study were unfamiliar with the concept of transcription, and they showed mixed reactions when they realized that transcripts of their utterances were used in the thesis. Some got excited, some thought it looked pretty messy and full of repetition. So, I clarified that the messiness of their utterances was natural and valuable.

Anonymity

Although the concept of anonymity was explained when the consents were obtained, and also revisited throughout the data collection, Leon's statement, 'You can find out [the identity of the respondent] from our handwriting', shows that some of the participants were still not convinced that the data collection could be done anonymously. Although it was impossible for me to recognize Leon's or any other students' handwriting, the fact that anonymity may not always be achievable in research is an important ethical issue. This also reflects children's own understanding of how a teacher will/can identify students. So, they are perhaps rightly doubtful that anonymity is possible in school-based research.

Another example is when Leon explains that he wanted to write his name on the questionnaire, but then decided not to be honest in answering some of the questions (Extract 11).

Extract 11

Leon	Like, I had an idea, but I couldn't say it, so I lied about it.
Researcher	Well, it's good that you mentioned this… why didn't you want to tell your initial idea?
Leon	I wrote my name [on the questionnaire]
Researcher	Well you had the option not to write your name.
Leon	Well…
Researcher	It's better not to lie in the questionnaire. Because it's not meant to collect fake results. You can choose not to answer the questions though.

This extract indicates that some children are unsure about anonymity, and this might be due to the traditional educational culture, which gives school staff automatic access to all data from students. Moreover, as Kuchah and Pinter pointed out in the introductory chapter to this book, the concepts of confidentiality and anonymity in child-focused research can be particularly ambiguous in educational settings. The fact that they brought this up in the follow-up session and were able to discuss this, along with their dilemma of disclosing ideas that were perhaps to be judged unacceptable with me is valuable. This conversation helped me to have a better understanding of children's concerns about research and I hope it also contributed to their better understanding of the nature of research. Although withholding information, or not writing what you really think, is not unique to children and can happen with adult partici-pants, the fact that children are rarely given a voice to talk about their views may well be a contributing factor. Moreover, children might be right that, especially in school contexts, they cannot express just any risky opinion or view because of possible negative consequences. Revisiting the research ethics and ground rules with participants and discussing it with them in detail, especially when they are not familiar with the concept of research, may be a possible way forward (Moore *et al.*, 2018). After all, as the researcher I can only encourage the participants to be honest with themselves and the researcher when they volunteer to participate in research, and hope they would provide truthful responses.

Another issue, which became clear in the follow-up session, was that children did not fully understand why they had been asked to choose pseudonyms. This is despite my explanation at the beginning of the group interviews, and despite the fact that they all happily selected a name at the beginning. Extract 12 illustrates this miscomprehension. Here, Bloom is explaining what the researcher did in the group interview.

Extract 12

Bloom	They chose new names for themselves... I was Bloom, she was Isabel, she was Nilou, and .. you?
Sara	Sara
	(...)
Bloom	You said.. if you want to go there [the imaginary context in the one of the interview activities] you have to change your names? I don't remember well.. you just said change your names.

After the participants learnt about the format of the final representation of the data (in a PhD thesis), and saw the extracts of their own contributions, it was clearer to them why pseudonyms were used in the research, and what the concept of anonymity meant. It seems that children's understanding of the research developed throughout the project and after seeing it in practice. At the beginning they only vaguely understood the purpose and nature of the research, but in the process they gained better understanding of some additional aspects of it. This is why going back to the child participants and sharing the findings of the study with them is an ethical decision, albeit one that is not always possible. For example, children may have changed school by the time the research is completed, and time and economic constraints may also hinder revisiting child participants after the completion of the study.

Discussion and Conclusion

Article 12 in the United Nations Convention on the Right of the Child emphasizes that children's views need to be heard and taken seriously. Believing that if child participants are informed of the research outcome and impact, they may have better realization of the adequate weight given to their views, I conducted these follow-up sessions to share the initial findings of the research with the child participants. Christensen and Prout (2002) also refer to 'dissemination' and 'impact' as key aspects of conducting ethical research with children. The children's reactions to these sessions revealed that despite the explanations and clarification provided in the beginning, and throughout, the project about the aims and process of the research, they did not fully understand what this study had been about and how they had contributed to it. Nonetheless, the follow-up sessions opened up a space to revisit children's developing views regarding the research process. These sessions also increased children's awareness about research in general and their roles in it. As Bloom's (one of the children) statement, 'But we've never seen what we did today before' illustrates, this was a new experience for the children. I believe that allocating enough time for the children to reflect, experience new things, and revisit their experiences in research is another valuable strategy and an ethical consideration.

Schools are commonly used as the venue for research with children, and are considered as a safe place for them to take part in research where the surroundings are familiar. However, the follow-up sessions revealed that the children were perceiving any activities taking place in the school to be ultimately aiming at assessing them. Consequently, many of them could not think of any other good reasons for ever participating in the research. It seems that schools as a venue for research can be problematic due to the social order of adult control (Barker & Weller, 2003). Children who never had the experience of participating in research are even more prone to associating research with assessment. The brief verbal feedback at the end of the administration of the questionnaires, and the more detailed discussions during the follow-up sessions, clarified that most of the respondents who initially had misinterpreted the questionnaire as a test, recognized its non-evaluative nature only afterwards, when re-reading the questions and reflecting together. Kostenius and Öhrling (2006) argue that follow-up meetings with the participating children and sharing the main points of the findings can alleviate the issue of distrust. I believe this is also a key point in research with children. In line with this, in the follow-up session, children realized that their participation was valued, and this strengthened their trust in the researcher and the research project. Although this happened in the later stage of this study, I believe it is still important and this will hopefully positively impact their experiences in future research.

Kuchah and Pinter (2012: 284) argue that 'children are aware that adults are in control of all aspects of their lives, and this expectation will naturally extend to the research content and procedures as well'. Children's comments in the follow-up sessions supported this claim. Children expected that their voices would be represented only minimally through the voice of the researcher. This indicates children's belief that the adult researcher would have control over their contributions to the research.

Such assumptions signal 'an assumed lack of authority and expectation to hand over power and responsibility to the knowledgeable and competent adult' (Pinter & Zandian, 2015: 243). Although in this study children were positioned as 'social actors' (Alderson, 2000; Christensen & Prout, 2002; Harwood, 2010), and their active participation was the core of the research design, their comments in the follow-up sessions revealed that children clearly considered themselves objects of the research rather than the active subjects. This also suggests that their automatic assumption is that the adult representations must be more reliable and valuable than their words. Lundy (2007) emphasizes that researchers who work with children need to acknowledge this issue and encourage children to express their views and show them that their views are taken seriously. Revisiting the participants and sharing the findings with them may contribute to developing children's understanding of their own crucial role in childhood research.

Lundy (2007: 938) rightly states that 'often children are asked for their views and then not told what became of them; that is, whether they had any influence or not'. The follow-up sessions opened up a space for reflection and the realization that the children's contributions mattered and this increased their sense of self-satisfaction and contributed to their empowerment, consequently boosting their confidence, particularly in the case of shy and less expressive participants.

Another ethical question concerns participant selection; that is, who we choose and who we leave out in research. It is important to include groups in the research who have little opportunity to express their ideas and have their voices heard (Matthews & Tucker, 2000), such as children who are less confident and those who usually remain in the shadow of the others. Mitra (2004) adds that providing opportunities for children to express themselves and be heard increases their sense of agency, belonging and competence. In this regard, Kostenius and Öhrling (2006) argue that even the interviews and the communication process in child-centred research projects can be an empowering experience for children. When children understand that their contributions to research are as valuable, they feel proud and important (Zandian, 2015a), and this can lead to their heightened sense of self-satisfaction and self-confidence. Engaging children in the design of the project, revisiting the child participants and sharing the findings with them in a child-friendly format will contribute to developing a culture of research amongst the students and staff in educational environments. Participants of this study claimed that this research broadened their own horizons about both concepts related to intercultural issues (the focus of the project) and research methodology.

In this chapter, I discussed some of the ethical dilemmas arising from children's levels of understanding of the research in which they are participants, and from having useful discussions with them explaining more about what research is all about. The central point emerging is that no matter how carefully we set up the research, in-situ dilemmas will always arise in everyday practice, which need further reflection and a reflexive attitude from the adult researcher. Future studies with child researchers could explore how children who have more active roles in research perceive their role in it. Participants of this study were 10–12 years old and did not have any experience of taking part in research before. Future studies could investigate children's perceptions of research in different age groups and could also explore how research knowledge grows when children have a chance to take part in research more frequently. The study discussed here was conducted in a school setting, and it would be interesting to explore how children's perceptions of research would be different in studies outside of school settings.

References

Alderson, P. (2000) Children as researchers. In P. Christensen and A. James (eds) *Research with Children: Perspectives and Practices*. London: Routledge Falmer.

Barker, J. and Weller, S. (2003) Geography of methodological issues in research with children. *Qualitative Research* 3 (2), 207–227. doi:10.1177/14687941030032004

Christensen, P. and Prout, A. (2002) Working with ethical symmetry in social research with children. *Childhood* 9 (4), 477–497. doi:10.1177/0907568202009004007

Davis, J., Watson, N. and Cunningham-Burley, S. (2000) Learning the lives of disabled children: Developing a reflexive approach. In P. Christensen and A. James (eds) *Research with Children: Perspectives and Practices*. London: Falmer Press.

England, K.V.L. (1994) Getting personal: Reflexivity, positionality, and feminist research. *The Professional Geographer* 46 (1), 80–89. doi:10.1111/j.0033-0124.1994.00080.x

Greene, S. and Hill, M. (2005) Researching children's experience: Methods and methodical issues. In S. Greene and D. Hogan (eds) *Researching Children's Experience: Approaches and Methods*. London: Sage Publications.

Grover, S. (2004) Why won't they listen to us?: On giving power and voice to children participating in social research. *Childhood* 11 (1), 81–93. doi:10.1177/0907568204040186

Harwood, D. (2010) Finding a voice for child participants within doctoral research: Experiences from the field. *Australasian Journal of Early Childhood* 35 (4), 4–13. doi:10.1177/183693911003500402

Hood, S., Kelley, P. and Mayall, B. (1996) Children as research Subjects: A risky enterprise. *Children and Society* 10 (2), 117–128. doi:10.1111/j.1099-0860.1996.tb00462.x

James, A., Jenks, C. and Prout, A. (1998) *Theorizing Childhood*. Cambridge: Polity Press.

Kellett, M. (2010) Small shoes, big steps! Empowering children as active researchers. *American Journal of Community Psychology* 46 (1–2), 195–203. doi:10.1007/s10464-010-9324-y

Kostenius, C. and Öhrling, K. (2006) Schoolchildren from the north sharing their lived experience of health and well-being. *International Journal of Qualitative Studies on Health and Well-being* 1 (4), 226–235. doi:10.1080/17482620600747485

Kuchah, K. and Pinter, A. (2012) 'Was this an interview?' Breaking the power barrier in adult-child interviews in an African context. *Issues in Educational Research* 22 (3), 283–297.

Kustatscher, M. (2014) Informed consent in school-based ethnography – using visual magnets to explore participation, power and research relationships. *International Journal of Child, Youth and Family Studies* 5 (4.1), 686–701.

Lundy, L. (2007) 'Voice' is not enough: Conceptualising Article 12 of the United Nations Convention on the Rights of the Child. *British Educational Research Journal* 33 (6), 927–942. doi:10.1080/01411920701657033

Mann, S. (2016) *The Research Interview: Reflective Practice and Reflexivity in Research Processes.* London: Palgrave Macmillan.

Matthews, H. (1998) The geography of children: Some ethical and methodological considerations for project and dissertation work. *Journal of Geography in Higher Education* 22 (3), 311–324. doi:10.1080/03098269885723

Matthews, H. and Tucker, F. (2000) Consulting children. *Journal of Geography in Higher Education* 24 (2), 299–310.

Mitra, D. (2004) The significance of students: Can increasing 'student voice' in schools lead to gains in youth development? *Teachers College Record* 106 (4), 651–688.

Moore, T.P., McArthur, M. and Noble-Carr, D. (2018) More a marathon than a hurdle: Towards children's informed consent in a study on safety. *Qualitative Research* 18 (1), 88–107. doi:10.1177/1468794117700708

Morrow, V. (1999) 'It's cool …Cos you can't give us detention and things, can you?!': Reflections on research with children. In P. Milner and B. Carolin (eds) *Time to Listen to Children: Personal and Professional Communication.* London: Routledge.

Morrow, V. and Richards, M. (1996) The ethics of social research with children: An overview. *Children and Society* 10 (2), 90–105. doi:10.1111/j.1099-0860.1996.tb00461.x

Pinter, A. (2014) Child participant roles in applied linguistics research. *Applied Linguistics* 35 (2), 168–183. doi:10.1093/applin/amt008

Pinter, A. and Zandian, S. (2015) 'I thought it would be tiny little one phrase that we said, in a huge big pile of papers': Children's reflections on their involvement in participatory research. *Qualitative Research* 15 (2), 235–250. doi:10.1177/1468794112465637

Pinter, A. and Zandian, Z. (2017) A questionnaire study of Iranian children's understanding of intercultural issues. In M.P. García Mayo (ed.) *Learning Foreign Languages in Primary School: Research Insights* (pp. 223–248). Bristol: Multilingual Matters.

Slepickova, L. and Bartosova, M.K. (2014) Ethical and methodological associations in doing research on children in a school environment. *The New Educational Review* 38: 84–93.

Zandian, S. (2015a) Children's perceptions of intercultural issues: An exploration into an Iranian sontext. (Unpublished PhD dissertation), University of Warwick.

Zandian, S. (2015b) Migrant literature and teaching English as an international language in Iran. In C. Kennedy (ed.) *English Language Teaching in the Islamic Republic of Iran: Innovations, Trends and Challenges.* London: British Council.

4 'Are you coming back? It was fun': Turning Ethical and Methodological Challenges into Opportunities in Task-based Research with Children

María del Pilar García Mayo

Introduction

There has recently been a growing interest in work concerning child second language acquisition (SLA) triggered by the premise that '[...] child SLA differs from adult SLA, having its own questions and issues' (Oliver & Azkarai, 2017: 62; see also Paradis, 2007; Philp *et al.*, 2017 for more information). In foreign language acquisition contexts, this interest has been fuelled by the fact that foreign languages are being introduced in the curriculum at very young ages (García Mayo, 2017; Murphy, 2014; Pinter, 2011) and there is a clear need for research-based evidence in order to make decisions about adequate educational provision and maximize children's opportunities for language learning. Working with children as participants of research projects is a challenging task as researchers have to face both ethical and methodological issues that may be very different to working with adult participants. Working with child participants means that adult researchers must carefully consider their social responsibility as research findings may have a real impact on pedagogy and teacher training.

The present chapter reflects on my experience in two funded research projects in which English as a Foreign Language (EFL) children's (ages

8–12) oral interaction and collaborative written production were elicited by means of communicative tasks. Couched within the backdrop of task-based language learning (Long, 2015, 2016), we were interested in a range of research issues with this group of young learners mostly informed by interactional (Long, 1996) and sociocultural perspectives (Swain, 2000). Among other things, our research has considered the impact of age and instructional setting (Azkarai & Imaz Agirre, 2016; García Mayo & Imaz Agirre, 2017; García Mayo & Lázaro Ibarrola, 2015), pair formation methods (García Mayo & Imaz Agirre, 2019) and task repetition (Azkarai & García Mayo, 2017; García Mayo & Imaz Agirre, 2016; Hidalgo & García Mayo, 2019; García Mayo et al., 2018) on language learning opportunities, the use of self-reported communication strategies (Martínez Adriáne et al., 2019) and the use of the children's shared L1 while interacting in English (García Mayo & Hidalgo, 2017; Martínez Adrián, 2020) – see García Mayo (2018) for a review. The current contribution will consider challenges at both the ethical and methodological levels. In particular, in this chapter I will focus on informed consent, the information actually provided to the child participants, and how some of the tasks used may have made them feel with regard to their performance relative to other participants. At the methodological level, I will focus on issues such as creativity in task design and task engagement (Philp & Duchesne, 2016). The chapter ends with a reflection on how challenges can be turned into opportunities to make researchers, parents and children aware of the benefits of research on child language learning in formal educational contexts.

Ethical Issues

On informed consent

Among the ethical issues that any researcher considers of utmost importance is informed consent (Alderson & Morrow, 2011; Greig et al., 2012; Harcourt et al., 2011; Schenk & Williamson, 2005). Thomas and Pettitt (2017) analyse the role it plays in second language (L2) research and state that '[informed consent] has not yet fully come of age in research on second language acquisition' (2017: 271). In the USA there have been Institutional Review Boards (IRBs) established by law since 1974 and other countries have their own guidelines (see for example the British Educational Research Association (BERA) guidelines (2011)) but, as Thomas and Pettitt (2017) acknowledge, it was not until the publication of the book by Mackey and Gass (2005) that informed consent was considered in L2 research methods (see also Porte, 2010 for more updated information). Previous guidelines were considered problematic as they had not evolved from a social sciences framework but, rather, they had been adapted from biomedical guidelines in which the participants were made aware of the risk of material and physical harm, for example. That is, previous guidelines were not adapted to the study of humans as social-psychological beings nor did they take into account children's perspectives.

Mackey and Gass (2005) devote a whole chapter to issues related to data gathering and ethics. They review ethical issues in second language research such as informed consent, IRBs and protocol preparation. These researchers emphasize the core elements that informed consent forms should contain procedures, purpose, and potential risks and benefits. Although apparently there is no risk in the type of research we carry out in schools or other educational institutions, they point out that if one wants to assess the impact of second language instruction a control group is needed, which will not receive the treatment of the experimental group, and this might be considered unethical. They also highlight the need to make clear that all information will remain confidential and anonymous. Another interesting issue Mackey and Gass raise is that in some linguistic research it may be necessary not to disclose all the information regarding the target feature under study because, for example, the data gathered will be unrepresentative if the participants know what the researcher is interested in.

Regarding participant comprehension in informed consent, and focusing on second language learners, Mackey and Gass follow the suggestion of the Office for Human Research Protections (OHRP) of the US Department of Health and Human Services (https://www.hhs.gov/ohrp/): the consent form should be understandable to people who have not graduated from high school. They also suggest providing a translation of the consent document for low-proficiency language learners. As for child participants, they indicate that the consent form should be understandable and meaningful to them. In addition, the researcher has to inform and obtain consent from parents/legal guardians and school boards.

Greig et al. (2012) remind us that the UN Convention on the Rights of the Child (1989) established the fundamental rights to which each child is entitled and that UNICEF (2002) provided recommendations for researchers carrying out studies with children and young people. Greig et al. (2012: 247–248) review commonly held ethical principles that should be used as a point of reference when working with children. These principles are beneficence (researchers should assess benefits and potential risk of the study for the child), non-maleficence (obligation to do no harm), justice (participants need to be treated fairly), equity and autonomy, which refers to the fact that researchers should make sure that young participants:

> […] are able to consent through free choice, without fear or worry that they will be disadvantaged if they refuse. It also requires that the researcher makes the information available in a form and at a level that is understandable to every child or adolescent so that they fully understand what they are required to do, should they agree to be part of the study, including what will happen to information gathered about them. (Greig et al., 2012: 247)

According to the principle of autonomy, child participants should voluntarily give informed consent before being involved in any study. As Gallagher *et al.* (2010: 147) point out, if consent is truly informed, participants need to understand what the purpose of the study is and that they will be allowed to withdraw at any time. We might add that truly informed consent should also provide information about the nature of the child's participation and the benefits they will obtain as well as those obtained by the researcher(s).

Informed consent in a foreign language setting

In my capacity as principal investigator (PI) I have been involved in data collection from adults and young people for over 20 years. In our first research projects data were gathered at different educational institutions with the school principals' permission. Issues of informed consent have only been seriously considered in the most recent research projects that I have coordinated, those dealing with children and funded by the Spanish Ministry of Economy and Competitiveness. The first project was entitled *Oral interaction among young EFL learners: Negotiation and feedback strategies in communicative tasks and their impact on learning* (2013–2016). Its main goal was to assess whether young EFL learners (8–12), with a beginner proficiency level, were able to negotiate for meaning, provide feedback and focus on formal aspects of the language while carrying out several communicative tasks. My research team collected cross-sectional and longitudinal data from three schools (approximately 450 participants during the four years the project lasted). The second research project, entitled *Interaction and written production: The potential of collaborative writing in the learning of English as a Foreign Language by primary school learners* (2016–2020) had an overall aim to explore the potential of collaborative writing in EFL learning and to document collaborative interaction among 5th and 6th year primary school children (10–12 year old) while they carried out communicative tasks that lead to a written product. My team is currently collecting data from five schools so the final database will also be large. In both projects we have administered background and motivation questionnaires and standardized language proficiency tests that the learners complete, and specially designed tasks that would elicit the information we are interested in.

As PI I need to contact potential participating schools, talk to their principals, explain the project and make sure that I appropriately convey the team's interest in improving the children's language learning in our foreign language setting. Language learners' exposure to English in this setting takes place mainly in the classroom so it is of great importance to document how actual learning unfolds in order for measures to be taken to improve it. In short, our role is to convince the principals of the likely benefits of our research for their pupils.

Once the project is awarded, it has to go through our University Ethics Committee, which examines the proposal and issues the final approval. At that time, we make appointments again in the schools, this time not only with the principals of the participating schools, who will themselves ask for approval from their School Councils, but also with the EFL teachers. The teachers' role is crucial because we need to involve them in task design and task choice so that the final research tool can be used and be of use in their classroom routines. One should not lose perspective of the fact that primary school teachers have their own busy schedule, overloaded with administrative work and a curriculum they need to cover. In order to make our research as relevant as possible, we regularly offer seminars in which we explain the findings from our studies and explain the impact they have on teachers' pedagogical practices, in line with recent research in the SLA field (Sato & Loewen, 2019).

We also prepare a document for parents/legal caregivers in which the main goal of the project as well as the procedure to be followed are explained. The document emphasizes that (a) participation will be on a voluntary basis and that the child can withdraw from the project at any time if the parents/legal caregivers consider that appropriate; (b) the data to be gathered (in audio and video) will be coded and anonymized; (c) the procedures have been approved by the University Ethics Committee and that (d) they could request information about the findings obtained.

Many people believe that children should be asked to give consent, an idea shared by Pinter et al. (2013) as well (see also Pinter, 2014, 2015). They should be informed about the general aim of the study in their L1, using age-appropriate consent forms with language that is meaningful to them. Once the project is finished, they should be informed about what the general findings were, again using language that is age-appropriate (e.g. see Zandian, this volume). This could be done by attending one of their EFL classes and taking a bit of time from one of their regular sessions. It is true, though, that not all authors agree that ethical problems can be solved by adopting 'child-friendly techniques' (see Gallagher et al., 2010).

Going through the different steps to obtain permission that I have outlined above for our projects, one wonders about our child participants. Has anyone asked them? In our projects we do not directly ask the children but the parents/legal caregivers might ask them and make the decision together based on the information in the consent form. We also administer motivation questionnaires about the children's experience in learning English, about their likes/dislikes of specific tasks before and after they carry them out; however so far they have not been asked about whether or not they really wanted to participate in the project. Not asking children will clearly go against the autonomy principle. In fact, UNICEF (2002: 5) already mentioned the need for children to be informed:

Researchers and M(onitor) & E(valuation) managers are responsible for ensuring that children receive the information they need to form and express their views as well as to decide whether they choose to express them at all. To 'inform' should be understood as meaning more than simply providing information. How information is conveyed must be appropriate to the context and to children's capabilities.

This could be considered a strong position, though. As Mackey and Gass (2005) already pointed out, information about the study cannot be disclosed in full in all types of research. Moreover, in a school context, asking students directly might place them in a difficult position. They are used to complying with what they think their teacher wants and, in this particular case, the teacher will support the researchers' activity because s/he has already been informed of its benefits for language learning. Besides, if the children see that their peers participate, it would be hard for them to say no just because of peer pressure. From a researcher's perspective, when large databases are needed in order to report robust findings, it could also be chaotic to form experimental and control groups when one would need to consider how many children return both consent forms (their parents and their own).

Even when adults (parents/legal caregivers) are the ones who decide about children's participation, researchers may find themselves in awkward situations. For example, some children may really want to participate but their parents/legal caregivers refuse to give consent. These days caregivers are worried about the possibility of their children's images (such as photos) ending up on social network sites or on the internet in general and, although they may agree with the overall benefits of the research, they do not want to run any risk so they simply refuse consent. Some other times, parents/caregivers do not see the point of having their children involved in the completion of tasks that they see as 'extra-tests' and as extra-work (see Kuchah & Pinter, this volume, on parents' not agreeing with their children's decision to participate or not participate). An immediate problem arises: what do these children do while their peers are taking part in a research project/a task? Sometimes the teachers prepare other activities that they will complete but that situation does not avoid the singling-out-feeling of the non-participating children.

The opposite scenario can also occur: parents/legal caregivers decide that the children need to participate and put pressure on them to do so. This situation is especially obvious in the case of EFL learning in Spain, where most children and teenagers attend extra-English classes in private academies because learning English is considered of utmost importance to have better job opportunities. The children participate even when they do not want to and the extra-pressure is filtered through questions such as '¿Esto cuenta para nota?' (Will this (=this task) be considered for my grade?). Such pressure could be influencing their performance in the task in a negative way (see also chapters by Zandian and Murphy in this volume). Therefore children have the right to know that their performance will be anonymous, only known to the researchers of the team and that their names would be changed to pseudonyms.

As Thomas and Pettitt (2017: 279) mention, authors such as Walkup and Bock (2009) reported that participants in research studies often do not want to have a lot of information in advance, in fact, too much information may also have a negative effect. Walkup and Bock (2009) refer to research that has shown that '[…] elaborate assurances of confidentiality and harmlessness (especially couched in the legalistic language of informed consent forms) can actually backfire, decreasing participants' confidence and comfort' (Thomas & Pettitt, 2017: 279). Granted, when compared to other research areas, participants in educational linguistics projects are less likely to be placed in situations that could be harmful or carry risk but it is true, especially when dealing with children (and teenagers undergoing peer pressure) that individual differences clearly play a role when oral production is being video-recorded. Some children really enjoy being in front of a camera, whereas others reflect in their expression that they struggle to overcome their innate shyness. In addition, probably due to the strong emphasis placed on the importance of exam grades, some children are reluctant to believe that their performance will not be considered for their final grade in the subject, even though their teachers have explained that this will not be the case.

Children can also gain important benefits from participating in research (see chapters by Butler and Zandian in this volume). Considering children's perspectives is crucial. Pinter *et al.* (2013: 486) conclude that '[…] it is clear that, as active participants in research, children themselves can benefit from a boost to their self-esteem and their motivation, quite apart from their insights being useful to researchers.' For example, in a recent study Butler (2017) assessed 82 Japanese 11–12 year old EFL learners' ideas about how to design digital instructional game (DIG) tasks. The study sought to identify motivational elements in DIGs based on young L2 learners' perspective on them. Although most task content in books for that age range tends to be limited to certain topics (such as animals, family, food, friends, sports), Butler points out that the children in her study chose a variety of topics as content of their game tasks (e.g. world of fairies and life styles). She concludes that teachers and curriculum designers might seriously consider children's voices when designing and selecting learning content '[…] so that tasks can promote children's personal investment in the learning process' (Butler, 2017: 747).

Children's participation should be rewarded as a way to show that their work is important and that their opinions count. In our particular case, we have rewarded the children who were given consent to take part in the different tasks but, in order to avoid the feeling of being singled out in front of their peers, we also rewarded those who had not participated (less than 5% in both projects). As a small token of our appreciation they were given coloured pencils, fancy rubbers and some attractive stationery.

Methodological Issues

This section considers some of the methodological issues that my research team has encountered while doing research with child participants in the two above-mentioned projects.

Once teachers and researchers agree on the types of tasks to be administered, a methodological issue that is potentially problematic depending on the school is the choice of venue for data collection. In our context it is highly unlikely that data can be gathered in the actual primary school classroom because of many different reasons like the one referred to in the previous section: not all children will be given consent to participate so if the data are collected in the classroom those without consent will feel they are bystanders. In our experience, finding appropriate rooms has never been a problem because the school principals have allowed us to use smaller rooms where they hold tutorials or meetings with parents/legal caregivers. The rooms are the perfect size for videotaping pair work. Although some researchers argue that children should choose the space they want within the school environment (Kuchah & Pinter, 2012), spaces such as the playground would not be a possibility due to the noise that would be generated in the recordings. Taking the children somewhere else outside the school would require a different type of permission by the school principal and the parents/legal caregivers, which will probably not be granted.

Even if one could gather data from all children in the same classroom, several research assistants would be needed to set up video cameras in strategic places and organize the different dyads, which leads us to another methodological problem, at least in our context: the recruitment of research assistants. Research assistants play a crucial role in this type of experimental studies. Their help is invaluable not just for data collection but also for data transcription and, if appropriately trained, for data codification as well. As mentioned above, we are currently working in collaboration with five primary schools located in two different major cities in the north of Spain. When the final data collection calendar is agreed upon by the school and the researchers (who obviously have to adjust to the school's requirements), the research team has to juggle things around to organize that data collection because most of us work full-time and our class schedules coincide with those of data collection. Due to reasons that are context-specific and whose explanation would go beyond the scope of this chapter, we have very few research assistants, which leaves most of the data collection, transcription and coding to our responsibility as full-time university lecturers.

Another methodological challenge in this type of research is child attrition. The average class size in the primary schools we are working with is 25–26 children. When we discuss the design of the different studies within our project, we count on a certain number of dyads per group (experimental group(s) and control group) in order to obtain data that can be considered robust in statistical terms. However, it is very common to face unexpected problems (mainly having to do with children's health issues) that will leave us with fewer participants than originally planned. Unfortunately, there is very little the research team can do about these situations and we will have to do without those missing school on the data collection days in longitudinal studies.

As already mentioned above, the research we carry out with child participants is mainly framed within a task-based language teaching (TBLT) approach (Long, 2016). We are interested in the extent to which peer interaction in foreign language contexts can foster language learning. Philp *et al.* (2014: 202) highlighted three strengths of peer interaction (see also Philp, 2016a): (a) peers provide a context for language practice that is not usually possible in whole-class interaction; (b) peers provide a context for experimenting with language and for discovering new words and structures that one of the members of the dyad may not know and (c) peer interaction can be beneficial to boost learners' motivation. In this type of research, relationships between peers are a critical issue and, as Philp (2016b: 377) points out in her epilogue for Sato and Ballinger's (2016) volume, '[…] we are left with a strong suspicion that peer relations might, for all our research in other directions, be a critical feature that mediates the relative effectiveness of peer interaction for learning.'

In recent work we have explored the impact of agency and pair formation on the degree of children's participation in collaborative dialogue (Imaz Agirre & García Mayo, 2020); children were divided into three groups: a (RA) group, a teacher-assigned (TA) group and a student-selected (SS) group. In the RA group, dyads were formed on the basis of the results of the proficiency test (i.e. those learners with the same level of proficiency). In the TA group, the teacher established the dyads with those pairs of students based on her intuition of who could best complete tasks together. In the SS group, students themselves selected who they were going to be working with. Our findings showed that dyad assignment had a clear impact on the children's contribution to the dialogue and on the language used during task completion. For example, in the RA group, students produced significantly more turns in English than in Spanish in both tasks used, whereas in the TA and the SS groups Spanish was the dominant language. When the members of the dyad were children who were working with their friends, the set-up had a clear impact on the overuse of their shared L1 and off-task talk, for example. When the children were working with classmates with whom they did not necessarily get along that well but who had the same proficiency level in the target language, they focused more on the task at hand. Peer relations did indeed matter: the RA group used the target language more frequently than the other two groups. One could wonder, though, whether establishing dyads based on results of standardized proficiency tests would not go against the idea of leaving children the possibility of choosing their partner, of providing them with the power to make their own decisions. The researcher faces the dilemma of having to decide what is beneficial for the children's foreign language development (RA groups) or what would be more interesting from the children's perspective (i.e. choosing the partner they want to work with).

Another one of the methodological challenges that researchers eliciting data from children face is the design of tasks that the participants find appealing, motivating and engaging. The teacher-researcher collaboration in this task design is key to success. In recent data collection with 6th year primary school children (11–12), García Mayo and Imaz Agirre (2019) designed tasks based on detective stories because that was one of the topics that the children had worked on in their English class. Thus, for one of the tasks, the researchers designed a story based on one of the adventures of the child detective 'Neat the Great' (© Marjorie Weinman Sharmat, 1975) and another in which the children had to decide who was the suspect of breaking into the school lab out of a group of four potential candidates. According to Philp (2016a: 159), when learners are engaged '[they] are typically cognitively, behaviourally, and affectively involved [...] Learners reflect involvement through on-task and collaborative behaviour, through language that is reciprocal and/or exploratory.' In collaborative behaviour we find children requesting assistance from their peer by asking direct questions *(how do you say...?)* seeking reassurance about how to use a particular lexical item *(is this correct?)*, or simply acknowledging they did not know how to express an idea in English. There is also a predominant use of the first person plural pronoun (Storch, 2002) to reflect a joint responsibility for the task. Consider example (1) – examples are transcribed verbatim from the children's oral production:

(1) Child B: this is the title so **we** have to see what is a problem.
     Child A: I think this.
     Child B: **which one?**
     Child A: this because first they do the shopping and then they go.
     Child B: and then this one .... **what do you think?**
     Child A: I think that the opposite because here the boy is in the house and here is going to the house.
     Child B: ok, so **we** have to put that the next one ... **do you follow me?**
     Child A: but here this cat? **Whose cat?**
     Child B: eh ..the girl's cat.
     (García Mayo & Imaz Agirre, 2019: 171)

As can be clearly seen, child B shows his interest in his partner's perspective *(what do you think?)*, in whether or not he is being understood *(do you follow me?)* and in considering the task as joint work *(this is the title so we have to see what is a problem)*. Child A is also involved in task completion and provides his point of view about what the story depicts and, in this short excerpt, requests assistance from his partner.

Sometimes, however, even when that collaboration exists, one is faced with unexpected results. For example, García Mayo and Lázaro Ibarrola (2015) analysed the oral interaction of 3rd (8–9) and 5th (10–11) year primary school children in mainstream EFL and Content and Language Integrating Learning (CLIL) (Dalton-Puffer, 2011) settings. The children completed a spot-the-difference task, which had been specifically designed for these groups on the basis of the vocabulary they had been working on in their classes and with their teachers' ideas. An unexpected finding when comparing 3rd and 5th year learners in both settings was the higher use of their shared L1 by the older learners. On the basis of this group's reaction to the task, the researchers speculated that the task might have been a bit easy/childish for them: as the older children did not find any challenge, they fell back on their L1 more frequently (see also García Mayo & Imaz Agirre (2016) for a passive-parallel interactional pattern in 10 year old children) compared to a collaborative pattern of 8–9 year old ones- collaborative patterns are those in which both members of the dyad contribute to the task and engage with each other's ideas (Storch, 2002); passive-parallel patterns are those in which no member of the dyad engages with the task (Butler & Zeng, 2015). García Mayo and Lázaro Ibarrola (2015) called for the use of motivation questionnaires when assessing task performance. We might also add that interviews with focus groups in this type of studies is an idea to consider in order to check what the children's interpretation of the task was.

Tasks have to be engaging for the children but should also elicit the target form the researchers are interested in. For example, in recent work by Calzada Lizarraga (2017) and Calzada and García Mayo (2020), the children were completing a dictogloss task that was designed to elicit instances of the third personal singular morpheme –s, a well-known problematic morphosyntactic feature for Spanish learners of English (Basterrechea & García Mayo, 2013). As example (2) illustrates, the children did focus on that form and, what is more important, resolved the problem they had with it:

(2) Child A: She do, no, *pon ahí* 'she', she does… (She do, no, put there 'she does')
     Child B: No.
     Child A: *Sí*, she does… (Yes, she does)
     Child B: She do…
     Child A: *No, porque es chica, o sea*, 'she does'… *¡es* 'does'! *Porque con* 'he', 'she' *and* 'it' *se pone* '-s', *y* 'do', *es*'does'. (No, because she is a girl, that means 'she does', it's 'she does'! Because with he, she and it, you have to put '-s', and 'do' is 'does')
     Child B: *Vale.* (Ok)
     Child A: *Y* 'do' *es* 'does', 'does' (And it's does, does)
     Child B: [giggles] She does lessons in the morning and training in the afternoon.
     (Calzada & García Mayo, 2020: 22)

Although there are other aspects in this example worth commenting on such as L1 use, pair dynamics and metalanguage, the excerpt in (2) shows that the children are engaged with the task and reflect on the verbal forms for third person singular subjects in English.

Conclusion

The main aim of this chapter was to reflect on some ethical and methodological issues that we have faced when collecting oral production data from young learners (8–12) in an EFL setting. I have considered ethical issues mainly having to do with informed consent and the extent to which children should be informed (see also chapters by Mourão and Mathew & Pinter in this volume). I have also mentioned how recording children may put them in potentially uncomfortable situations as they feel their performance is being measured against that of their peers. As researchers, I believe we should inform children using age-appropriate consent forms in which both the goal of the study and the benefits they will obtain are clearly explained but, as mentioned above, this decision is also challenging. I have also mentioned some methodological issues which my research group has faced and which I am sure are shared by others involved in studies with this age group. We should try to create a child-friendly environment so that these young learners feel at ease, consider their views on the task we design in collaboration with their teachers and make those tasks engaging both in content and format.

As Skelton (2008: 33) already pointed out, we should be working within a social science ethical research framework, not within one that has been adapted from medical research guidance. There is no easy solution to some of the problems referred to above but the challenges we face need to be turned into opportunities in order to advance in the research agenda with young populations. Thus, we should find our place in university ethic committees. Experience doing research with young learners and knowing their specific characteristics should be taken into account to modify and adapt some of the guidelines which directly do not apply to the type of population we do research on/with. In a recent article Robson (2018) reflects on debates between the ethics regulation systems operationalized by institutions and the practice of ethics-related reflection and action by critical researchers. Although I agree with her arguments against a universal requirement of evidence of Institutional Review Board approval because '[...] institutional review in itself cannot guarantee that research is conducted ethically' (2018: 476), I still believe that our voices should be heard in such committees. However, along the lines suggested by Robson herself, I would be more inclined to raise awareness of what ethical conduct in research is and to consider the participation of children in research design.

We should also establish firmer and long-term collaboration with schools to make teachers aware of the benefits of research. In foreign language teaching contexts, they need to be aware that, given the reduced access to the target language, children need to make the most of well-designed tasks that will allow them to use the language in meaningful conditions. Lightbown (2016) stated that 'It is essential to recognize the paramount importance of local teachers, students and learning contexts when we seek to "apply" research findings'. In fact, recent work in the SLA field has stressed the importance of critically engaging teachers with research evidence and researchers with practice throughout the research process (Marsden & Kasprowicz, 2017: 614). We should be able to convey the pedagogical implications of our research so that teachers assess our contributions and they themselves can provide feedback on our ideas (García Mayo, 2012).

The research we carry out is also a matter of social responsibility as research findings may have a real impact on pedagogy and teacher training. Thus, we should disseminate our research widely via holding information seminars and other events for stakeholders, teachers and parents/legal caregivers.

We do want to have children engaged with our work and hear the following, as we did once we were leaving one of the schools after a day of data collection: 'Are you coming back? It was fun!'

Acknowledgements

This article is part of the research activities conducted within a program of research on child L2 task-based interaction financed by the Spanish Ministry of Economy and Competitiveness (Research Grants FFI2012-32212-P and FFI2016-74950-P; AEI/FEDER/EU) and the Basque Government (IT904-16), which are hereby gratefully acknowledged.

References

Alderson, P. and Morrow, V. (2011) *The Ethics of Research with Children and Young People: A Practical Handbook*. London: Sage.

Azkarai, A. and García Mayo, M.P. (2017) Task repetition effects on L1 use in EFL child task-based interaction. *Language Teaching Research* 21, 480–495.

Azkarai, A. and Imaz Agirre, A. (2016) Negotiation of meaning strategies in child EFL mainstream and CLIL settings. *TESOL Quarterly* 50, 844–870.

Basterrechea, M. and García Mayo, M.P. (2013) Language-related episodes during collaborative tasks: A comparison of CLIL and EFL learners. In K. McDonough and A. Mackey (eds) *Second Language Interaction in Diverse Educational Contexts* (pp. 25–33). Amsterdam: John Benjamins.

British Education Research Association (2011) *Ethical Guidelines for Educational Research*. See https://www.bera.ac.uk/publication/ethical-guidelines-for-educational-research-2018 (accessed 4 January 2018).

Butler, Y.G. (2017) Motivational elements of digital instructional games: A study of young learners' game designs. *Language Teaching Research* 21, 735–750.

Butler, Y.G. and Zeng, W. (2015) Young foreign language learners' interactional development in task based paired assessment in their first and foreign languages: A case of English learners in China. *Education 3–13* (44), 292–321.

Calzada Lizarraga, A. (2017) Collaborative work among primary school children: Dictogloss and focus on form. MA thesis, University of the Basque Country.

Calzada, A. and García Mayo, M.P. (2020) L2 grammar learning through a collaborative writing task. In W. Suzuki and N. Storch (eds) *Languaging in Language Learning and Teaching* (pp. 19–39). Amsterdam: John Benjamins.

Dalton-Puffer, C. (2011) Content and language integrated learning: From practice to principles. *Annual Review of Applied Linguistics* 31, 182–204.

Gallagher, M., Haywood, S.L, Jones, M.W. and Milne, S. (2010) Negotiating informed consent with children in school-based research: A critical review. *Children and Society* 24, 471–482.

García Mayo, M.P. (2012) La formación del profesorado de lenguas extranjeras. In E. Alcón Soler and F. Michavila (eds) *La Educación Superior desde una Perspectiva Multilingüe* (pp. 203–221). Madrid: Tecnos.

García Mayo, M.P. (ed.) (2017) *Learning Foreign Languages in Primary School: Research Insights*. Bristol: Multilingual Matters.

García Mayo, M.P. (2018) Child task-based interaction in EFL settings: Research and challenges. *International Journal of English Studies* 18, 119–143.

García Mayo, M.P. and Hidalgo, M.A. (2017) L1 use among young EFL mainstream and CLIL learners in task-based interaction. *System* 67, 132–145.

García Mayo, M.P. and Imaz Agirre, A. (2016) Task repetition and its impact on EFL children's negotiation of meaning strategies and pair dynamics: An exploratory study. *The Language Learning Journal* 44, 451–466.

García Mayo, M.P. and Imaz Agirre, A. (2017) Child EFL interaction: Age, instructional setting and development. In J. Enever and E. Lindgren (eds) *Early Language Learning: Complexity and Mixed Methods* (pp. 249–268). Bristol: Multilingual Matters.

García Mayo, M.P. and Imaz Agirre, A. (2019) Task modality and pair formation method: Their impact on patterns of interaction and LREs among EFL primary school children. *System* 80, 165–175.

García Mayo, M.P. and Lázaro Ibarrola, A. (2015) Do children negotiate for meaning in task-based interaction? Evidence from CLIL and EFL settings. *System* 54, 40–54.

García Mayo, M.P., Imaz Agirre, A. and Azkarai, A. (2018) Task repetition effects on CAF in EFL child task-based interaction. In M.A. Ahmadian and M.P. García Mayo (eds) *Recent Perspectives on Task-based Language Learning and Teaching* (pp. 9–28). Berlin: De Gruyter.

Greig, A., Taylor, J. and MacKay, T. (eds) (2012) *Doing Research with Children: A Practical Guide* (3rd edn). Los Angeles: Sage.

Harcourt, D., Perry, B. and Waller, T. (eds) (2011) *Researching Young Children's Perspectives: Debating the Ethics and Dilemmas of Educational Research with Children*. London: Routledge.

Hidalgo, M.A. and García Mayo, M.P. (2019) The influence of task repetition type on young EFL learners' attention to form. *Language Teaching Research* https://doi.org/10.1177/1362168819865559

Imaz Agirre, A. and García Mayo, M.P. (2020) The impact of agency in pair formation on the degree of participation in young learners' collaborative dialogue. In C. Lambert and R. Oliver (eds) *Using Tasks in Second Language Teaching: Practice in Diverse Contexts* (pp. 306–323). Bristol: Multilingual Matters.

Kuchah, K. and Pinter, A. (2012) 'Was this an interview?' Breaking the power barrier in adult–child interviews in an African context. *Issues in Educational Research* 22, 283–297.

Lightbown, P. (2016) All politics is local … and so is language teaching. Plenary talk delivered at the Sixth International Conference on *Immersion and Dual Language Education*, University of Minnesota, October, 19–22 October.

Long, M.H. (1996) The role of the linguistic environment in second language acquisition. In T. K. Bhatia and W.C. Ritchie (eds) *Handbook of Language Acquisition* (pp. 413–468). New York: Academic Press.

Long, M.H. (2015) *Second Language Acquisition and Task-Based Language Teaching.* Oxford: Wiley-Blackwell.

Long, M.H. (2016) In defense of tasks and TBLT: Non-issues and real issues. *Annual Review of Applied Linguistics* 36: 5–33.

Mackey, A. and Gass, S.M. (2005) *Second Language Research: Methodology and Design.* Mahwah, NJ: Lawrence Earlbaum.

Marsden, E. and Kasprowicz, R. (2017) Foreign language educators' exposure to research: Reported experiences, exposure via citations, and a proposal for action. *The Modern Language Journal* 101: 613–642.

Martínez Adrián, M. (2020) ¿Los juntamos? A study of L1 use in interactional strategies in CLIL vs. Non-CLIL primary school learners. *International Review of Applied Linguistics in Language Teaching* 58: 1–27.

Martínez Adrián, M., Gallardo del Puerto, F. and Basterrechea, M. (2019) On self-reported use of communication strategies by CLIL learners in primary education. *Language Teaching Research* 23: 39–57.

Murphy, V. (2014) *Second Language Learning in the Early School Years: Trends and Contexts.* Oxford: Oxford University Press.

Oliver, R. and Azkarai, A. (2017) Review of child second language acquisition (SLA): Examining theories and research. *Annual Review of Applied Linguistics* 37, 62–76.

Paradis, J. (2007) Second language acquisition in childhood. In E. Hoff and M. Shatz (eds) *Blackwell Handbook of Language Development* (pp. 387–406). Malden, MA: Blackwell.

Philp, J. (2016a) Eliciting oral production of a target form in peer interaction: Challenges and options. In A. Mackey and E. Marsden (eds) *Advancing Methodology and Practice: The IRIS Repository of Instruments for Research into Second Languages* (pp. 149–175). New York and London: Routledge.

Philp, J. (2016b) New pathways in researching interaction. In M. Sato and S. Ballinger (eds) *Peer Interaction and Second Language Learning: Pedagogical Potential and Research Agenda* (pp. 377–395). Amsterdam: John Benjamins.

Philp, J. and Duchesne, S. (2016) Exploring engagement in tasks in the language classroom. *Annual Review of Applied Linguistics* 36, 50–76.

Philp, J., Adams, R. and Iwashita, N. (2014) *Peer Interaction and Second Language Learning.* New York: Routledge.

Philp, J., Borowczyk, M. and Mackey, A. (2017) Exploring the uniqueness of child second language acquisition (SLA): Learning, teaching, assessment and practice. *Annual Review of Applied Linguistics* 37, 1–13.

Pinter, A. (2011) *Children Learning Second Languages.* London: Palgrave Macmillan.

Pinter, A.M. (2014) Child participants roles in applied linguistics research. *Applied Linguistics* 35, 168–183.

Pinter, A.M. (2015) Task-based learning with children. In J. Bland (ed.) *Teaching English to Young Learners: Critical Issues in Language Teaching with 3–12 Year Olds* (pp. 113–128). London: Bloomsbury Academic.

Pinter, A.M., Kuchah, K. and Smith, R. (2013) Researching with children. *ELT Journal* 13, 484–487.

Porte, G. (2010) *Appraising Research in Second Language Learning: A Practical Approach to Critical Analysis of Quantitative Research.* Amsterdam: John Benjamins.

Robson, E. (2018) Ethics committees, journal publication and research with children. *Children's Geographies* 16, 473–480.

Sato, M. and Ballinger, S. (eds.) (2016) *Peer Interaction and Second Language Learning: Pedagogical Potential and Research Agenda*. Amsterdam: John Benjamins.

Sato, M. and Loewen, S. (2019) Towards evidence-based second language pedagogy: Research proposals and pedagogical recommendations. In M. Sato and S. Loewen (eds) *Evidence-based Second Language Pedagogy: A Collection of Instructed Second Language Acquisition Studies* (pp. 1–24). New York: Routledge.

Schenk, K. and Williamson, J. (2005) *Ethical Approaches to Gathering Information from Children and Adolescents in International Settings: Guidelines and Resources*. Washington, DC: Population Council.

Skelton, T. (2008) Research with children and young people: Exploring the tensions between ethics, competence and participation. *Children's Geographies* 6, 21–36.

Storch, N. (2002) Patterns of interaction in ESL pair work. *Language Learning* 52, 119–158.

Swain, M. (2000) The output hypothesis and beyond: Mediating acquisition through collaborative dialogue. In J.P. Lantolf (ed.) *Sociocultural Theory and Second Language Learning* (pp. 97–114). Oxford: Oxford University Press.

Thomas, M. and Pettitt, N. (2017) Informed consent in research on second language acquisition. *Second Language Research* 33, 271–288.

UNICEF (1989) Convention on the Rights of the Child. See www.unicef.org/crc. (accessed 4 January 2018).

UNICEF (2002) Evaluation Technical Notes. Children Participating in Research, Monitoring and Evaluation (M&E) – Ethics and your Responsibility as a Manager. See http://www.gyerekesely.hu/childpoverty/docs/TechNote1_Ethics.pdf (accessed 1 March 2020).

Walkup, J. and Bock, E. (2009) What do prospective research participants want to know? What do they assume they know already? *Journal of Empirical Research on Human Research Ethics* 4, 189–203.

Weinman Shartman, M. (1975) *Nate the Great and the Lost List*. London: Penguin.

Part 2

Research with Children in Multilingual Contexts

5 Social Justice and Questions of Marginalization in Research with Linguistically Diverse Children

Victoria A. Murphy

Introduction

Linguistic diversity in its very essence refers to the range of different languages or linguistic systems represented in any given context. In relation to children, and school in particular, linguistic diversity typically refers to the range of different languages represented by the school population. The focus of this chapter is on primary school children who have linguistically diverse (LD) backgrounds. There are different terms used for identifying this population. Internationally, the term minority language (or language minority) children has been used to indicate that children from LD backgrounds typically speak a language in the home that is in the minority relative to the majority language context. In France, for example, a child from an Arabic-speaking community will have Arabic as a minority language in relation to French, the language spoken by the wider society and, importantly, the language of education and governance. Arabic in this sense is a minority language despite the fact that Arabic is one of the world's most important languages spoken by hundreds of millions around the world. I use the term 'linguistically diverse' in this chapter simply to highlight that there is no pejorative connotation intended in describing the language status of any individual or group of individuals.

Understanding the needs of, and any challenges faced by, LD children is critical for numerous reasons. First, they themselves represent a large (and growing) proportion of primary school populations around the world. For example, in the UK, one fifth of the primary school population is categorized as EAL (English as an Additional Language) – the term used in the UK to designate LD status. Some countries have higher proportions, others lower, but one thing many countries have in common is

that the proportion of LD children is growing. With increased globalization, migration and the international refugee crisis, more children than
ever before are being educated in a linguistic context that is not the same
as their home language setting. For this reason alone understanding the
linguistic, educational, personal and social development of LD children is
important. However, there are other reasons as well. As I have articulated
elsewhere (Murphy, 2014, 2017, 2018, 2019), from an international perspective, children from LD backgrounds *tend* to under-perform academically. I emphasize *tend* because this is by no means a given, and indeed
there are numerous counter-examples. Indeed, for the first time in England
in 2018 children tagged as EAL in the National Pupil Database were at the
top of the league table academically as they left formal education
(Hutchinson, 2018). Unfortunately, however, the international trend suggests that a more typical pattern is that LD pupils have lower academic
scores on reading, maths and science relative to majority language speaking peers. As highlighted by Kuchah and Pinter in the introductory chapter to this volume, it becomes an ethical issue if we see that sub-populations
of school children are systematically under-performing yet fail to do anything about it. Therefore, it is an ethical duty to better understand the
complex problem that is often faced by LD pupils so as to provide them
with the most effective support possible. LD pupils' pattern of academic
performance highlights another major characteristic of this population
that warrants more detailed and comprehensive investigation: heterogene-
ity. Within any given setting, children with LD backgrounds will not all
perform alike on language or academic assessments (e.g. Hutchinson,
2018). In much the same way that children from majority language speaking backgrounds are not all the same, neither are children from LD backgrounds. Hence generalizing across such a highly diverse population can
be problematic. Consequently, we have another reason for understanding
this population better – we need to be able to identify those variables
which predict success (both linguistically, academically and socially) so as
to be able to provide the settings in which these variables can exert their
influence. Not doing so is unethical.

In short, there are theoretical (what does typical bilingual development in minority language contexts look like), educational/pedagogical
(what are the most effective educational programmes and pedagogies for
LD pupils) and socio-political (how can societies best support LD families) reasons for needing to understand key developmental features of
children with LD backgrounds. Working with LD pupils and families in
both research and educational settings is therefore increasingly important. In order to maximize the potential impact of this research, however, we need to have a careful and comprehensive understanding of
challenges associated with working with LD children so as to work
towards finding appropriate resolutions and ensuring our research has
maximum potential to benefit all its stakeholders. In this chapter, I focus

on three specific issues (but there are of course many more) that can present challenges to working with LD pupils and their families.[1] The first concerns ethics and research with young LD pupils. The second relates to measuring the complete linguistic repertoire of LD pupils and the third issue addressed in this chapter is the linguistic landscape within educational settings and a discussion of which are more (and less) conducive to supporting multilingualism.

Ethics and Research with Young Linguistically Diverse Pupils

Most professional organizations have guidance on how to carry out research with young participants. For example, the British Education Research Association (BERA https://www.bera.ac.uk/) has clear guidance on how to conduct ethical research when participants are not considered old enough to freely give their informed consent.[2] Furthermore, a number of researchers who work with young children have written about unique and particular ethical issues, offering frameworks of reference and suggestions on how to provide and support a maximally inclusive and informative research setting (e.g. Cowie & Khoo, 2017; Lastikka & Kangas, 2017; Pinter, 2013; Pinter et al., 2013; Pinter & Zandian, 2014). The opening chapter to this volume introduced some of the key principles that underpin ethical research in working with children. General issues related to working with young children in research projects include ensuring that children are as informed as possible about the nature of the research (see also García Mayo in this volume), ensuring that children do not feel uncomfortable in any way in participating in the research (i.e. do they feel they are being formally assessed or judged which can be stressful for many children), ensuring that they are not fatigued – a particular issue with very young children, and of course given that young children are cognitively immature, they are less likely to be able to understand the full ramifications of agreeing to participate in research. This is one of the main reasons why it is important that the child's parent or legal guardian provides their informed consent for their child to participate even if the child or the child's teacher has given their assent.

All of the issues related to carrying out ethical research with young children are equally relevant to working with young LD children. However, LD pupils present further dimensions to consider regarding research ethics. For example, a parent sending their child to school at one level hands over their responsibility for their child during the school day to the school and teachers. In other words, schools and teachers have responsibility over the child *in loco parentis* – for some of the functions and responsibilities of a parent – during the school day. As such, it often transpires that in seeking consent to participate in schools, teachers will say that, given they agree to the research, we (the researcher) do not need to ask the parents. This has happened to us on more than one occasion with our research, where a teacher has told us that we don't need to send home the information sheets describing the study to the parents and seek consent, because they (the teacher) grant permission *in loco parentis*. However, while this may often be the school's view, it is not the view of educational research organizations such as BERA or the stance taken by higher education settings like universities who are typically responsible for the research. We must, therefore, seek out the *informed* consent of the parent or legal guardian. There are typically two protocols in obtaining this consent. Usually, we provide the parents with an information sheet or letter which outlines in detail the nature of the research, why it is being carried out, why their child is being asked to participate and what will happen to their child and their data.

We also make it clear that the child's data will be kept securely and anonymized, and of course, that participation is voluntary, issues regarding ethical research that were discussed in the introductory chapter to this volume. Therefore, the scenario for a typical research study is one where this information sheet outlining this information appears on formal (often university) letter head which is sent home with the parents or distributed to parents in some way. Parents then have to read through this information sheet and are given the contact details of the researchers, should they wish to raise any concerns. They then typically have to sign a consent form agreeing that they understand what the research is all about and that they agree for their child to participate.

Given this disconnect between what is required of us as researchers from an institutional and/or organizational point of view, and what some teachers and schools expect, an important lesson to be learned here is the value of working closely with teachers as collaborators, and helping teachers understand better (when necessary) what constitutes rigorous and ethical research. There is a difference between teaching in classrooms and carrying out research in classrooms and there is scope therefore for teachers to become more involved in research as collaborators so they can gain a better understanding of research processes, and we as researchers can in turn gain a better understanding of classroom-based practice (see García Mayo in this volume). A good example for this type of collaboration can be found in the Educational Endowment Foundation's (EEF) Research Schools network (https://educationendowmentfoundation.org.uk/scaling-up-evidence/research-schools/). In this network, schools sign up to become a designated research school where the aim is for these schools to implement evidence-based approaches to teaching. As part of their collaboration with the EEF, research schools tend to become much more aware of the processes underpinning rigorous research and benefit from being able to learn about and access the most up-to-date research findings in their schools.

In working with LD pupils, there are (at least) two problems with this scenario for obtaining informed consent. First, the formal nature of seeking out informed consent can be off-putting to many parents from ethnic minority backgrounds. The information is typically somewhat complex no matter how simply we may attempt to present it, and its presentation on formal letterhead contributes to the sense that this is a serious, formal request. It can be intimidating for families to receive such notification and invitation to participate in research, particularly if the family is newly arrived from a context where official institutions might not be as ethical as one would hope. As a brief anecdotal example – I was once lecturing a class of undergraduate psychology students and at the end of the class one (mature) student came up to me with a letter from a university (different to the one we were in), seeking my opinion on whether 'it was OK' for her child to participate in this. While she did not explain in any great detail why she was concerned, I did get the impression from our conversation that she was somewhat intimidated by the invitation, and was not entirely clear about what the invitation to participate in the research was really asking of her and her child. This was a parent of a child who themselves were being educated at university and yet who was uncertain about receiving this letter. Imagine then how a parent might react who has never dealt with universities before and who may indeed be intimated by the authoritarian nature of the invitation and consent forms. In this case, the parent may either feel pressure to acquiesce OR might feel threatened in some way and hence not feel comfortable in offering their consent. Both possibilities are problematic. The second problem in obtaining informed consent from LD families is one of *language*. In obtaining informed consent we typically are required to use certain, often formal, wording which might not be accessible to the parents if they have low levels of English (see also Mathew & Pinter in this volume). For example, we typically have to explain how we will 'anonymize' their child's identity, how their participation is 'voluntary' and so forth. These are low-frequency words that may not be accessible to individuals with lower levels of proficiency in English. Parents may not feel able to ask for help in understanding more complex wording, particularly if they feel intimidated by the request as indicated above.

Fortunately, there are ways to mitigate against these problems. One way is to offer leaflets to either accompany, or if possible replace, the formal letters. We often use these in our research, which include pictures that make the invitation much more user friendly (see Figure 5.1 for an example).

We also regularly hand these out to parents at the school gates, giving the parent the opportunity to meet us and ask any questions about what we're doing in the school. Through the school we can create other opportunities to talk to the parents about the research project either at a meeting after school, a time during school assemblies, or one-on-one – which is often more accessible to parents with lower levels of English (or whatever the majority language is). If there is a language barrier that is substantial enough that aural/oral communication is still unhelpful, we can either

To learn to read is
to light a fire

A research project by

WHAT SHOULD YOU DO NEXT?

If you would like to discuss the project, please do not hesitate to contact me:

[contact details removed]

If now or at any time you have any concerns about this research and you are not satisfied with the answers I have given you, you can contact my supervisor, [contact details removed]

If you are happy for your child to take part, please tick the box on the slip at the bottom of this page, fill in your child's name and return the slip to your child's teacher. If you would like a general summary of the results of the project, please put your email or postal address on the slip at the bottom of this page and return it to your child's teacher.

Yours sincerely,
[name removed]
X

I would like to have a summary of the results of this project.
My email or postal address is:

☐ I am happy for my child to participate in this project.
My child's name is

Signed by parent or guardian:

Name of parent/ guardian:

Date:

Name of researcher:

UNIVERSITY OF OXFORD
DEPARTMENT OF EDUCATION
[contact details removed]

Figure 5.1 Example leaflet

[name removed], reading with her daughter.

LEARNING TO READ PROJECT

My name is [name removed]. In partnership with the University of Oxford and Jacari, your child's school has agreed to take part in my project on children's language learning.

I am trained as a school teacher and language researcher, and I am carrying out this project as a part of my PhD research in Education. I would like to invite your child to participate in my project. Before you decide whether you are happy with this, please read this letter carefully, and ask me any questions you would like.

WHAT IS THIS PROJECT TRYING TO FIND OUT?

We think that children learn to read at different paces, and that this learning is influenced by additional languages they speak.

For example, eight-year-old children might learn to read well in general, but they might have problems with reading some types of figurative phrases (such as *to learn to read is to light a fire*) because they do not speak English at home. While a lot of research has been carried out on reading figurative language in in adults with one language, not much research has been done on how young children learning an additional language read figurative phrases.

WHY AM I INVITING YOUR CHILD TO TAKE PART?

I am inviting two groups of eight-year-old children to take part in this research: one group of children who speak English at school and at home with their parents, family and friends, and another group of children who speak English at school and an additional language at home. This is so I can see whether there are differences between the groups in their reading.

I am inviting your child to take part because they are 8 years old, and because they speak either English at school and at home, or English at school and an additional language at home.

DOES YOUR CHILD HAVE TO TAKE PART?

Your child does not have to take part in this project. If you or your child decide against taking part, they will not be at any educational disadvantage.

You can even change your minds later: your child can stop participating at any time, without having to give me a reason – you just need to let me know.

[name removed] and her daughter, using a camera that films her daughter's eye movements.

WHAT WILL HAPPEN IF YOUR CHILD DOES TAKE PART?

If you choose for your child to take part, I will come to the school and do some individual activities with them, in a quiet room. Before working with your child, I will ask them whether they are happy to do the activities. I will let them know that they can stop the activities at any time.

The two sessions will last about 30 minutes each. Your child will do three short tasks: a vocabulary task, a word reading task, and a story reading task. During their reading of the stories, their eye movements will be filmed with a little camera like the one in the picture to the left. This is to observe how they read in real-time.

If at any time your child gets tired or loses interest, I will stop the session and arrange to meet them again at another time.

WHAT WILL HAPPEN TO THE RESULTS OF THE PROJECT?

All the information I collect will be kept strictly confidential. I will give each child a code number, and only this code number will be written on the test papers. I will keep the list of children's names and numbers in a password-protected computer file, and I will erase this file at the end of the project. When I have finished the project, I will give a general summary of findings about all children to the school, and you are welcome to have this summary too. However, I cannot give you or anyone else any information about your child's individual results.

Who is supervising this project?
The project is supervised by [name removed]. The project has received ethics clearance through the University of Oxford's ethical approval process (Central University Research Ethics Committee).

Figure 5.1 Example leaflet (*continued*)

have the information translated into the families' home language, or collaborate with assistants who can speak the language and liaise with the parents. Indeed, in many schools with high proportions of LD pupils, schools themselves sometimes have individuals with the requisite linguistic skills to communicate with LD families. Another oft-used approach within ethnic minority families is for older siblings to take on the role of a language broker – someone who acts as a kind of translator for the parents thus facilitating interaction with schools, health care workers and financial institutions. There is a great deal of research on this approach and the concomitant identity and pressure placed on a relatively young child (the older sibling) as they help their family navigate through a novel linguistic landscape (e.g. Cline *et al.*, 2011; Hua & Costigan, 2012). Important in all of this is to secure the cooperation of the schools and teachers. These are the key collaborators and the gateway to facilitate good communication between the school and the family. It may also be possible to seek assistance from professional bodies. In England, the National Association for Language Development in the Curriculum (NALDIC: www.naldic.org.uk) is the charitable professional organization for teachers of EAL pupils. Contacting and working with such associations may also be fruitful because teachers working in schools may be members of these professional organizations and hence can help facilitate the process of doing research in classroom settings – both in terms of recruitment and also in terms of making research accessible to teachers.

In summary, there can often be real obstacles in gaining appropriate informed consent in carrying out research with young LD pupils. These problems can be all the more challenging when we consider that often it is the most hard-to-reach pupil that we might want to include in our studies. As an example, newly arrived refugees are an important population to work with so we can best understand how to support these families as they learn to adapt to a new linguistic, social and educational environment. While it can be sometimes quite challenging to obtain informed consent to work with such families and young children we must ensure that we do our best to understand, and then meet, their needs. With careful planning, patience and perseverance we can work to mitigate against these challenges.

First Language Assessment and Use in Linguistically Diverse Pupils

A key characteristic of LD pupils is that they have another language in addition to the majority language. If we want to know who our LD pupils are (and from both a research and educational perspective it is difficult to imagine not ever wanting to know this), we need to assess their language proficiency. Indeed, LD pupils' English (or majority) language proficiency has been shown repeatedly to be a major, significant predictor in an LD pupils' academic achievement. Demie and Strand (2005), Strand and Demie (2006), Whiteside *et al.* (2016) and most recently Strand and Hessel (2018) have each demonstrated clear links between an LD pupils' proficiency in English and their academic achievement. Understanding the importance of this link prompted the British government to initiate the mandatory assessment of EAL pupils' Proficiency in English (PiE) using a five-level scale in 2016/17. Unfortunately, the government then rescinded this requirement[3] despite the fact that the Strand and Hessel (2018) report shows clearly that performance in English based on these scales is a significant and reliable predictor of children's academic attainment and thus could be a vital source of information for teachers as they support LD pupils' language and learning in classrooms.

In addition to supporting the majority language development of LD pupils, increasingly the importance of developing the child's first (home) language is being recognized. It is not a new idea however. In the 1970s and 1980s Cummins put forward two influential theories that attempt to explain how supporting both an LD pupils' home and majority language can be mutually supportive. In his linguistic interdependence hypothesis he argued that the underlying skills which are required for school success can be improved in the L2 if they are equally supported in the L1. In other words, well-developed L1 skills will positively influence the development of those same skills in the L2 (the language of schooling). He also argued for a distinction between surface-level linguistic features and underlying linguistic proficiencies that enable the child to use these features effectively in his Common Underlying Proficiency hypothesis – illustrated by his now famous iceberg metaphor. The notion is that the part of an iceberg that is under water is the foundation (or underlying proficiency) that enables an emergent bilingual to use their surface-level features of language most effectively. Importantly for the LD pupils they will have two 'peaks' to their iceberg above water level, representing their two linguistic systems, but both peaks are part of the foundational (submerged) underlying proficiency that is common across both linguistic systems (Cummins, 1979, 1980, 2001). More recently, these ideas have been explored further and have led to increased interest in the importance of a child's ability to use their L1 in school-based settings. A recent report published by Oxford University Press presents a review of research carried out in English Medium Instruction (EMI) educational programmes around the world (Chalmers, 2019). One of the main findings of this report is that those EMI programmes that also include appropriate language arts instruction in the child's L1 yield the highest performance in both English language and academic outcomes. One of the report's key messages is that 'Ensuring that students' L1 is maintained and developed alongside English Medium Instruction is associated with: better acquisition of English, beneficial outcomes in other academic areas, higher proficiency in L1' (2019: 31).

This recognition of the importance of the L1 in classroom settings has extended beyond EMI programmes. Multilingual classrooms are increasingly prevalent internationally. In a context like England for example, where over 20% of the primary school population is EAL (DfE, 2016), it is not an unlikely occurrence for teachers to have multiple students in their class who speak a wide variety of different home languages. How best to support the L1 in these contexts? The concept of *translanguaging* is being championed as a way for teachers to be able to allow students to use both their L1 and their L2 in L2 (majority) classrooms. Translanguaging is a complex concept that has been used in a variety of ways but in its essence it encourages the use of all languages available to an LD pupil in any given learning situation. The argument is that use of the child's home language(s) in majority language classrooms helps support multilingual language development (García, 2014, 2017). More research is needed to be able to precisely show both how and when use of the home language has direct (causal) benefits on improved L2 and academic outcomes, but minimally the increased interest in this approach signals the importance of home language use and development for LD children.

If we are to adopt a multilingual pedagogy for LD pupils, in the same way that assessing their majority language proficiency has been shown to be helpful and predictive of language and academic achievement, assessing the child's home language proficiency would be equally informative. Herein lies a significant challenge for educators and researchers working in LD contexts. Whereas in contexts like the US where there are significant proportions of the population who speak the same minority language (e.g. Spanish), in other contexts like the UK over 360 different home languages are represented by the LD pupils in British schools (see NALDIC (www.naldic.org.uk)). Two very big questions arise here. How to effectively adopt a multilingual pedagogy when there might be many different home languages in the classroom, and how to assess home language proficiency, which is likely to be an important predictor in determining a child's success? This latter question about assessing home language proficiency is of particular import for researchers who aim to understand the developing linguistic proficiency of LD pupils. Assessing home language proficiency can, and no doubt should, be viewed also as an ethical concern because without being able to accurately measure the child's linguistic proficiency in the round – including both their home language and majority language estimates – we underestimate what the child can do with language and hence we are disadvantaging them (see also Kuchah & Milligan in this volume).

Some of the issues related to measures that we might use in research with children, particularly if they have lower levels of linguistic proficiency, were highlighted in the introductory chapter to this volume. Linguistic proficiency can often be assessed either through standardized tests, or through experimental measures designed by a researcher. There are advantages and disadvantages to both (see Faitaki & Murphy, 2020; Menken, 2008) but assessing bilingual or multilingual proficiency becomes increasingly complicated because we need to (a) have the tests available that are accepted as reliable and valid measures of the aspect of proficiency we are assessing and (b) typically we need to have speakers of those languages to enable us to accurately code the responses. In researching contexts where multiple languages are spoken, it becomes increasingly difficult within one research study to adequately assess home language skills. One way to deal with this issue is through the administration of detailed questionnaires. The notion here is that instead of a direct, objective measure of a child's home language proficiency, detailed questionnaires are used with the parents to be able to gauge how much the child uses the home language, in which contexts, with whom, etc. and thus gain some insights into the likely proficiency that child has in the home language (see Paradis et al., 2010 as an example). This approach can be really helpful, however, if the parents themselves do not speak much of the majority language, then the problem of finding appropriate language brokers or translators becomes again relevant here. Of course, questionnaires like these, as detailed and informative as they can be, are ultimately also self-report and hence subject to all the subjectivity that may be associated with self-report measures. Another possibility then to dealing with the challenge of measuring home language proficiency is to develop tests that can be administered easily and reliably. Many established measures that were developed in English have versions in many other languages. For example, the Peabody Picture Vocabulary Test (PPVT) (Dunn, 2018) which measures receptive vocabulary in young children is available in a variety of different languages (and dialects). However, even if a version is available in the many languages a researcher or educator might need, it is likely to still be a test norm-referenced against a monolingual population and hence potentially inappropriate for use with bilingual pupils (see Faitaki & Murphy, 2020). There are some advances, however, where online measures of receptive vocabulary in a variety of languages are being developed specifically for multilingual children (e.g. Schaefer et al., 2015). The idea here is that a receptive vocabulary measure can be easily used in a variety of languages online (where the administrator does not need expertise in the language itself to administer the task as it is automated online through a tablet) that can help identify the breadth of receptive vocabulary available to a given child. Initiatives such as these are most welcome as they will go a long way in helping educators and researchers alike in the challenge to measure developing languages that are relevant in a LD pupil's life. Being able to rely on measures of home language proficiency will enable us to have a more comprehensive and accurate assessment of children's linguistic skills, and hence make more equitable judgements about a given child's capabilities.

In summary with regards to the LD child's developing home language proficiency, increasingly researchers and educators are recognising the need to support the L1 through educational settings, though much work is yet to be done on identifying the most effective approaches that teachers can use in multilingual classrooms. Furthermore, and associated with actively encouraging the development of the L1, is the issue of validly and reliably assessing the L1 for both research and educational purposes. We have clearly seen from previous research that the developing English (or majority) language proficiency of LD pupils is an important predictor of their academic success. It is very likely to be the case then, that their developing home language is an equally powerful predictor. However, the challenge of adequately measuring the home language in LD settings is real. As long as we are not accurately measuring the child's full bilingual competence, we are not capturing their abilities properly which can have negative consequences on their educational development (Robertson *et al.*, 2014). Advances such as the ones described in this section will allow us to tap into the LD child's full 'funds of knowledge' (cf. Conteh, 2015) and hence gain a more comprehensive understanding of their linguistic skills at different stages of development.

Linguistic Landscapes within Education

A final issue worth discussing within the context of this chapter is the way(s) in which different educational settings accommodate multilingual pupils. As has been mentioned elsewhere in this chapter, many countries around the world have seen a significant increase in the proportion of children who are being educated in a majority language that is not their home language. It is a real issue and concern therefore about how to best support multilingual pupils.

One first question to ask is whether our educational systems should be doing anything to support the multilingualism in these pupils. Certainly, many countries do not have any formal policy for supporting multilingualism. In the UK, for example, children have no statutory right to be educated in any language other than English – though there are a few examples of bilingual education programmes in various languages around the country, and of course in Wales, Ireland and Scotland children can be educated in the regional ethnic minority languages relevant to those countries (Welsh, Irish and Scottish Gaelic). Generally, however, the typical LD pupil in England is unlikely to receive any support for their home language through their educational experience.[4] There is definitely a view, unfortunately widely held, that the educational environment should focus only on the development of English (or the majority language of the context). Again in the UK, certain media outlets have expressed outrage that schools have so many EAL pupils and suggest that the high incidence of EAL has a deleterious effect on the native-speaking English pupils.[5]

Unfortunately this type of rhetoric, which has led to a strong anti-immigrant discourse, has done little to help support multilingual pupils, nor native-speaking English ones for that matter, as mostly they obfuscate the reality that immigration is actually a fiscally positive aspect to societies.[6] From an educational standpoint, research has shown that native speakers of the majority language can actually do as well, or even better, academically in schools in which there are high proportions of LD pupils. Strand *et al.* (2015) compared academic achievement of pupils with EAL and non-EAL pupils in schools with high, medium and low proportions of EAL pupils. Their analysis indicated that non-EAL pupils had marginally higher scores on formal assessment outcomes in schools where there were high proportions of EAL in comparison to schools with lower numbers of EAL pupils. We have clear evidence, then, that LD pupils do not in and of themselves create difficulties in educational settings, nor do they cause lower academic attainment in non-EAL pupils. Furthermore, we also have evidence that LD pupils themselves can be at the top of the academic attainment league table. As previously mentioned, in 2018 in the UK children tagged as EAL in the National Pupil Database (NPD) topped the academic league table in England (Hutchinson, 2018) so we know that being EAL in and of itself does not mean that students will under-perform academically. Therefore, there is plenty of evidence (in the UK and beyond) to highlight that children from LD backgrounds do not represent a burden on our educational systems and can be well-represented in the highest achievement bands of our schools. Does this mean, though, that we should actively support their multilingualism? Indeed, should we view this issue as an ethical concern?

Many of the ideas expressed already in this chapter should point to the affirmative. Citing again the work from Cummins, from a theoretical point of view, supporting the child's home language should have a manifestly positive impact on their developing English (and by extension academic attainment) due to the Linguistic Interdependence Hypothesis and the Common Underlying Proficiency hypothesis (Cummins, 1979, 1980, 2001). Again, as previously mentioned, reviews of EMI programmes where the focus is not exclusively on English but where the children's home language is also supported also yield higher linguistic and academic outcomes (Chalmers, 2019). Hence we do have evidence that suggests pupils would benefit from targeted support in their home language. Furthermore, with the increased interest in translanguaging (García & Li Wei, 2014) educators are spending more time exploring ways to include home languages into the classroom settings. It is worth noting, however, that there is still a dearth of research that has been able to empirically demonstrate, through controlled experimental manipulation (i.e. with a randomized control trial) what specific ways translanguaging can work. I would argue we need this type of research before we can truly know how and when the use of the L1 is effective in LD classrooms. Nonetheless, this is a burgeoning area of educational research and no doubt the coming years will bear fruit on this issue. For now, we have good reason to believe it is effective based on the performance of children in bilingual education programmes. If educators are charged with the responsibility of helping all children reach their full academic potential, and if there is evidence that supporting the home language of LD pupils helps fulfil this potential, then we are ethically bound to do so.

From a social justice perspective the argument to promote multilingual development in LD pupils is sound. Many researchers and educators alike have discussed the human rights and social justice issues which relate to the education of children from different linguistic backgrounds. Some researchers have argued passionately that a failure to educate a child through their home language constitutes a violation of the child's human rights. This issue has been argued most strongly from the perspective of providing dual language education models for children from regional minority language groups such as Maori immersion (e.g. Harrison, 1998), dual language programmes for Latino children in the US (García, 2005; Hornberger, 2007), ethnic minority pupils in North America more generally (Cummins, 2000) and indigenous languages in Canada (e.g. Richards & Burnaby, 2008; Sarkar & Metallic, 2009). The argument is that denying a child the right to be educated through their heritage language – particularly if it is an endangered language like many regional minority languages around the world – is a violation of that child's human rights as it denies the child access to key aspects of their culture and heritage (Fishman, 1997; Skutnabb-Kangas, 2012). As a result of research in this area, many more immersion models, and specifically language maintenance immersion models have emerged over the years (see Murphy, 2014). What about ethnic minority LD pupils who do not speak an ethnolinguistically minority language that is endangered, like the Urdu speaking student in England? Are these social justice issues through education equally applicable? How would one go about facilitating their 'human right' to be educated through the medium of their home language? Indeed, can that even be feasible in a LD context where many different home languages are spoken – as is increasingly the case around the world? No doubt many scholars would strongly argue that the human rights issues remain the same. The practicality, however, of being able to offer every child the opportunity to be educated through the medium (at least in part) of their home language becomes increasingly hard to conceive in multilingual societies with many different home languages.

This is where the notion of multilingual pedagogy comes in. If we were able to establish a clear evidence base for how to develop pedagogical approaches that did not rely on the teacher's knowing the home language of all their pupils, and which can be promoted through the classroom and indeed the whole school, then in theory not only would the LD pupil benefit, but so too would the monolingual (majority language speaking) child.

Increasingly, scholars have proposed different strategies to harness the linguistic resources of LD pupils in mainstream classes, and where there may be multiple languages represented by the student population. Cummins (2005) for example argues for a range of different pedagogical practices that can serve to empower LD pupils. These include the creation of identity texts (e.g. Cummins & Early, 2010; Cummins *et al.*, 2015) where students work on texts which help affirm their identities and supports their engagement with literacy; focusing on cognate relationships between the L1 and L2 which the teacher can ask the child to do whether they know the L1 of the child or not (e.g. 'How would you say that in your home language?') which also provides opportunities for LD pupils to bring their home language into the classroom, and the work of the classroom in particular. Student-authored dual language books and student collaboration within multiple languages are all ways that cross-linguistic awareness can be enhanced and in particular, ways to challenge monolingual hegemony within mainstream classrooms (Cummins, 2005). Issa and Hatt (2013) also present a detailed discussion of different pedagogical practice in relation to LD pupils in the early years – widely recognized to be the most important grade (Barnett & Hustedt, 2003). As I've already mentioned, what is lacking here is (a) a more detailed account of how to offer multilingual pedagogical approaches and (b) a strong evidence base, one which rests on a foundation of rigorous empirical data, which illustrates which of these approaches causally leads to improved linguistic and educational outcomes.

The final point to make here is that not only is it likely that adopting such multilingual approaches in the classroom will benefit LD pupils, but they are also likely to support the metalinguistic awareness of non-LD pupils, those who speak the majority language and who may not have much linguistic competence in any other language (particularly likely in contexts where English is the majority language). By being exposed to many different ways of communicating the sounds, structures, vocabulary and cultural features that are represented in different languages, *all* children could develop greater inter-cultural awareness and importantly from a linguistic perspective, greater language awareness which would support language learning later on in their lives, and also help support their literacy development in the majority language. In summary, there do not seem to be (m)any disadvantages to working towards developing evidence-based multilingual strategies to support the home language development of LD pupils, and which could also support the development of metalinguistic awareness in non-LD pupils.

Summary and Conclusions

In this chapter, I have briefly discussed three issues which are related to research and education of LD pupils. In the first section on research ethics I identified how it is often difficult to recruit LD pupils into research studies, despite the fact that often these potentially vulnerable or at-risk children need to be better represented in research. I also highlighted a few possible ways which might help resolve some of the difficulties. It is an area that demands further attention however, because while the importance of upholding the highest ethical standard of research cannot be under-estimated, it is also true that we need to find appropriate and possibly more flexible ways, of ensuring that our participants are welcomed into our studies, viewed more collaboratively, and supported as research partners. The problem of measuring the home language proficiency of LD pupils was also discussed, identifying how administering standardized tests that have been norm-referenced on a monolingual population can be difficult in assessing competence of bilingual pupils, and how difficult it can be to assess the L1 of students where there is a significant range of languages represented in the research sample. Again, there are advances in these areas too and hopefully as this work develops it will become easier to measure objectively the full range of linguistic skills of LD pupils. Finally, the chapter turned to the issues of promoting multilingualism through educational settings, identifying that advances had been made in this area with the development of dual language immersion programmes throughout the world, particularly with respect to the maintenance of indigenous languages. The problem of how to develop and implement a multilingual pedagogy in a mainstream classroom, particularly in diverse linguistic contexts was also discussed, highlighting that there are already a number of approaches that researchers argue are helpful. More research needs to be carried out, however, in order to be able to unambiguously identify what constitutes best practice.

Despite various political discourses around the world that might seem to promote more insular approaches to education and society more generally, the reality is very likely that we are not going to regress to a time when people did not move around the globe. Multilingualism is a real, global, phenomenon and one that is here to stay. An important question for us as we move forward is how will we ensure that we maximize the potential of all our children so they can become global citizens in this world? More than ever we need a citizenry that is inter-culturally aware and linguistically and academically equipped to face the challenges of the future. Close collaboration between researchers and teachers and multilingual families will provide fruitful opportunities to work towards resolving many of these issues.

Notes

(1)   Note that given the context in which I carry out most of my own research is the UK, and England in particular, many of the examples from which I draw will be taken from this particular setting. I will highlight where I believe the setting is particularly unique and cannot be readily generalizable to other contexts.

(2) (https://www.bera.ac.uk/researchers-resources/publications/
ethical-guidelines-for-educational-research-2018)
(3) See NALDIC's response to this decision and the Strand and Hessel (2018) report here:
https://naldic.org.uk/about-naldic/campaigns-and-reports/responses/
strand-hessel-2018/#the-report
(4) One small caveat to this statement is of course participation in complementary
schools, which are voluntary and attended outside the school day, and certainly not
attended by all children from LD backgrounds.
(5) https://www.dailymail.co.uk/news/article-2944102/Only-one-10-pupils-east-
London-primary-speaks-English-language-nine-10-1999-speak-SIXTY-different-
languages.html
(6) https://www.economicshelp.org/blog/6399/economics/
impact-of-immigration-on-uk-economy/

References

Barnett, W.S. and Hustedt, J.S. (2003) Preschool: The most important grade. *The First
Years of School* 60 (7), 54–57.

Chalmers, H. (2019) *The Role of the First Language in English Medium Instruction.* OUP
ELT Position Paper. See https://elt.oup.com/feature/global/expert/emi?cc=gb&sel
Language=en

Cline, T., Crafter, S., O'Dell, L. and de Abreu, G. (2011) Young people's representations
of language brokering. *Journal of Multilingual and Multicultural Development* 3
(32), 207–220. doi: 10.1080/01434632.2011.558901

Conteh, J. (2015) 'Funds of Knowledge' for achievement and success: Multilingual pedagogies for mainstream primary classrooms in England. In C.J. Jenks and P. Seedhouse (eds)
International Perspectives on ELT Classroom Interaction (pp. 49–63). London: Palgrave.

Cowie, B. and Khoo, E. (2017) Accountability through access, authenticity and advocacy
when researching with young children. *International Journal of Inclusive Education*
21 (3), 234–247. doi: 10.1080/13603116.2016.1260821

Cummins, J. (1979) Linguistic interdependence and the educational development of bilingual children. *Review of Educational Research* 49 (2), 222–251.

Cummins, J. (1980) The construct of language proficiency in bilingual education. In
J. Alatis (ed.) *Current Issues in Bilingual Education* (pp. 81–103). Washington, DC:
Georgetown University Press.

Cummins, J. (2000) *Language, Power and Pedagogy: Bilingual Children in the Crossfire.*
Clevedon: Multilingual Matters.

Cummins, J. (2001) Bilingual children's mother tongue: Why is it important for education? *Sprogforum* 7 (19), 15–20.

Cummins, J. (2005) A proposal for action: Strategies for recognizing heritage language
competence as a learning resource within the mainstream classroom. *The Modern
Language Journal* 89 (4), 585–592.

Cummins, J. and Early, M. (2010) (eds) *Identity Texts: The Collaborative Creation of
Power in Multilingual Schools.* Stoke-on-Trent: Trentham Books.

Cummins, J., Hu, S. Markus, P. and Montero, M.K. (2015) Identity texts and academic
achievement: Connecting the dots in multilingual school contexts. *TESOL Quarterly*
49 (3), 555–581.

Demie, F. and Strand, S. (2006) English language acquisition and educational attainment
at the end of secondary school. *Educational Studies* 32, 215–231. doi:10.1080/
03055690600631119

Department for Education (DfE) (2016) *Schools, pupils and their characteristics: January
2016.* See https://www.gov.uk/government/uploads/system/uploads/attachment_
data/file/552342/SFR20_2016_Main_Text.pdf

Dunn, D.M. (2018) *Peabody Picture Vocabulary Test* (5th edn) Boston: Pearson.

Faitaki, F. and Murphy, V.A. (2020) Oral language elicitation tasks in applied linguistics research. In H. Rose and J. McKinley (eds) *The Routledge Handbook of Research Methods in Applied Linguistics*. Abingdon: Routledge.

Fishman, J.A. (1997) *In Praise of the Beloved Language: A Comparative View of Positive Ethnolinguistic Consciousness*. Berlin & New York: Mouton de Gruyter.

García, O. (2005) Positioning heritage languages in the United States. *The Modern Language Journal* 89 (4), 601–605.

García, O. (2014) What is translanguaging? Expanded questions and answers for U.S. educators. In S. Hesson, K. Seltzer and H.H. Woodley. *Translanguaging in Curriculum and Instruction: A CUNY-NYSIEB Guide for Educators*. New York: CUNY-NYSIEB.

García, O. (2017) Translanguaging in schools: Subiendo y bajando, bajando y subiendo as afterword. *Journal of Language, Identity & Education* 16 (4), 256–263.

García, O. and Li Wei (2014) *Translanguaging: Language, Bilingualism and Education*. New York, NY: Palgrave MacMillan.

Harrison, B. (1998) Te Wharekura o Rakamangamanga: The development of an Indigenous language immersion school. *Bilingual Research Journal* 22 (2/4), 297–316.

Hornberger, N. (2007) Literacy, language maintenance, and linguistic human rights: Three telling cases. *International Journal of the Sociology of Language* 127, 87–103

Hua, J.M. and Costigan, C.L. (2012) The familial context of adolescent language brokering within immigrant Chinese families in Canada. *Journal of Youth and Adolescence* 41 (7), 894–906. DOI 10.1007/s10964-011-9682-2

Hutchinson, J. (2018) *Educational outcomes of children with English as an additional language*. Report produced by the Bell Foundation, Unbound Philanthropy and the Education Policy Institute. https://epi.org.uk/wp-content/uploads/2018/02/EAL_Educational-Outcomes_EPI-1.pdf

Issa, T. and Hatt, A. (2013) *Language, Culture and Identity in the Early Years*. London: Bloomsbury.

Lastikka, A.L. and Kangas, J. (2017) Ethical reflections on interviewing young children: Opportunities and challenges for promoting children's inclusion and participation. *Asia-Pacific Journal of Research in Early Childhood Education* 11 (1), 85–110.

May, S. (2013) Indigenous immersion education: International developments. *Journal of Immersion and Content-Based Language Education* 1 (1), 34–69.

Menken, K. (2008) *English Learners Left Behind: Standardized Testing as Language Policy*. Clevedon: Multilingual Matters.

Murphy, V.A. (2014) *Second Language Learning in the Early School Years: Trends and Contexts*. Oxford: Oxford University Press

Murphy, V.A. (2017) Literacy development in children with English as an additional language (EAL). In J. Enever and E. Lindgren (eds) *Early Language Learning: Complexity and Mixed Methods* (pp. 41–61). Bristol: Multilingual Matters.

Murphy, V.A. (2018) Literacy development in linguistically diverse pupils. In D. Miller, F. Bayram, J. Rothman and L. Serratrice (eds) *Bilingual Cognition and Language: The State of the Science across its Subfields*. Amsterdam: John Benjamins.

Murphy, V.A. (2019) Multilingualism in primary schools. In S. Garton and F. Copland (eds) *The Routledge Handbook of Teaching English to Young Learners*. Abingdon: Routledge.

Paradis, J., Emmerzael, K. and Sorenson Duncan, T. (2010) Assessment of English language learners: Using parent report on first language development. *Journal of Communication Disorders* 43, 474–497.

Pinter, A. (2013) Child participant roles in applied linguistics. *Applied Linguistics* 35 (2), 168–183. https://doi.org/10.1093/applin/amt008

Pinter, A. and Zandian, S. (2014) 'I don't ever want to leave this room': Benefits of researching 'with' children. *ELT Journal* 68 (1), 64–74.

Pinter, A., Kuchach, K. and Smith, R. (2013) Researching with children. *ELT Journal* 67 (4), 484–487.

Richards, M. and Burnaby, B. (2008) Restoring aboriginal languages: Immersion and intensive language program models in Canada. In T.W. Fortune and D.J. Tedick (eds) *Pathways to Multilingualism: Evolving Perspectives on Immersion Education* (pp. 221–241). Clevedon: Multilingual Matters.

Robertson, L.H., Drury, R. and Cable, C. (2014) Silencing bilingualism: A day in a life of a bilingual practitioner. *International Journal of Bilingual Education and Bilingualism* 17 (5), 610–623, DOI: 10.1080/13670050.2013.864252

Sarkar, M. and Metallic, M.A. (2009) Indigenizing the structural syllabus: The challenge of revitalizing Mi'gmaq in Listuguj. *The Canadian Modern Language Review* 66 (1), 49–71.

Schaefer, B., Bowyer-Crane, C., Hermann, F. and Fricke, S. (2015) Development of a tablet application for the screening of receptive vocabulary skills in multilingual children: A pilot study. *Child Language Teaching and Therapy* 32 (2), 179–191.

Skutnabb-Kangas, T. (2012) Indigenousness, human rights, ethnicity, language and power. *International Journal of the Sociology of Language* 213, 87–104.

Strand, S. and Demie, F. (2005) English language acquisition and educational attainment at the end of primary school. *Educational Studies* 31, 275–291. doi:10.1080/03055690500236613

Strand, S. and Demie, F. (2006) Pupil mobility, attainment and progress in primary school. *British Educational Research Journal* 32 (4), 551–568.

Strand, S. and Hessel, A. (2018) English as an additional language, proficiency in English and pupils' educational achievement: An analysis of Local Authority Data. Report published by The University of Oxford, Unbound Philanthropy and The Bell Foundation. See https://www.bell-foundation.org.uk/wp-content/uploads/2018/10/EAL-PIE-and-Educational-Achievement-Report-2018-FV.pdf

Strand, S., Malmberg, L. and Hall, J. (2015) English as an additional Language (EAL) and educational achievement in England: An analysis of the National Pupil Database. Research Report for the Education Endowment Foundation, Bell Foundation and Unbound Philanthropy.

Whiteside, K.E., Gooch, D. and Norbury, C.F. (2016) English language proficiency and early school attainment among children learning English as an additional language. *Child Development* 88 (3), 812–827. https://doi.org/10.1111/cdev.12615

6 Reframing Expertise: Learning with and from Children as Co-investigators of their Plurilingual Practices and Experiences

Gail Prasad

Cultural and linguistic diversity have become defining features of classrooms around the world today. In the North American context, for example, the National Association for the Education of Young Children (NAEYC, 2009) has projected that 'the biggest single child-specific demographic change in the United States over the next twenty years is predicted to be an increase in children whose home language is not English' (2009: 2). Similarly in Canada, Statistics Canada (2017) projects that immigrant children will make up 39% to 49% of all children in Canada by 2036. Many Canadian school districts, particularly in major urban centres like Toronto, Montreal and Vancouver, report their student populations speaking more than 100 different home languages. Today, this linguistic and cultural diversity cuts across English, French-immersion and French-language schools in Canada (Mady & Arnett, 2019; Prasad, 2015).

The European Commission (2017) also notes growing linguistic and cultural diversity in schools as a result of the rise in migrant children moving to the European Union, as well as between countries in the European Union. For some European countries, such as Austria, Belgium, Luxemburg, Germany, Spain and Malta, growing numbers of students speak different languages at home than at school. While linguistic diversity has often been conceptualized as a problem for schools and for multilingual students themselves, shifting paradigms to conceptualize linguistic diversity as a resource for teachers and learners alike can help us to see classrooms and schools as key sites of encounter in which students and educators from a range of cultural, linguistic and social backgrounds come together by design to negotiate their complex identities and leverage dynamic ways of living and learning together within a shared community of practice (Wenger, 2009).

Tsing (2005) uses the metaphor of the river and its riverbed to highlight the ways in which seemingly fixed structures such as riverbeds are actually reshaped by the rivers that flow through them. While we may not perceive any change to be taking place at first, the current of the river gradually (re)shapes its riverbed over time. In a similar manner, while schools, as riverbeds, may appear to be fixed structures of immobility, the dynamic flow of diverse students and their families invariably reshapes classrooms and by extension what teaching and learning look like in the context of such dynamic and heterogeneous mobility. How do children, both dominant language speakers and minoritized language speakers, make sense of the linguistic diversity they encounter within their classrooms and beyond the walls of the school? Further, how can language education researchers capture, analyse and represent children's ways of knowing, seeing and being in ways that inform equitable practice with and outcomes for minoritized language speakers? I use the term *minoritized* rather than the more commonly used term 'minority' to foreground hegemonic forces that ascribe value to certain languages and their speakers while devaluing others. 'Minority' languages are socially and politically constructed in ways that purposefully privilege some speakers and not others. Children are doubly minoritized relative to their adult counterparts who have reached the age of maturity. It is critical to highlight power relations at work in this discussion of expertise of children, particularly language-minoritized children. In this chapter, I reflect on my classroom-based language research with culturally and linguistically diverse children in multilingual schools to argue for a reframing children's expertise and to honour the inside(r) knowledge that only children can possess during the limited time in which they grow and remain children.

Following a New Childhood Studies approach (Christensen & James, 2008; Clark, 2005; Prout, 2005) as outlined by Kuchah and Pinter in the opening chapter to this book, I recount why and how I have moved from doing research *about* children to doing research *with* children as co-investigators of their plurilingual practices and experiences. I consider how positioning children as active co-investigators of their own language practices and literacies creates the opportunity to reframe children as embodied experts of their lived experience rather than as language-minoritized learners who cannot speak for themselves. I argue that adult researchers must adopt a disposition of humility in order to reframe children as experts of their plurilingual language and literacy practices. I use the two Greek words for time – *chronos*, the quantitative term and *kairos*, the qualitative term – to describe the ways in which adult researchers engage with children in the research process. As Miller (1992: 313) discusses, 'chronos reflects measureable time, the background that kairos presupposes... Against that background, kairos appears as a critical occasion for decision or action (or revelation in the biblical sense)'. I argue that in doing research *with* children, adult researchers must be sensitive to critical 'kairos moments' that unfold, sometimes seemingly as interruptions or divergences, along the research process.

Drawing on a multi-site study that I conducted with 9–11 year olds as co-ethnographers of their language and literacies practices, I present three 'kairos moments' to illustrate how children have taught me to foster a disposition of humility that has allowed me to learn to pay exquisite attention to both child-generated artefacts and to children as experts of their own experience, to prioritize curiosity over skepticism; and, to hold loosely to research tools in order for them to be shared with and adapted by children. I conclude the chapter by considering how facilitating research with children as co-investigators and child-led language inquiry necessitate further exploration of alternative modes of inquiry such that children's voices, identities and experiences are honoured throughout the process of data collection, analysis and dissemination.

Shifting Paradigms: From Research on Children Towards Research with Children

Long before I became a university-based language education researcher, I began studying children's language and literacy development as an English Language Arts and English-as-a-Second Language (ESL) teacher in a French elementary school. All students received instruction in French for core subjects, as well as English Language Arts from Kindergarten (age 5) through grade 5. As a novice teacher, I had many questions as I endeavoured to teach culturally and linguistically diverse kindergarteners, as well as first and second graders to read and write in English. My questions eventually led me to graduate school where I conducted a case study of elementary teachers' perspectives and practices supporting culturally and linguistically diverse learners' literacy development in a French-language school in Toronto, Canada (Prasad, 2012).

Towards the end of my data collection, which included classroom observation, teacher interviews and focus groups over a six-month period, I observed a kindergarten class responding to a read-aloud story by drawing a picture on a worksheet in response to the prompt: *'Je suis comme Nicolas* [the protagonist of the story]. *Je lis mon livre pour avoir un moment de plaisir.'* (I am like Nicolas. I read my book to experience a moment of pleasure. [English gloss]) As I circulated and talked with children about their drawings, I became aware that while most children produced a self-portrait with a book in their hands, many children had further added details to contextualize where and/or with whom they engaged in reading. These 'extra' details often spilled into the margins of the worksheet; these extra details revealed stories of important family members and special spaces within their homes or in the community that were in fact central to students' developing literacy practices and how they saw themselves becoming readers and writers.

As I got in my car at the end of the day, I still recall that I found myself wondering how many times I, as a teacher, was more focused on getting work(sheets) finished, rather than lingering to listen to the stories children had to share. I kept three students' drawings out of the many that I received over those six months of data collection. They serve as reminders of this *kairos* moment that interrupted my thinking and broke through my careful chronicling of teachers' practices to support the language and literacy development of young culturally and linguistically diverse students. I came away from my observations that day wondering how children *themselves* made sense of themselves as multilingual readers, writers and speakers. I had seen and heard first-hand that children had ideas to share about what made reading meaningful and enjoyable for them. Sparks from this original kairos moment in my journey of becoming a researcher were fanned into flame as I began to explore in theory and practice epistemological, methodological and ethical, empirical questions related to engaging with children themselves in collaborative language and literacy research.

Extant research regarding cultural and linguistic diversity in schools has largely focused on adult perspectives: on issues such as teachers', administrators' and parents' perspectives on and goals for minoritized language learners (Stagg-Peterson & Heywood, 2007; Wiltse, 2006). Children's accounts of their own plurilingual experiences, however, have until recently remained marginal in language education literature (Prasad, 2013, 2018a, 2018b) and applied linguistics research more generally (Pinter, 2014). Traditionally, children have been excluded from participating in research based on historical conceptions of childhood that have positioned the child as 'developmentally immature and incomplete, and therefore unreliable respondents' (Freeman & Mathison, 2009: 2). Since the international adoption of the Convention on the Rights of the Child in 1989, interdisciplinary New Childhood Studies researchers have advocated for a shift from conducting research on and about children as objects and subjects respectively to engaging in research with children as social actors and co-researchers (Albanese, 2009; Belanger & Connelly, 2007; Bucknall, 2012; Christensen & James, 2008; Freeman & Mathison, 2009; Mason & Hood, 2010; Kellet, 2005; Pinter, 2014; Prout, 2005). As social scientists have focused on how children and youth construct meaning in and through their lives, they have come to acknowledge children's active role in society, 'as cocreators of... society, not just absorbers of it' (Freeman & Mathison, 2009: 4).

Brooker (2001) has outlined four main principles that underpin New Social Studies of Childhood:

(1) Childhood is a distinct and intrinsically interesting and important phase in human experience, valued for its own unique qualities rather than for its resemblance to adulthood.

(2) Children are viewed, therefore, as fully formed and complete individuals with a perspective of their own rather than as partially developed, incompletely formed adults.
(3) Children are autonomous subjects rather than members (or even possessions) of their family; their parents' and family members' interests and views are no longer assumed to be identical to their own.
(4) Children have rights of their own, including the right to protection from harm and the right to voice opinions and influence decisions in matters relating to their own lives. (2001: 162–163)

These four principles position children as experts with privileged 'insider' knowledge about childhood. It is important to recognize, however, that the nature of children's expertise on childhood is bounded by their lived experience as children only for as long as they remain children. Children's expertise then is *embodied,* a unique quality that is inextricably tied to the temporality of childhood. Unlike cognitive expertise that develops cumulatively over time, with training, mentorship and practice, children ultimately outgrow their *embodied expertise* as insider 'knowers, do-ers and be-ers' of childhood when they move on through adolescence into adulthood. Thus, while adult researchers can develop (meta) cognitive expertise to do research respectfully with children as social actors and co-researchers, adults cannot by definition ever (re)enter the embodied expertise that is a property of childhood alone. Such expertise is something that children have intrinsically by virtue of being children and members of the culture of childhood. As such, children warrant the privilege of sharing their expertise on their own terms and it behoves the adult researcher to find ways of adapting and adopting alternative ways of accessing children's ways of knowing, doing and being that resonate with children themselves.

Research in language education and applied linguistics has traditionally focused on using language-based methods that rely on a single mode, that of the verbal. When working with children, particularly culturally and linguistically diverse children, a more expansive approach is required: rather than conceptualizing the research process as one of data collection, Bucknall (2012) advocates that we move towards a process of data generation with children through which they may produce a variety of multimodal research artefacts or products. When we shift from data collection as a linear process towards data generation the process and its products may be non-linear. What I seek to bring to the foreground by suggesting a shift from conceptualizing the research process and its products as a linear one towards the research process and its products becoming increasingly non-linear is that multimodal and multilingual data generation with participants can be unpredictable. The data generation process, particularly when combined with the creative, can get messy. This is even more the case regarding the interpretative process since a photo, drawing,

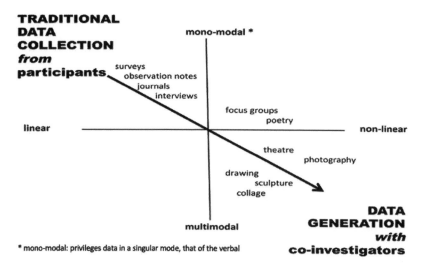

Figure 6.1 Towards data generation with co-investigators

collage or performance, or other artefacts offer multiple entry points of interpretation.

Figure 6.1 offers a schematic representation of how various continua intersect in the classification of methods as we move from data collection to data generation.

In the context of my journey as a researcher investigating children's language and literacy practices, my focus has shifted from doing research *on* multilingual children and the ways in which the adults in their lives (parents, teachers, administrators, etc.) support and/or constrain their language practices and literacy development to doing research *with* children as social actors and co-investigators of their plurilingual lives. This shift has involved taking up creative visual and multimodal methods that engage children as co-ethnographers of their language and literacy practices through data generation. More than being active participants, I understand the role of children as co-investigators because they engage both in data generation and its interpretation based on their insider perspectives as culturally and linguistically diverse children. I have previously described children as co-ethnographers of their own lives (Prasad, 2013). While I have come alongside children as an adult researcher with questions about children's sense-making and social representations of multilingualism, children are the ones who offer thick descriptions of their perspectives and practices by generating photos, drawings, multiliteracy texts and collages. None of these research artefacts are transparent and they rely on children as community insiders to interpret their meanings.

As an adult researcher, it would be easy for me to position myself as the principal investigator and driver of our collaborative inquiry because

I laid out the 'chronology' of the research process. While I necessarily negotiated timelines with teachers, parents and administrators that made it possible for children to engage in data generation, children provoked kairos moments throughout the data generation, interpretation and dissemination process that shape the quality and authenticity of our joint research.

In what remains in this chapter, I want to further develop the notion of the kairos moment in researching with children. I conceptualize kairos moments as powerful interruptions along the chronology of the research process – interruptions of thought, and self-awareness that provoke adult researchers to make critical ethical choices that privilege children's voices and ways of knowing, seeing and being.

Several *kairos* moments have led and continue leading me deeper into questioning how children's 'expert' perspectives can be seen, heard and represented by children themselves in research about their lives and experiences. As outlined earlier, I use the two distinct notions of time in Greek (*kairos* versus *chronos*) to make clear the transformative nature of critical reflexive *kairos* moments that interrupt the steady *chronos* of the inquiry process and radically shift relations of power among children and adults. Kairos moments come as a whisper inviting the adult researcher to lay down the mantle of scholarly expertise and to lean in to learn from children as experts of their own lives and experiences.

L'Engle (1992) explains the Greek distinction between chronos and kairos in the following way:

> Kairos is not measurable. Kairos is ontological...Kairos can sometimes enter, penetrate, break through chronos: the child at play, the painter at his easel... [t]he burning bush before which Moses removed his shoes... In kairos that part of us which is not consumed in the burning is wholly awake. We too often let it fall asleep, ...dully, bluntingly. (1992: 245)

The idea of being wholly awake is central to listening to and learning with children as co-investigators in the research process. In the midst of chronic scholarly pressure to research and publish more and more quickly, it can be easy for adult researchers to miss or hastily bulldoze over *kairos* moments. Research with children necessarily takes time and cannot be rushed precisely because children intuitively linger in spaces of wonder, reflection and imagination. The child at play is not aware of time marching on because the creative, embodied world of play encourages children to step outside of real time into the imaginary. By contrast, adulthood is characterized not by play but rather by work. And, the world of work is strictly governed by *chronos*, tasks, deadlines and calendars. *Kairos* moments whisper invitations to adult researchers to pause long enough to look and to listen closely and deeply to children. These invitational moments, however, can never force us to heed them; in fact, the risk is always present for adult researchers to miss them all together.

In the following section, I recount three *kairos* moments that unfolded over the course of a two-year multi-site case study involving five different schools in Canada and in France in which I examined children's social representations of plurilingualism. Three main research questions guided this collaborative research:

(1) If we shift from doing research about children's plurilingualism to engaging with children as co-ethnographers of their own plurilingual languages and literacies, what might such an approach reveal that we would not discover otherwise?
(2) Methodologically, how can children develop and express their representations of plurilingualism?
(3) In terms of teaching and learning, how does understanding children's representations of plurilingualism inform inclusive mainstream classroom practice and policy?

Drawing on Clark and Moss' (2011) Mosaic approach, I designed a number of visual and multimodal tasks for children to complete individually or in groups as co-ethnographers of their own language and literacy practices. Tasks included reflexive drawings (Prasad, 2018a), digital photography (Prasad, 2013), creating collaborative multilingual and multimodal texts (Prasad, 2015) and collages (Prasad, 2018b). Children in the five participating classes engaged in completing each of these tasks over a 4–6 month period per school. Table 6.1 outlines the characteristics of students from each participating class / school.

Each task provided insight into children's sense-making and social representations of plurilingualism. Taken together, this mosaic of research artefacts contributes to a holistic understanding of children's sense-making about their language and literacy practices and their plurilingual identities, while not losing individual differences and specificities.

Figure 6.2 illustrates the research timeline and mosaic of tasks completed at each of the five participating schools.

I focus in this chapter on three kairos moments that unfolded during the collaborative data generation and analysis processes with children as co-investigators of their plurilingual lives. I have selected these moments because they continue to be vivid signposts that remain continuously in my mind's eye as I have continued engaging with children in collaborative language inquiry. I am acutely aware that these vignettes do not generally paint me in a positive light; my reflections candidly portray my adult biases. At the same time, these touchstone kairos moments have been (trans)formative in terms of how I conceptualize child-led inquiry. In each case, a child invited me to pause and to take on (or not) a disposition of humility that would help me better see, hear and understand how children themselves make sense of their plurilingual experiences and identities.

Table 6.1 School and class features (Prasad, 2018b: 5)

School model	Location	Participating teachers	Number of participating students	Grade level	Curriculum	Languages of instruction *indicates principle language of instruction	Home languages
Public English school	Toronto, Canada	1 teacher	25/28 Students	Grade 5	Ontario Ministry of Education	* Enalish + French-as-a-second language: 45 min / day (taught by another teacher)	17 Languages
Public French immersion school	Toronto, Canada	1 teacher	17/20 Students	Grade 5/6	Ontario Ministry of Education	* French-as-a-second language: 50% am) * English: 50% (pm)	11 languages
Public French-language minority school	Toronto, Canada	1 teacher	26/29 Students	Grade 4/5	Ontario Ministry of Education	*French + English: 45 min /day (taught by another teacher)	14 languages
Private French school	Toronto, Canada	2 teacher	12/12 Students	CM2 (French equivalent of grade 5 in Canad)	National French curriculum [France] locally-developed English curriculum	* French+ English: 5h/ week (taught by 2nd participating teacher)	7 languages
French school	Toronto, Canada	1 teacher	26/27 Students	CM2 (French equivalent of Grade 5 in Canada)	National French curriculum (France)	*French + Occtian as a regional language: 1h / week (taught by participating teacher) + English as a foreign language: 1 h / week (taught by another teacher)	11 languages

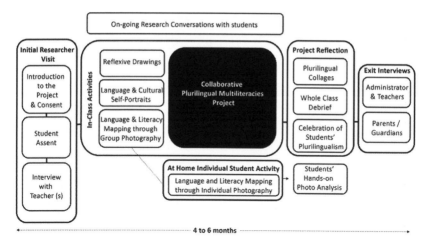

Figure 6.2 Research process mosaic

Vignette 1: Exquisite attention

At the outset of a classroom-based case study at *l'école internationale*[1], asked a class of fifth grade students, ages 10–11 years old, to engage in generating a series of four sequential reflexive drawings related to key vocabulary about linguistic identity categories. I asked students to draw a series of four pictures including: (a) a picture of someone who was monolingual; (b) someone who was bilingual; (c) someone who was plurilingual; and (d) a picture of themselves. Before students completed their drawings, we discussed the meaning of the prefixes mono-, bi- and pluri- in relation to language speakers. The first three drawing prompts were crafted to help students develop visual metaphors that would help them distinguish between each category and the fourth drawing was designed for students to be able to use their own visual metaphors to share how they saw their own linguistic identities. While the majority of students' drawings revealed positive representations of being bilingual or plurilingual, there was one student in particular whose drawings and his description of them precipitated a kairos moment in which I became aware of how my bias as a former classroom teacher was shaping how I read students' drawings. Figure 6.3 shows the student's four drawings. The first drawing depicts a happy monolingual, the second drawing shows an ambivalent bilingual and the third drawing shows an unhappy plurilingual. The fourth drawing then strays from the sequential metaphor and the student depicts himself as a moderately happy bilingual. Because I saw this fourth drawing in contradiction to the visual metaphor he had developed, I asked him to tell me more about his pictures.

In my analysis of the students' drawings (Prasad, 2018a: 324), I recounted this student's description of his drawings:

Figure 6.3 Richard's sequential reflexive drawings

he thought that it might be easier in just one language...His father was French and his mother was Australian so their family life as well as his school life at the French private school focused around negotiating two languages ... this student used his drawings to voice his struggle at home and at school.

I go on to note that drawing his representations seemed to provide this student with an alternative mode – a visual one (rather than a verbal one) in which he felt more free to express mixed emotions about his language development. In my research journal notes from that day in class, I reflected:

Honestly I wasn't ready for [Richard's] explanation of his drawings...His teachers had said that he struggled with reading and writing in both English and French – so I don't know why I was totally caught off guard when he began to explain that he found it difficult to have to work in two languages at school and at home. And then it kind of all came pouring out. What a confession... how often are kids asked how they *feel* about their language development? Especially in a context where there are two languages of instruction. It almost felt like he was relieved to get it off his chest that he found navigating both languages so difficult. Like he had just let me in on a secret that he had been keeping inside. I don't know that he actually would have explained his feelings if he hadn't drawn them. There seems to be something to the artefact — like we were both focused on his drawing and maybe because I was so interested in his pic-tures, he really opened up. My heart really went out to him.

In Abric's (2003) discussion of the study of social representations, he highlights that it is often difficult to access 'the silent zone' (la zone muette) of an individual's social representations through discourse because individuals can use various non-discursive strategies to hide personal, negative representations that vary from dominant collective social norms. Busch (2010) has similarly argued that 'processes that influence language use tend to operate unconsciously and cannot easily be verbalized. The switch in mode of representation from word to image helps deconstruct internalized categories, to reflect upon embodied practices and to generate narratives that are less bound by genre expectations' (2010: 286). Engaging children in drawing their social representations of monolingual, bilingual, and plurilingual speakers as well as themselves offered visual space for more nuanced, hidden and even negative representations to become visible. Moreover, the time necessarily allotted to producing these representational artefacts supported children expressing themselves without being limited to or by language, particularly the dominant language of instruction in school settings.

In this *kairos* encounter with Richard, his description of his drawings challenged me to adopt a disposition of humility because I realized my own limitations in interpreting Richard's drawings without Richard himself cluing me in on his thinking and feelings. It would be easy for adults to believe that simply engaging children in drawing their perspectives and ideas produces transparent child-generated research artefacts. My interview with Richard revealed, however, that it is not just important to listen to the child sharing their research artefacts but also to pay 'exquisite attention' to the artefact itself (Lather, 2007). The collaborative act of focusing together on something created by and of value to the child opens up a space for them to interpret their drawings on their own terms. Richard was willing to share his drawings with me because I took an interest in him and paid 'exquisite attention' to his work. Richard taught me not to hurry, but rather to linger in the story-telling moments and to pay attention to both what is said and unsaid, seen and invisible.

Vignette 2: Curiosity over skepticism

After spending six months working with teachers and students at *l'ecole international* to generate drawings, photos and collaborative multilingual and multimodal texts, I asked students to engage in generating a final photo-collage in response to the prompt: What does it look like and feel like to be plurilingual? Students used images from magazines as source material for their collages. The only restrictions that students were given included that there should be no white space left on their 8.5 by 11 inch collage and that they should avoid using words/text in their collage (i.e. it should be image-based). Overall students' collages were not only visually compelling but also they displayed a sophistication of personal reflection about their plurilingualism. (For further discussion of collage as method, see Prasad, 2018a.)

While I was observing students sort through magazine photos and compose their collages, I caught sight of one student, Alex, flipping hastily through magazine pages. From the outside, he did not seem to really care about how carefully he was cutting out images. I noted the following in my researcher journal after observing in class that day,

> I really thought Alex had completely missed the point of the collage exercise. I can't believe how skeptical I was that he had actually taken the task seriously. I was entirely expecting that he was going to say that he had randomly chosen the dog in the Santa suit to be funny. I was way off base. Alex really opened my eyes – like he removed the blinders I had on as an adult, as a teacher, and even as 'researcher' — I clearly had been waiting for a specific type of response and I was ready to write Alex off as soon as it appeared that his collage didn't conform to what I had anticipated. I was really humbled when he began sharing. The whole time that I was watching Alex thinking about how he had missed the point of the collage task. I had [even] started stewing over whether collage as method was such a good idea if students weren't going to take it seriously – all the while, [Alex] was entirely on task – and not just on task but also very insightful.

Figure 6.4 depicts Alex's collage. He included a picture of a lizard because there are 'lots of lizards and in Miami, [where] we speak Spanish

Figure 6.4 Alex's collage

and also English. And I picked the Montreal Canadians shirt and the Montreal Canadians hat because in Montreal we speak French there' (Prasad, 2018: 13). Alex had clearly associated specific images with specific locations and their languages. He then went on to explain that he had purposefully included a dog in a Santa suit because 'Santa Claus has to travel around the whole world and he has to ask the kids in different languages what they want.' Santa Claus personified plurilingualism at its finest as Santa was not only able to read children's letters in different languages but he was able to respond and deliver the hearts' desires of children around the world each Christmas (Prasad, 2018a: 13).

Alex's explanation exemplifies the strength of children's creative imagination not being limited to the literal here and now. I had instinctively written Alex's collage off because in my adult mind, I could not imagine how a dog in a Santa suit could relate in any way to looking and feeling plurilingual. I found myself humbled again – but in this kairos moment, the lesson I took away was that I needed to foster curiosity over skepticism especially at the stage of engaging with children in data generation. Simply shifting from verbal data collection to an alternative visual or multimodal form of data generation with children does not guarantee that children's perspectives and voices will be seen and heard in research and in the world. In fact, if as adult researchers, we do not cultivate genuine curiosity and reserve judgment regarding children's generation of research artefacts until children themselves have been given time and space to offer their interpretations, we run the risk of completely missing out on learning with and from children as experts of their own experience. As Bochner (2000) has argued, our concern should not be whether or not child-generated research artefact are true but rather if child-generated research artefacts are true, then what? What does this mean for the future of research with children and youth? How do we prepare for and even provoke kairos moments among adults and children so that both groups come to new understandings of themselves and one another?

Vignette 3: Holding tools loosely with an open mind

This third vignette unfolded in the participating English school while facilitating a group interview with two students (Raj and Marten) about their final plurilingual collages. The case study at the English School followed a similar design to that of *l'ecole internationale,* except that instead of audio recording students' analysis of their collages, I had amended the research protocol to use an iPad app 'Explain Everything' to produce a video recording of students' collages and their analysis. We began by taking a picture of students' finished collages and then we used the video record function in the app to record pairs of students sharing their collages with one another. As I had switched from digitally audio-recording students' discussion of their collages to producing a video-recorded retelling, I tried to model for students how to use the Explain Everything App before we started the interview. At the time, the app was new to me so I tried to keep things simple and I only demonstrated one tool within the app. As I set up to have Raj and Marten share their collages, I started to explain how to use Explain Everything. I was having difficulty modelling how to use the pointer, when Raj interjected, 'Can I just show you *my own way?*'

Raj's question caught me off guard. I had been rather proud of myself for learning how to use the new app and felt with some continued practice that I would get the hang of it. But his question struck a chord:

> 'Can I just show you *my own way?*' Raj's words echoed in my head for the rest of the afternoon. Here, I had been so intent that I was going to implement this new change in protocol that would allow me to capture talk along with photos – I hadn't even thought to ask the students if they already knew how to use the app! I'm still so quick to take on the position as 'expert' even when it comes to technology where I clearly have a big learning curve ahead. Of course [these students] knew how to use it! That's why their teacher had recommended it! You would think by this stage in trying to do research *with* children that I would be mindful at least of how to help children bring their creativity and expertise to our research … Still, it's hard to let go and get out of the way. (Researcher notes)

I have often returned in my mind to this moment with Raj because I so distinctly recall being destabilized by his question to use the app 'his own way'. Indeed, he showed me 'his own way' which included using a wider range of tools within the app. In retrospect, if I had let myself be put off by his request to use the app 'his own way' or by the fact that he was more proficient with the app than me, I might have missed out on hearing his insights about being plurilingual and asking questions to clarify his reasoning. Figure 6.5 depicts Raj's collage and the interview that follows elaborates on his choices of images.

Raj: I have soil [top left corner] due to the fact that for soil I think that when I learn a different language it feels like I'm in a different land. And like I have the car on the clock [watch], that's because when I learn a new language time drives by. The graduation picture, it feels like I earned something when I learn a new language.
… [exchange with another student]

Gail: And I think it's really interesting that you have graduation. Can you talk a little bit about what you earn; what's valuable for learning a language?

Raj: What's valuable is that you get to learn something brand new that you don't know. And you feel like you've done something that matters, that I learned something!

In this exchange with Raj, it is clear that he has a well-developed response to the collage prompt about being plurilingual. He is able to

Figure 6.5 Raj's collage

explain at least three different images in relation to being plurilingual and learning new languages. The images support him in articulating the rationale for his choices. He was not at all phased by navigating the Explain Everything app to explain his choice of images – in fact, in the transcript, that he is using a pointer and zooming in and out do not even appear. The significance of this vignette then is that it serves as a reminder that when doing research with children as co-investigators, adult researchers need to foster a disposition of humility in order to respond flexibly to children's requests and suggestions to adapt and adopt tools in a collaborative way. Rather than maintaining a firm grip on research tools, adult researchers need to be open to releasing them into the hands and abilities of children as co-investigators.

In each of these three vignettes, I have highlighted how a disposition of humility is key to fostering collaborative research relationships with children as co-investigators. It can be difficult within the context of scholarly research to advocate for cultivating a disposition of humility when researchers and scholars see themselves as experts in their fields. We must remember, however, that humility is not the absence of expertise, it is the absence of self-importance and self-promotion. Thus, to continue to push the boundaries of collaborative research with children towards collaborative child-led inquiry, we need to continue to make space for alter(n)ative ways of knowing, being and doing research.

Creating Space for Alter(n)ative Ways of Knowing, Being and Doing: Towards Child-led Research

In the case of language-minoritized (im)migrant children, in particular, it is crucial that children's own perspectives are seen, heard and represented in research about their lives and experiences. The paradox of (im) migrant children is that they often become language brokers (experts) within their families while being positioned as language-minoritized learners within classrooms and schools. Students' rich linguistic repertoires have often remained overlooked, if not completely rejected by schools (Chumak-Horbatsch, 2012; Cummins, 2001; García & Li Wei, 2013; García et al., 2006; Kenner & Ruby, 2012; Wong-Fillmore, 2005).

Creative multimodal research methodologies draw on alternative ways of knowing and being and as such offer insights and opportunities for engagement that may not be revealed through traditional approaches to inquiry. Cahnmann Taylor (2011) traces the emergence of arts-based methods across the social sciences and in language education in particular to the 1980s as a result of the postmodern turn and the crisis in representation in qualitative inquiry (Denzin & Lincoln, 2008). One of the hybrid forms of artistic and scientific scholarship has been described by Neilsen (2002) as scholartistry. By drawing on the arts, 'scholartists bring to inquiry an understanding and sedimented knowing of schooling, education, and learning. They bring to inquiry the artistry of their imaginative powers in the literary and visual arts. These combine to become the skills and insight that unleash the spirit into new territory' (2002: 212).

Through previous arts-informed inquiry (Prasad, 2012), I conceptualized alter(n)ative modes of inquiry as forms of inquiry that draw on alternative or creative methods that privilege voices and perspectives that have traditionally been excluded in scholarly representation. By placing the (n) of alter(n)ative in parentheses, I highlight parenthetically how setting up 'in-between' creative third spaces in which inquiry can unfold makes room for the transformation of thought and experience. Alter(n)ative modes of inquiry foster an alteration or change of the status quo; they can produce a shift in power and privilege to allow previously unheard voices and unseen perspectives to be seen and heard. As with visual researchers such as Thomson (2008) and classroom-based researchers such as Thiessen (2007), transformative change is an intended outcome of alter(n)ative inquiry. Researching with children and by children invites the use of alter(n)ative modes of inquiry as they offer the opportunity to empower children as co-investigators of their plurilingual practices and lived experiences, as well as to enable them to have their creative research representations seen and their voices heard.

Throughout this chapter, I have argued for the need for adult-researchers to cultivate a disposition of humility, particularly when they engage with children and youth during the research process. I have shared four *kairos* moments that have interrupted my research journey to make me more mindful of my assumptions, positionality and my limitations as an adult researcher who seeks to understand children's social representations of their lived experiences with language and literacies. I have argued that it is easy to miss the kairos moments that occur along the research way – this risk is also present in research with adults, but perhaps even more acutely in research with children where the power differential is significantly greater. Humility and respect for children as insiders of childhood can help all researchers tune into new ways of truly speaking, listening and facilitating the representation of children's experiences from their own perspectives.

Note

(1) All participating schools in the study were identified by a pseudonym.

References

Abric, J.C. (ed.) (2003) Méthodes d'étude des représentations sociales. Ramonville, Saint-Agne: ERES.

Albanese, P. (2009) *Children in Canada Today*. Toronto, ON: Oxford University Press.

Bélanger, N. and Connelly, C. (2007) Methodological considerations in child-centered research about social difference and children experiencing difficulties at school. *Ethnography and Education* 2 (1), 21–38. doi: 10.1080/17457820601158994

Bochner, Arthur P., 'Criteria Against Ourselves' (2000) *Communication Faculty Publications*. 12. See https://scholarcommons.usf.edu/spe_facpub/12

Brooker, L. (2001) Interviewing children. In G. Mac Naughton, S.A. Rolfe and I. Siraj-Blatchford (eds) *Doing Early Childhood Research: International Perspectives on Theory and Practice* (1st edn, pp. 162–177). Crows Nest: Allen & Unwin.

Bucknall, S. (2012) *Children as Researchers in Primary Schools: Choice, Voice and Participation*. New York, NY: Routledge.

Busch, B. (2010) School language profiles: Valorizing linguistic resources in heteroglossic situations in South Africa. *Language & Education* 24 (4), 283–294. doi: 10.1080/09500781003678712

Cahnmann-Taylor, M. (2011) When poetry became ethnography and other flying pig tales in honor of Dell Hymes. *Anthropology & Education Quarterly* 42 (4), 393–396. doi: 10.1111/j.1548-1492.2011.01146.x

Christensen, P.M. and James, A. (2008) *Research with Children: Perspectives and Practices* (2nd edn). Abingdon: Routledge.

Chumak-Horbatsch, R. (2012) *Linguistically Appropriate Practice: A Guide for Working with Young Immigrant Children*. Toronto: University of Toronto Press.

Clark, A. and Moss, P. (2011) *Listening to Young Children: The Mosaic Approach*. London: Jessica Kingsley Publishers.

Clark, A. (2005) Listening to and involving young children: A review of research and practice. *Early Child Development and Care* 175 (6), 489–505. See https://doi.org/10.1080/03004430500131288

Cummins, J. (2001) *Negotiating Identities: Education for Empowerment in a Diverse Society* (2nd edn). Ontario, CA: California Association for Bilingual Education.

Denzin, N.K. and Lincoln, Y.S. (2008) *The Landscape of Qualitative Research* (Vol. 1). New York, NY: SAGE.

European Commision (2017) COMMUNICATION FROM THE COMMISSION TO THE EUROPEAN PARLIAMENT AND THE COUNCIL: The protection of children in migration. Brussels, Belgium. Retrieved on December 13, 2020 from https://ec.europa.eu/home-affairs/sites/homeaffairs/files/what-we-do/policies/european-agenda-migration/20170412_communication_on_the_protection_of_children_in_migration_en.pdf

Freeman, M. and Mathison, S. (2009) *Researching Children's Experiences.* New York, NY: Guilford Press.

García, O. and Li Wei (2013) *Translanguaging: Language, Bilingualism and Education.* New York, NY: Palgrave Macmillan.

Garcia, O., Skutnabb-Kangas, T. and Torres-Guzmán, M.E. (eds) (2006) *Imagining Multilingual Schools: Languages in Education and Glocalization.* Clevedon: Multilingual Matters.

Kellett, M. (2005) *How to Develop Children as Researchers: A step by step guide to teaching the research process.* London: Sage.

Kenner, C. and Ruby, M. (2012) Co-constructing bilingual learning: An equal exchange of strategies between complementary and mainstream teachers. *Language and Education* 26 (6), 517–535. doi:10.1080/09500782.2012.666248

L'Engle, M. (1992) *A Circle of Quiet.* San Francisco, CA: Harper & Row.

Lather, P. (2007) *Getting Lost: Feminist Efforts toward a Double(d) Science.* Albany, NY: SUNY.

Mady, C. and Arnett, K. (2019) Novice teachers' perspectives on the use of languages in French as a Second Language classes that include English Language Learners. *Brock Education: A Journal of Educational Research and Practice* 28 (2), 82–95. Retrieved on December 13, 2020 from https://files.eric.ed.gov/fulltext/EJ1220026.pdf

Mason, J. and Hood, S. (2010) Exploring issues of children as actors in social research. *Children and Youth Services Review* 33 (4), 490–495. doi:10.1016/j.childyouth.2010.05.011

Melo-Pfeifer, S. (2015) Multilingual awareness and heritage language education: Children's multimodal representations of their multilingualism. *Language Awareness* 24 (3), 197–215. doi: 10.1080/09658416.2015.1072208

Miller, C.R. (1992) Kairos in the rhetoric of science. In S. Witte, N. Nakadate and R. Cherry (eds) *A Rhetoric of Doing: Essays on Written Discourse in Honor of James L. Kinneavy* (pp. 310–327). Carbondale, IL: Southern Illinois UP.

NAEYC (National Association for the Education of Young Children) (2009) Developmentally appropriate practice in early childhood programs serving children from birth through age 8: A position statement of the National Association for the Education of Young Children. Washington, DC: National Association for the Education of Young Children.

Neilsen, L. (2002) Learning from the liminal: Fiction as knowledge [Scholartistry]. *Alberta Journal of Educational Research* 48 (3), 206–214.

Pinter, A. (2014) Child participant roles in applied linguistics research. *Applied Linguistics* 35 (2), 168–183. See https://doi.org/10.1093/applin/amt008

Prasad, G. (2018a) 'But do monolingual people really exist?' Analysing elementary students' contrasting representations of plurilingualism through sequential reflexive drawing. *Language and Intercultural Communication* 18 (3), 315–334, doi: 10.1080/14708477.2018.1425412

Prasad, G. (2018b) 'How does it look and feel to be plurilingual?': Analyzing children's representations of plurilingualism through collage. *International Journal of Bilingual Education and Bilingualism.* AOP. https://doi.org/10.1080/13670050.2017.1420033

Prasad, G. (2015) Beyond the mirror towards a plurilingual prism: Exploring the creation of plurilingual 'identity texts' in English and French classrooms in Toronto and

Montpellier. *Intercultural Education* 26 (6), 497–514. doi: 10.1080/14675986. 2015.1109775

Prasad, G. (2013) Children as co-ethnographers of their plurilingual literacy practices: An exploratory case study. *Language and Literacy* 15 (3), 4–30. doi: https://doi.org/10.20360/G2901N

Prasad, G. (2012) Multiple minorities or culturally and linguistically diverse (CLD) plurilingual Learners? Re-envisioning allophone immigrant children and their inclusion in French-language schools in Ontario. Canadian *Modern Language Review/La Revue canadienne des langues vivantes* 68 (2), 190–215. doi: 10.3138/cmlr.68.2.190

Prout, A. (2005) *The Future of Childhood: Towards the Interdisciplinary Study of Children*. London: Routledge.

Ramachandran, V.S. (May, 1992) Blind spots. *Scientific American* 266 (5), 86–91. https://www.jstor.org/stable/24939062

Stagg-Peterson, S. and Heywood, D. (2007) Contributions of families' linguistic, social, and cultural capital to minority-language children's literacy: Parents', teachers', and principals' perspectives. *Canadian Modern Language Review* 63 (4), 517–538. doi: 10.3138/cmlr.63.4.517

Statistics Canada (2017) Census in Brief: Linguistic diversity and multilingualism in Canada homes. Retrieved on December 13, 2020 from https://www12.statcan.gc.ca/census-recensement/2016/as-sa/98-200-x/2016010/98-200-x2016010-eng.cfm

Thiessen, D. (2007) Researching student experiences in elementary and secondary school: An evolving field of study. *International Handbook of Student Experience in Elementary And Secondary School* (pp. 1–76). New York, NY: Springer.

Thomson, P. (ed.) (2008) *Doing Visual Research with Children and Young People*. New York, NY: Routledge.

Tsing, A.L. (2005) *Friction: An Ethnography of Global Connection*. Princeton University Press, Princeton.

Wenger, E. (2009) Communities of practice. *Communities* 22 (5). See http://hdl.handle.net/1794/11736

Wiltse, L. (2006) 'Like pulling teeth': Oral discourse practices in a culturally diverse language arts classroom. *Canadian Modern Language Review/La Revue canadienne des langues vivantes* 63 (2), 199–223. doi : 10.3138/cmlr.63.2.199

Wong-Fillmore, L. (2005) When learning a second language means losing the first. In M. Suàrez-Orozco, C. Suàrez-Orozco, D. Baolian Qin and D. Qin-Hilliard (eds) *The New Immigration: An Interdisciplinary Reader*. New York, NY: Routledge.

7 Artefactual Narratives of Multilingual Identity: Methodological and Ethical Considerations in Researching Children

Nayr Ibrahim

Introduction

Researching multilingualism and identity in the age of superdiversity (Vertovec, 2007) requires new theoretical concepts of language and more appropriate methodological tools (García *et al.*, 2017; Martin-Jones & Martin, 2017). Despite the growing body of research into multilingualism, the one domain that has been ignored until recently is the study of objects or physical artefacts that connect our meaning-making to the symbolism of the material world around us. In research with children, material tools offer interesting avenues for investigating early multilingualism through the creative ways in which children communicate (see also Prasad in this volume). From an ethical perspective, this methodological approach has the potential to position children as knowledgeable and active agents in the research process, thus respecting their insights into their experience of multilingual living.

This chapter presents a study that included artefacts, that is, physical objects and children's multimodal texts, as data collection tools. This study was a PhD thesis that elicited from the participants, thirteen trilingual children living in Paris, their perceptions of identity in multilingual contexts. The overall methodological approach included children and parent interviews, children's writing, drawings and physical objects. This ensemble aimed to give children multiple modes of exploring their emotional and experiential connections to their languages. In this chapter, I focus on the methodological and ethical implications of asking children to choose objects to represent their languages. The inclusion of objects added a material dimension to the study and acknowledged the importance of concrete processes in helping children engage with the research process.

I start by outlining my theoretical framework on the methodological and ethical implications of integrating an artefactual or material perspective when researching with children. This is followed by a description of the research design, which includes: an overview of the complex sociolinguistic context of children's emerging multilingualism; a short description of the data collection and analysis; and a detailed discussion of the procedures. The procedures section highlights two main areas: the ethical issues around *access* and *choice* in the research process; and the role of the artefacts in facilitating children's narrative on the complexity of living between fixed monolingual and hybrid multilingual spaces. In the discussion I consider the following points: the benefits of including an artefactual component in prompting and validating children's voices on language and identity; the research design, created and initiated by the researcher, versus the children's agency in the process; and children's appropriation of the research tools to construct their own identity narratives.

Theoretical Background: Ethical Considerations in Researching Children in Multilingual Contexts

In the social study of children over the last few decades new theoretical perspectives have emerged that conceptualize the child as 'strong, competent and active' (Clark, 2004: 143). Children are seen as 'social actors' (Qvortrup *et al.*, 1994: 2) and 'experts in their own lives' (Langsted, 1994: 42). This movement, better known as the 'New Sociology of Childhood' (James & Prout, 1997), emphasises the importance of accessing children's views on different aspects of their lives. It promotes the idea of involving, informing, consulting with and listening to children, in a dialogical process of hearing, interpreting and co-constructing meaning around their lived experiences.

Consequently, research with children necessitates a multifaceted approach, which elicits children's unique ways of communicating and reflects their creativity in conveying meaning. It calls for flexible, participatory and inclusive approaches that address children's 'dialectical relationship with other people' (Greig *et al.*, 2007: 45) and break down 'the generational power barrier between adults and children' (Kuchah & Pinter, 2012: 283). Fernqvist (2010: 1310) suggests that an (inter)active approach, offering 'various forms of communication – words and pictures – increases children's scope for action, which is an ethical demand crucial from the perspective of the sociology of childhood'. Visual methodologies are becoming more prevalent in researching multilingualism as evidenced by Kalaja and Melo-Pfeifer's (2019) recently edited volume. These authors place visual methodologies at the forefront of the 'visual turn' (Kalaja & Pitkänen-Huhta, 2018) in researching multilingualism as lived experience, thus giving the multilingual voice multiple modes of expression.

Besides the traditional verbal, and more recent visual approach, the material culture of multilingualism (Aronin & Ó Laoire, 2013) offers another possible response to the silencing of children's voices. I included a deliberate focus on the materialities of language, that is, the realm of physical items, embracing everyday objects that we use or produce, in order to elicit children's voices of experiencing multilingualism. Not only do these material tools, or artefacts, contribute to the multiple ways children create meaning but they also connect to their individual biographical trajectories (Blommaert & Backus, 2012) by eliciting biographical narratives (Busch, 2017: 46–59). Aronin and Hornsby (2018: 1) describe material culture as 'dynamic, changeable in space, time, form and value thus linking languages with the physical environment where they are used'. In transnational contexts, objects and their inherent significance in a static pre-defined socio-cultural space are displaced and imbued with the meaning that individuals bestow on them. As products of children's creative performance, these artefacts become children's identity texts (Cummins & Early, 2011), representing powerful research tools. They embody the multilingual experience, afford agency and promote the co-construction of meaning in research with children.

Aim of the Main Study

The main aim of the overall study was to uncover children's attitudes, perceptions and interpretations of an emergent multilingual identity. The impetus for choosing language, literacy and identity as a research focus was to obtain a deeper understanding of how children negotiate an identity position in all their languages. The research questions explored the child's perspectives on developing a multilingual identity across different educational and linguistic contexts. It included the role of the adults (parents, relatives and educators) as well as siblings and friends in nurturing children's multiple literacies and identities. Even though both the children and their parents participated in this study, in this chapter I focus on the children's role in the research process.

This chapter explores, in more depth, the methodological and ethical implications of employing an artefactual perspective when researching children. I will analyse the challenges and benefits of this approach in an attempt to show how objects and the creation of multimodal artefactual texts constitute an appropriate vehicle for eliciting children's complex identity narratives. This material approach advances our understanding of children's experiences of living and learning in multilingual contexts and meets ethical requirements in working with children.

The Research Design

The sociolinguistic context

This study was set in France, which is an officially monolingual context with a highly multilingual population. Despite the status of French as the one and only official language of the country (Article 2 of the Constitution, 1958), France is a multilingual society, as stated by former Minister of Education, Jack Lang in 2001: 'contrary to widespread belief, France is not a monolingual country' (Hélot & Young, 2006: 72). Harding-Esch and Riley (2003) wrote that, with a multitude of regional and immigrant languages in the French territory, over 20% of the population is bilingual. This is corroborated by a number of studies: Cerquiglini (1999) identified 26% of French people as being raised by parents speaking other languages; Akinci (2003) found that 53% of the 12,000 primary school participants in his study in Lyon declared using a language other than French at home and 67 languages were identified in these schools; official birth registrations indicated that 27.2% of children born in France in 2010 had at least one parent of foreign origin (Young, 2014). The latest report on the state of language learning (Manes-Bonnisseau & Taylor, 2018) acknowledged that many children in French classrooms have first languages other than French. However, no concrete measures were stipulated to support children's heritage languages.

Even though there is consensus in France around the concept of multilingualism, formulated by the Council of Europe as the one-mother-tongue-plus-two-foreign-languages policy, it describes a utilitarian view (Garcia, 2015): it focuses on foreign language education policies, is centred on European standard languages, and disregards, and even marginalizes immigrant and regional languages. Also, any initiative to recognize children's languages and value their identity as multilinguals in the classroom has been left on the shelves of academia; for example, The Didenheim Language Awareness Project (Hélot & Young, 2002) or *Comparons nos Langues* (Comparing our Languages) (Auger, 2005). These policies pose an ethical challenge as they exclude the numerous languages spoken in the French territory and render invisible the heritage languages and identities of the school population today. As these multilingual voices are silenced, we fail to give due weight to the knowledge and experience of children developing their identity in contradictory, contested and sometimes conflictual spaces (see also Murphy in this volume).

The participants

The children in this study, aged 5 to 16, were all living in the Paris region at the time of the data collection. They were first and foremost 'socialized into multilingualism' (Auleear Owodally, 2014: 17–40) in a tandem of personal multilingual experiences, in monolingual or bilingual educational, and mostly monolingual political contexts, over time and space. The thirteen children represented nine family units, including four sibling pairs with very similar (Oscar-Maru and Anna-Arra; Kiana and Tala; Edwin and Victor) or differing (Melinda and Lily) linguistic journeys. Table 7.1 gives an overview of the children's family language situation at the time of the study. The names of the children are pseudonyms in order to meet ethical standards and ensure anonymity. I decided to give the children names, as opposed to

Table 7.1 Children's sociolinguistic background

Pseudonym	Age at time of interview	Place of birth	Age of arrival in France	Heritage language(s)		Main home language (s)	Additional language(s)	Foreign languages at school
				Father's language	Mother's language			
Anna-Arra Oliver-Maru (Twins)	5:11	England	2.5 years old	French	Korean	English	Not mentioned	Not mentioned
Melinda (Lily's half-sister)	7:6	France	Born in France	English	English	English	Italian German	Not mentioned
Victor (Edwin's brother)*	8:6	England	3 years old	Russian	English German	Russian English	French	Chinese
Tala (Kiana's sister)	10:3	France	Born in France	Farsi	Farsi	French	English	Not mentioned
Kiana (Tala's sister)	11:11	France	Born in France	Farsi	Farsi	French	English	Not mentioned
Mathieu	11:8	France	Born in France	French	Spanish	Spanish French	English	German
Taku	11:10	France	Born in France	Japanese		Japanese	English French	Spanish
Edwin (Victor's brother)*	12:2	England	7 years old	Russian	English German	Russian English	French	German Chinese
Anaka	13:11	France	Born in France	Bangla	Bangla	Bangla English	French	German Italian Arabic Korean
Lily (Melinda's half-sister)	14:6	England	6 years old	German Italian	English	German Italian English	French	Spanish
Keiko	14:6	England	7 years old	French	Japanese	Japanese English	English	Japanese
Thalya	16:6	Sri-Lanka	4 years old	Sinhala	Sinhala	Sinhala	English French	German

*Edwin and Viktor's father was a Russophone Ukrainian, so the children identified as Russian-speakers with very little knowledge of Ukrainian.

participant numbers, in order to give them an identity, and not reduce them to a mere code.

All of the children had had access to education in their three languages in different educational spaces from the pre-primary years. At the time of the study, they were learning to read and write their three languages in language-specific educational sites:

The mainstream French school

Regardless of the children's time of arrival in France they were all following the age-appropriate French curriculum.

Community-based heritage language programmes (Korean, German, Russian, Farsi, Spanish, Japanese, Bangla and Sinhala)

These languages were crucial for maintaining a linguistic relationship with their families, within and across national borders. However, children's access to heritage language education varied the most and depended on the following factors: finding opportunities for real language use in a minority context; procuring material in the language, which was difficult or non-existent in some cases; and the parents' efforts to find and finance an after-school programme. As parents did not expect any support from the national education system, they proactively sought alternative solutions to maintain the children's languages. These efforts entail time, dedication and financial investment and, therefore often exclude children from low socioeconomic status (SES) backgrounds. The parents in this study were all educated to at least undergraduate level, held positive attitudes towards multilingualism and had the means to invest in their children's language education.

The out-of-school English literacy course

Children's access to English had been more heterogeneous and can be divided into four, often overlapping, experiences: having English as a heritage language (Victor and Edwin; Melinda and Lily); using English as a chosen family/home language (Oliver-Maru and Anna-Arra, Keiko); learning English as a language of instruction in bilingual French-English schools (Mathieu, Taku, Victor and Edwin, Kiana and Tala); and adopting English as an additional language as part of the family's language policy (Kiana and Tala, Anaka, Thalya).

I discovered these children in the English after-school programme at the British Council (Ibrahim, 2004) in Paris, where they were all developing English literacy in a two-hour-a-week class and where I was the Head of the Bilingual Section. The children in this programme were primarily English/French bilinguals. However, I had learned from a previous survey on the Bilingual Section (Ibrahim, 2010) that 39% of the children were actually tri-/multi-lingual. This was a practical and opportunistic, as well as purposive choice of participants, yet this choice highlighted ethical implications in terms of who is given a voice in research, that is, children from families who could not afford the private after-school tuition fees at the British Council where I worked were automatically excluded from the study (see also Mathew & Pinter in this volume regarding inclusion/ exclusion). However, my intention was not to identify social inequalities in multilingual contexts but to focus on children who self-reported as being trilingual, were learning to be literate in three languages and seemed comfortable within this complex situation. I wanted to discover how they had successfully developed their trilingualism and what helped them to readily identify with their multiple languages.

Data collection

In order to allow children to engage fully in the research process it was imperative to give them appropriate tools to express themselves. I chose both verbal (interviews and writing) and non-verbal (drawing and objects) tools that were familiar to the child's world of learning and communication. The study also included a parent survey, which aimed to contextualize sociolinguistic information on the parents' background and elicit their attitudes towards multilingualism and developing literacy in three languages.

All of the children were interviewed at different times over a period of nine months in small age-related groups:

- Mathieu, Taku and Anaka – aged 11–13
- Keiko and Thalya – aged 14–16

or in sibling pairs:

- Oliver-Maru and Anna-Arra – aged 5
- Lily and Melinda – aged 14 and 7
- Victor and Edwin – aged 11 and 7
- Tala and Kiana – aged 9 and 10

Children's selected objects were discussed at the end of the interview. They were also asked to draw a picture or write a text about their perceptions of their own identity in their three languages.

Data analysis

The study used primarily a content analysis approach which captured the elements children foregrounded as important in constructing a multilingual identity. The artefacts, grouped into eight categories in Table 7.2, evoked the children's cultural origins or geographical placement and captured their representations through multisensory activities (food, weather), sociocultural experiences (school, playground, canteen) and abstract notions (justice). Some objects were language-defined with

Table 7.2 Categories of children's chosen objects/artefacts

Cultural objects	Transport	Food	People	Abstract concepts	Monuments	Multi-Literacy	Places
Spanish bull;	Tokyo metro;	French baguette;	Mother; English teacher;	Justice; *Liberté, Egalité, Fraternité*	Eiffel Tower; Big Ben; Motherland monument in Kiev.	Books; Newspapers; Tablets; Workbooks; DVDs/film; Internet.	Scotland; Ukrainian landscape; Brasserie; WHSmith (British retailer selling books, news, stationery and convenience items).
Camel and Arab figurine;	Double-decker bus;	*Pain au raisin* (a raisin pastry);	American father;	*(Liberty, Equality, Fraternity).*			
Japanese fan;	Lada (a car, first built in Russia in 1970).	Italian restaurant;	Friends; Family.				
Persian carpet;							
Italian musical box;		*Ras malai* (an Indian dessert);					
Flags.		*Zereshk Polo* (an Iranian dish -barberry rice with chicken);					
		Peanut butter.					

inscriptions in a language or several languages or non-language-defined, that is, without inscriptions. The latter was not studied in isolation, but rather 'viewed in their interactions with, and interrelations to the multilingual situation' (Aronin, 2018: 25).

Analysis of the choice of, and narrative around the artefacts revealed the contradictions and conflicts that children constantly experienced as they negotiated an identity between 'polarized perspectives' (Ibrahim, 2016: 78–79): fixed (essentialist, national, unique and narrow) and hybrid (multilingual, multilayered, overlapping and complex) positions. Subsequently, I classified the meanings children afforded their artefacts into these two overarching categories to show this constant pull between opposing ways of life.

Procedures: Searching for the Children's Voices

In this section I present my reflections, from an ethical perspective, on the research process, including selecting, accessing and obtaining consent from multilingual children. I also analyse a limited selection of children's objects and artefactual narratives as they 'illustrate the dynamic, active, negotiated process of generating data with young children' (Crump & Phipps, 2013: 142).

Ethical considerations in the research process

Despite attempts to include the child in every step of the process, the study was heavily biased towards the adult (parent and researcher) in the initial stages. As the children, all under 18, were selected from an out-of-school programme and were in different classes on different days, the logistics of the research project, namely, participation and gaining consent, interview times and dates, were negotiated by email with the parents. Hence, in the process of identifying potential participants, I was confronted with three ethical dilemmas: (a) how to access the children; (b) how to obtain their consent; (c) how to elicit narratives on the abstract concepts of multilingualism and identity.

Selecting multilingual children and negotiating access

In order to identify the trilingual/triliterate children, I analysed the results of a First Day Questionnaire, which we administered in class on the first day of the course. This questionnaire aimed to establish children's linguistic profile, by asking them about other languages they spoke, how and where the children learned these languages, who they spoke the languages with, literacy in the three languages, and their attitudes towards multilingualism. As this questionnaire was completed by the children, it was an opportunity to acknowledge and give weight to their self-reporting on knowledge of reading and writing in their three languages and their attitudes to being trilingual. I identified an initial 29 children, representing 26 families. After liaising with the parents by email for further details and to negotiate their availability or willingness to participate, I ended up with 13 child participants, aged 5–16.

Asking for and giving consent

Accessing the children had to happen via the parents, but giving consent could not exclude the children's voice. I created separate participant information sheets and consent forms for the parents and the children. The information was similar on both documents, that is, participants were reassured of their physical and emotional well-being and were guaranteed confidentiality throughout the process; they were given the choice to withdraw at any time; and I listed the different data collection tools. However, the children's document differed from the adult's form as I tried to adapt both the language and the format (see also Mourão in this volume). I went even a step further and decided to cater for the age differences in my child participants. I produced two age-specific consent forms for the children (ages 5–8 and 9–16), which varied in language, conceptual difficulty and format. For example, instead of boxes, I added smiley faces

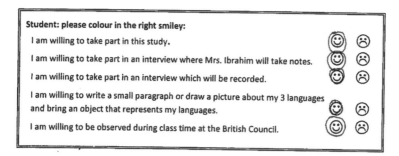

Figure 7.1 Extract of Anna-Arra's completed Consent Form (age 5–8)

(Figure 7.1), a recognisable visual method, for children aged five to eight to express their agreement to participate in the different data collection procedures. In retrospect, I question the validity and appropriateness of smiley faces as they evoke feelings (*happiness, sadness*) or *likes* and *dislikes*, and are not necessarily indicative of informed decision-making.

My intention was to make the study more accessible to the younger children with limited literacy and render procedures more child-friendly. I wanted to acknowledge the way children interact and make sense of the written word and to give the children a sense of ownership. Inevitably, the language was still too difficult for the younger children and required the support of the parent, which I had anticipated: the parents were asked to read the participation information with the children and decide together. Not only did the form give the parents simpler language to explain the research project to the children, but it created a dialogue about the research process, which started with the parent in the home and continued with the researcher in an attempt to co-construct meaning about identity.

The first completed child consent forms I received were from the twins, who had signed them in their three languages, including the Korean script, a first example of the children making visible their multilingual identity (Ibrahim, 2014). As consent was negotiated at home with the parents, and the initial research information was filtered by the parent, it is difficult to confirm whether this was a spontaneous response from the children or a suggestion or even instruction from the parents. This poses the ethical question of the child's agency versus the role of the parent and home influence in the initial decision to participate. However, as children could not participate without explicit parental consent, I chose not to question this so as not to undermine the children's potential role in the decision-making process. Despite this uncertainty, there was evidence of consent from the child at some level as all of the children's consent forms were returned and signed by them and they engaged actively in the different processes they encountered in the study. I also believe that the parents' likely influence was counteracted by the child-focused tools employed in the study, which I describe below.

The interview: Listening to children's voices

The interviews took place at the English school or in the home, depending on which location suited the parents best, as they had to accompany the younger children. They were conducted in groups, with peers, classmates or siblings, in familiar surroundings, which created a natural and reassuring environment and encouraged the children to communicate openly.

The interviews were recorded and consisted of three main parts. Firstly, I thanked the children for their participation and reiterated the objective of the study. I informed them I was going to ask them questions about learning their languages, how they felt about speaking, reading and writing multiple languages and their identity. I started the interview with a topic the children could grasp immediately and would feel confident discussing: *Which languages do you know and how did you learn them?* This served as a springboard for questions on identity. I nuanced the concept of identity with the younger children by asking them how speaking, reading and writing these languages made them feel about who they were. If I felt children were struggling with a question or concept I would rephrase or move on to another topic to avoid any kind of pressure.

Even though the children were given the choice of expressing themselves in French or in English, or both, all of the children automatically used English in the interview. I believe this is because they associated the research site and the researcher, whom the children knew as the Head of the School, with the English language. These factors established English as the language of the research and the children remained in English-mode throughout the study. This could be viewed as an ethical issue as children were not necessarily using their perceived strongest language. However, as a result of their educational access to English they all had excellent skills in English to be able to communicate easily.

Although the choice of English denies the idea of eliciting children's multilingual voices, there was evidence of translingual practices during the interview and in children's multimodal texts. For example, Tala's drawing representing Farsi (Figure 7.2) included a combination of verbal explanation, drawing, writing and symbols. She drew a Persian carpet and an Iranian chicken dish, barberry rice with chicken. She included the name of the dish in Farsi, written in the Arabic script and transcribed into Latin [*zereshk polo*], within square brackets, for the benefit of the researcher and/or the

Figure 7.2 Tala's drawing representing Farsi

non-Iranian context of France and the English context of the interview. Her oral narrative included her three languages: the name of the dish in Farsi, and code-switching between English and French as she searched for the correct word in English for saffron: *Zereshk Polo … it's rice with little red things with … how do you say <safran>? (French pronunciation).*

Hence, when code-switching involved the heritage language, the children decided to explain or translate for the sake of the researcher, attesting to children's metalinguistic awareness and expert management of their multilingual resources. In this artefactual space, the children controlled the narrative: they displaced the perceived hegemony of English, switched to multilingual mode and consolidated their linguistic resources to reflect their multilingual identity.

Artefacts, Objects and Multimodal Texts: Negotiating Identity in Fixed and Hybrid Spaces

When inviting the children to the interview, the parents were reminded to ask the children to choose and bring objects that represented each language. At the end of the interview, the children brought out their objects and were asked to say why they chose those objects and in what way they represented their languages. Seven children brought objects and the other six were encouraged to, or offered to describe them orally and/or made drawings of their objects instead. As the objects were chosen at home it is most likely that some parents helped the children in making their choices. For example, Victor and Edwin mentioned that their mother chose the objects that represented English (books) and Russian (Figure 7.3): a grey *Lada* and three T-shirts with inscriptions (an image of a Russian cartoon character, <*Cheburashka*>; a well-known personality, Gagarin, written in Latin script; an inscription in Ukrainian in Cyrillic script). Edwin probably found it difficult to find an object as he stated: *I don't really have objects that represents…,* without terminating the sentence. Despite the parents' potential involvement, the children connected to the objects at a personal level through the narrative around the artefact, as Edwin explains later: *Yeah, but they kinda do associate…* and then the boys proceeded to describe their connection to their language through the objects. For instance, the grey *Lada,* evoked visits to Ukraine and his relationship with his grandfather.

The object offered the children an alternative means to express their identity. It was when the children explored their reasons for choosing a particular object to represent each language that intricate identity narratives were generated. For example, Mathieu chose a camel and an Arab figurine (Figure 7.4), signifiers of the Middle East, to represent English.

Mathieu: *The Arab because … in Dubai … in the street there are only men dressed like that … and the camel … because when I went in the desert there were camels.*

Figure 7.3 Victor and Edwin's objects representing Russian

> Researcher: *So, your link to English is the place … seeing that you brought the camel and the Arab … so your link to English is when you picked up English in Dubai, that's important to you.*

This choice was both surprising and disconcerting and required my deductive skills to understand the connection. Even though Mathieu never

Figure 7.4 Arab figurine and camel – Mathieu's objects representing English

mentioned English in his explanation above, he had described his experience in Dubai at the beginning of the interview when he introduced his connection with English: *I learnt English when I went to Dubai from 3 years to 5 years and there I learnt to speak English.* The camel and the Arab figurine were not only symbols of English, but became a sign of his multi-layered and subjective experience of language: he described his link to English through a spatio-temporal journey that started in the Middle East and culminated in his English classes in Paris. When I asked if he felt he had an English identity, Mathieu replied empathically: *I do, because I lived a part of my life in an English country [...] I went to an English school in Dubai and my best friend is still English ... he's like me ... French, English and Spanish.*

The pictorial representations of the children's objects were multimodal: they included drawings, written words, different scripts and languages as well as symbols (Ibrahim, 2016). My initial intention was to give the younger children the option of drawing, as they obviously could not engage in writing texts. I expected the younger children to draw and I had asked the teenagers to write. However, as from the age of 7 the children chose to mix writing and drawing, and in this way, they created their personal multimodal identity texts. These artefactual texts reflected children's agency and creativity in expressing themselves, as these were spontaneously produced. Away from the immediacy of the interview, where children felt obliged to respond promptly and constantly interact with the researcher, the writing and drawing gave children the space to reflect on their representations of language and identity. From an ethical perspective, these introspective tools allowed children to choose and focus on aspects of their multilingualism and its impact on identity that were not dependent on the researcher's probing questions, thus allowing them to explore and express their own voice.

Finding their voice reflected a constant pull between belonging and non-belonging as is evident from Kiana's two drawings. In Figure 7.5, Kiana depicted a positive life-long relationship with her languages (the girl

Figure 7.5 Kiana's drawing of her future multilingual repertoire

Figure 7.6 Kiana's drawing of her questioning her identity

is smiling) and included an expanded multilingual repertoire. Figure 7.6 denotes hesitation and uncertainty (the girl is frowning), as she doubted or questioned who she was.

The artefactual space afforded children creative ways to present the quest for coherence and synergy, which is epitomized in Melinda's drawing (Figure 7.7). Melinda had created an imaginary world, called Melinda World, which was mediated by 'Melinda language', an invented language with sounds, a visual written form and translated for the sake of the

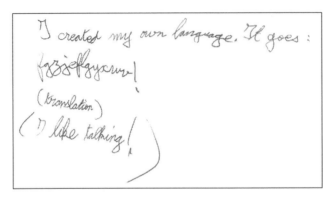

Figure 7.7 Melinda's drawing of Melinda Language

uninitiated. All of Melinda's experiences and identities existed simultaneously in Melinda World, where she took refuge from the contradictions of her multilingual life and where she could be and experience her fragmented self fully. In this 'third space' she could safely be her multifaceted self and she could *'keep them all'*, all her languages and identities. Melinda World/Language did not surface in the interview, so the artefactual component in this study offered her a space to foreground her hybrid living. Her artefact gave shape to her imaginary world and became a potent visible metaphor for her multilingual reality.

Inviting children to comment on the research process

Flexibility in the interview process, acknowledging a genuine interest in children's expert insights and accepting children's different ways of presenting their objects was key to the success of the project and placed me in the 'humble researcher position' (Crump & Phipps, 2013: 132). Children were active meaning-makers during the interview and asked for clarification which prompted me to repeat or rephrase my questions, especially those related to identity. For example, Victor checked his understanding with the following question: *Do you mean like ... when I think about English, what do I see in my head?*

At the end of the interview I asked the children if they had any further comments or questions. This was another opportunity to give children a more active role in the research process, to encourage them to reflect on the themes generated by the different tools, to engage with the researcher at an equal level and hand over the questioning to them. Keiko identified commonalities between her narrative and Thalya's, her co-interviewee, and expressed surprise at the similarities in their multilingual experiences. The research process itself offered her a space for discovering their shared multilingual identity experiences:

> **Keiko:** *When I was thinking about the interview I thought ... I'm sure there would be different opinions ... but there is so much in common ... it's really surprising.*

Edwin asked me three questions about my reasons for interviewing the brothers: *Are you going to write an article about this? What about? Are you bilingual?* He expressed his curiosity about the process and forced me to reveal my own multilingualism, making me very much aware of my role as a multilingual researcher (see also Zandian about reflective spaces at the end of research projects, in this volume). Eventually, he stated: *So, you kinda know what it feels like,* making analogies and connecting his experience to that of the researcher and drawing me into the contested lives of multilinguals.

Discussion: Expanding Children's Multilingual Voice

This study placed on centre stage the children, the experts in their lives and validated their perceptions and opinions of multilingualism and identity. Despite a pre-determined research framework, and the parents' roles as gatekeepers, concrete measures were taken for children to take on a more active and informed role (Kuchah & Pinter, this volume) and make children's multilingual voices heard. From a methodological and ethical perspective, this study gave children a voice by (a) acknowledging them as creative storytellers, (b) expanding children's discursive repertoires, (c) creating the symbolic space of artefacts (objects and multimodal texts) for their complex stories of belonging to thrive and (d) positioning children as agentive meaning-makers.

Acknowledging children's creative storytelling

To ensure good ethical practice it is important to position children as exercising agency in the research process. This does not negate the role of the adult in a particular research context or in the wider development of children's multilingualism. However, when adjustments are made to acknowledge and enhance the ways children make meaning, the conversation is enriched and deeper knowledge is gained. In this study I made a conscious effort to adapt question formats, introduced multiple multimodal data collection tools and ensured flexible interview processes. The children engaged with and appropriated the tools at their disposal: they may not have chosen or brought the objects, but they created their own; their narrative dislocated these objects from their cultural and political positionings, thus constructing a more personalized story of a lived multilingual identity.

Expanding children's discursive repertoires

The artefactual component of this study, in its physical and pictorial form, created 'new opportunities for story telling' (Fernqvist, 2010: 1310). It expanded the children's repertoire of discursive possibilities and offered them an alternative, concrete and agentive tool for exploring their multilingual identity. Objects offered the children a symbolic space for deconstructing monolithic and fixed representations of language and reconstructing a complex, dynamic and multifaceted multilingual identity. Children used the objects and texts to create links to past memories (Mathieu's English experience in Dubai), present emotions (Kiana's doubts about her identity) and built bridges to an imagined (Norton, 2013) multilingual future (Kiana's expanding language repertoire). Even though this was not a longitudinal study, the children's artefactual narratives embodied the linguistic history of the child in the space of the research study. It respected the 'being' of childhood (James *et al.*, 1998) as it captured the 'presence' of children's multilingual and transnational living.

The symbolic space of artefacts

Artefacts are not value-free. They already possess a political and cultural narrative with a narrow symbolism and limited interpretative possibilities. For example, most objects were stereotypical representations of a national identity (Table 7.2). Some generated very little in terms of a personal identity narrative, for example, the Spanish bull or the Japanese fan. Other objects gained meaning beyond their narrow, predicable associations in the experiential and narrative space provided in the research process. Taking into account the prompt to bring objects that represent children's three languages, it is important to consider the dilemma of interpretation, that is, allowing the object to speak for itself versus eliciting an oral or written explanation or interpretation of the children's choice. In anticipation of this ethical dilemma, I provided a narrative space around the object, which gave children the means to deconstruct the surface-level stereotypes of an object and create a complex story of belonging. These multimodal narratives subverted the conventional symbolism of belonging, destabilized the status quo and empowered children to tell their multilingual identity stories through *their* choices and voices. Ultimately, these symbolic artefacts offered the children additional material tools to negotiate a place in multilingual contexts and provided a lens through which the researcher viewed their world.

Children as agentive meaning-makers

This approach also gave the child the power to mean as opposed to relying on the researcher's bias in relation to the objects and her interpretation of the children's drawings. When we listen carefully to children's narratives, the way multilingual children reclaimed these artefacts reconceptualized children as social actors in their own right. This expanded repertoire included cross-linguistic and transnational representations and created a rich mosaic of narrative possibilities in a fluid and integrated manner. For example, the narrative around Tala's drawing of the Persian carpet, a stereotypical image of Iran, is more revealing of her experience of her mother's Parisian flat and her relationship with her mother than of the established symbolism of Iran: *Yeah ... because Iran is ... in my mum's house there is just carpets* .... When the children took hold of the research tools, they were able to control the narrative and express their constructions of language and identity.

These unique perspectives help the adult gain new insights, and even challenge the researcher/practitioner's own beliefs and practices. Giving the children a voice in this study broadened the perspective of the researcher: it made me listen more attentively, provided me with a plethora of personal narratives on the complexity of multilingual living and moved the research agenda from an exclusively adult enterprise to a rich and complex personal story.

Conclusion

Our understanding of the multilingual child is enriched when the voice of the child is respected, valued and heard. Hence, we need processes and tools that centre-stage the child's perspective. Children in this study combined verbal, visual and concrete tools to express powerful and imaginative ideas. They were thus conceived as skilful users of linguistic-semiotic resources which are embedded in the world of the child. This approach acknowledged children's right to be heard (UNCRC, 1989), gave them the means to speak for themselves and thus established the children as active subjects and not passive objects in the research process (Christensen & James, 2008: 1). The result was a rich conversation about growing up multilingual.

References

1958. *La Constitution du 4 Octobre 1958*. Le Gouvernement de la République Française. Available from: https://www.conseil-constitutionnel.fr/le-bloc-de-constitutionnalite/texte-integral-de-la-constitution-du-4-octobre-1958-en-vigueur

Akinci, M.-A. (2003) France Multilingue : Richesse ou Danger ? Résultats d'une enquête dans les écoles élémentaires de Lyon. *Écarts d'identité: Mobilité – Egalite – Interculturalité* 102, 41–47.

Aronin, L. (2018) The theoretical underpinnings of the material culture of multilingualism. In L. Aronin, M. Hornsby and G. L. Kilianska-Przybylo (eds) *The Material Culture of Multilingualism* (pp. 21–45). Switzerland: Springer International Publishing.

Aronin, L. and Hornsby, M. (2018) Introduction: The realm of material culture of multilingualism. In L. Aronin, M. Hornsby and G.L. Kilianska-Przybylo (eds) *The Material Culture of Multilingualism* (pp. 1–20). Switzerland: Springer International Publishing.

Aronin, L. and Ó Laoire, M. (2013) The material culture of multilingualism: Moving beyond the linguistic landscape. *International Journal of Multilingualism* 10, 225–235.

Auger, N. (2005) Comparons nos Langues: Démarche d'apprentissage du français pour les enfants nouvellement arrivé [Comparing our languages: Guide for learning French for newly arrived children in France], DVD et guide pédagogique (15 pages). In CNDP (ed.) *Ressources Formation Multimédia*. CRDP Languedoc-Roussillon, CDDP du Gard: Editions CNDP.

Auleear Owodally, A.M. (2014) Socialised into multilingualism: A case study of a mauritian pre-school. In J. Conteh and G. Meier (eds) *The Multilingual Turn in Languages Education: Opportunities and Challenges* (pp. 17–40). Bristol: Multilingual Matters.

Blommaert, J. and Backus, A. (2012) Superdiverse repertoires and the individual. *Tilburg Papers in Cultural Studies,* Paper 24, 1–32.

Busch, B. (2017) Biographical approaches to research in multilingual settings: Exploring linguistic repertoires. In M. Martin-Jones and D. Martin (eds) *Researching Multilingualism* (pp. 46–59). Abingdon: Routledge.

Cerquiglini, B. (1999) *Les Langues de France : rapport au ministre de l'éducation nationale, de la recherche et de la technologie et à la ministre de la culture et de la communication*. France: Ministère de l'éducation nationale, de la recherche et de la technologie.

Christensen, P. and James, A. (2008) *Research with Children: Perspective and Practices*. Routledge: Oxon.

Clark, A. (2004) The mosaic approach and research with young children. In V. Lewis, M. Kellet, C. Robinson, S. Fraser and S. Ding (eds) *The Reality of Research with Children and Young People* (pp. 142–161). London: Sage Publications.

Crump, A. and Phipps, H. (2013) Listening to children's voices: Reflections on reserching with children in multilingual Montreal. *LEARNing Landscapes* 7 (1), 129–148.

Cummins, J. and Early, M. (2011) *Identity Texts: The Collaborative Creation of Power in Multilingual Schools*. Stoke-on-Trent: Trentham Books.

Fernqvist, S. (2010) (Inter)Active interviewing ion childhood research: On children's identity work in interviews. *The Quarterly Report* 15 (6), 1309–1327.

Garcia, N. (2015) Tensions between cultural and utilitarian dimensions of language: A comparative analysis of 'multilingual' education policies in France and Germany. *Current Issues in Language Planning* 16, 43–59.

García, O., Flores, N. and Spotti, M. (2017) *The Oxford Handbook of Language and Society*. Oxford: Oxford University Press.

Greig, A., Taylor, J. and Mackay, T. (2007) *Doing Research with Children*. Los Angeles, CA: Sage Publications.

Harding-Esch, E. and Riley, P. (2003) *The Bilingual Family: A Handbook for Parents*. Cambridge: Cambridge University Press.

Hélot, C. and Young, A. (2002) Bilingualism and language education in French primary schools: Why and how should migrant languages be valued? *International Journal of Bilingual Education and Bilingualism* 5: 96–112.

Hélot, C. and Young, A. (2006) Imagining multilingual education in France: A language and cultural awareness project at primary level. In O. García, T. Skutnabb-Kangas and M. Torres-Guzmán (eds) *Imagining Multilingual Schools: Languages in Education and Glocalization* (pp. 69–90). Clevedon: Multilingual Matters. https://doi.org/10.21832/9781853598968-004

Ibrahim, N. (2004) A bilingual adventure in Paris. *YLT Sig: Cats: Children and Teenagers* 2, 29–32.

Ibrahim, N. (2010) Bilingualism: A child's perspective. *YLT Sig: Cats: Children and Teenagers* 1, 29–32.

Ibrahim, N. (2014) Perceptions of identity in trilingual 5-year-old twins in diverse pre-primary educational contexts. In S. Mourão and M. Lourenço (eds) *Early Years Second Language Education: International Perspectives on Theories and Practice* (pp. 46–61). Routledge: Abingdon.

Ibrahim, N. (2016) Enacting identities: Children's narratives on person, place and experience in fixed and hybrid spaces. *Educational Enquiry* 7 (1), 69–91.

James, A. and Prout, A. (eds) (1997) *Constructing and Reconstructing Childhood: Contemporary Issues in the Sociological Study of Childhood* (2nd edn). London: Falmer Press.

James, A., Jenks, C. and Prout, A. (1998) *Theorising Childhood*. Cambridge: Polity Press.

Kalaja, P. and Pitkänin-Huhta, A. (eds) (2018) Double special issue 'visual methods in applied language studies.' *Applied Linguistics Review* 9 (2–3), 157–473.

Kalaja, P. and Melo-Pfeifer, S. (2019) *Visualising Multilingual Lives: More Than Words*. Bristol: Multilingual Matters.

Kuchah, K. and Pinter, A. (2012) Was this an interview? Breaking the power barrier in adult-child interviews in an African context. *Issues in Educational Research* 22 (3), 283–297.

Langsted, O. (1994) Looking at quality from the child's perspective. In P. Moss and A. Pence (eds) *Valuing Quality in Early Childhood Service: New Approaches to Defining Quality*. London: Paul Chapman.

Manes-Bonnisseau, C. and Taylor, A. (2018) *Propositions pour une meilleure maîtrise des langues vivantes étrangères : Oser dire le nouveau monde.* Rapport remis le 12 septembre 2018. Paris: Ministère de l'Éducation.

Martin-Jones, M. and Martin, D. (eds) (2017) *Researching Multilingualism.* Abingdon: Routledge.

Norton, B. (2013) *Identity and Language Learning: Gender, Ethnicity and Educational Change* (1st edn). Essex: Pearson.

Qvortrup, J., Bardy, M., Sgritta, G. and Wintersberger, H. (1994) *Childhood Matters, Social Theory, Practice and Politics.* Aldershot: Avebury.

UNCRC. (1989) *The Convention on the Rights of the Child.* Geneva: United Nations.

Vertovec, S. (2007) Super-diversity and its implications. *Ethnic and Racial Studies* 30, 1024–1054.

Young, A. (2014) Looking through the language lens: Monolingual taint or plurilingual tint? In J. Conteh and G. Meier (eds) *The Multilingual Turn in Languages Education: Opportunities and Challenges* (pp. 89–110). Bristol: Multilingual Matters.

8 'I don't want to talk any more': Reflecting on Research into Young Children's Perspectives on their Multilingual Lives

Jane Andrews

Introduction

Brooker (2011) warned educators and researchers that there was still a long way to go if we wanted to truly value children's perspectives and take them seriously, as enshrined in the United Nations Convention on the Rights of the Child (1989). This chapter aims to address Brooker's concern which, it is argued here, may also be applied to educational research and research into children's multilingual experiences where children's own perspectives are less evident. The chapter offers a reflexive account of a research study, which engaged with young children about their multilingual lives, giving specific attention to ethical and methodological design features and research experiences in the field. The focus for the research study was to (a) develop an understanding of how children, who access and use a range of linguistic resources in their daily lives, reflect on those experiences, (b) explore what children's linguistic preferences might be, in their English medium primary schools in England and (c) to make these insights available to feed into educational practices for all multilingual children in similar contexts. The chapter begins with a description of the research study, including its rationale, research questions, context, methodological approach and finally the findings. There then follows a selective review of published research into ethical and methodological issues raised in studies of young children who use several languages in school and in daily life. Then, four vignettes of researcher and research participant engagement and interaction are explored in terms of their impact on the methodology and ethics of the study. The chapter ends with a concluding discussion of issues for research, and, potentially, educational practice, relating to the challenges surrounding valuing and seeking out children's perspectives while being responsive to their preferences and willingness to engage in the moment.

Background to the Research

The research reported here was conducted in the school year of 2009–2010 and data were gathered in primary schools in two cities in England. The motivation for conducting this study was to respond to continuing linguistic diversity in the population and to add children's voices to educators' understandings of children's multilingual lives and address the implications for their learning in schools. There is a wealth of research into multilingualism and bilingualism with children undertaken from a range of linguistic perspectives, for example Painter (1998) using systemic functional linguistics and Babayigit (2014) using psycholinguistic theory. However, it is suggested here that the majority of these studies tend to prioritise adults' perspectives on children's multilingualism, whether in their roles as parents, teachers or educational practitioners such as early years staff. Such research situates children as objects of research (by being observed or recorded in interaction) rather than as informants on their own experience and expertise. So, the research reported here sought to foreground children's perspectives on their multilingualism and learning and it also paid heed to Article 30 of the United Nations Convention on the Rights of the Child (1989):

> In those States in which ethnic, religious or linguistic minorities or persons of indigenous origin exist, a child belonging to such a minority or who is indigenous shall not be denied the right, in community with other members of his or her group, to enjoy his or her own culture, to profess and practise his or her own religion, or to use his or her own language.

This research study, therefore, sought to explore perspectives and experiences of being multilingual 'with' children (in a collaborative ethos) rather than 'on' children (with an overt or covert hierarchy between researcher and participants). Children's actual experiences and future hopes were explored in small discussion groups which were designed to allow children to pursue ideas of interest to them, facilitated by open-ended prompts. The two main research questions were as follows: (1) what are children's perspectives on their multilingualism? and (2) what is the potential for children's learning if they access all of their languages?

The findings from data gathered from the discussion groups to respond to the first question provide the material in Vignettes 1–3 explored below and data gathered to respond to the second research question provide the material for Vignette 4.

Research Design

As noted above the research was conducted in two primary schools in England where the age range of children is from 4 to 11. The two schools were in cities which both reflect superdiverse communities (Vertovec, 2007), some of whom are recently arrived, others of whom have been settled for one or more generations. The participating schools, known to have a linguistically diverse intake of pupils, were approached to elicit their interest in the research, which represented an opportunistic approach to school sampling. The relevant background details of the pupils who participated in the research are set out below, with pseudonyms used for both the pupils and the name of their school.

The research methods used were qualitative in nature and informed by the Mosaic Approach (Clark & Moss, 2000). The Mosaic Approach was developed in the context of research with mainstream educational settings, rather than for applied linguistics research in particular. It lays out ideas for research which are particularly tailored for working with young children. They could include walking and talking or using visual techniques such as providing opportunities for children to lead conversations by taking photographs or drawing. Regardless of the specific technique used to implement the Mosaic Approach, the emphasis is always on a participatory ethos, which allows the child to lead in documenting their experience and it conceptualizes the child as a competent meaning-maker.

With the Mosaic Approach informing my research practice, I sought to engage children in my study using activities which could be expected to be familiar and easily accessible. To explore research question 1, above, the medium of drawing was used as a starting point for initiating small group conversations about languages and everyday interests between myself as researcher and groups of between 3 to 5 children. In total I had conversations with 14 groups of children, aged between 5 and 10.

Audio recordings and transcriptions were made of the small group conversations and after each research encounter I wrote up a research diary record about every aspect of my school visits and the conversations with the children. The data discussed in this chapter are offered as vignettes, using an approach which shares characteristics with the work of Blodgett et al. (2011). In the case of this research, the vignettes are composed of elements of the recorded data together with my diary writing.

The four vignettes discussed in this chapter were taken from the full set of data from the study based on their relevance to considerations of ethics and methodologies in research with children. The main home language and ages of the children who took part in the research addressing research question 1 (noted below) are summarized in Table 8.1, based on information provided by the children themselves and by the class teachers.

Table 8.1 Children's pseudonyms, year groups, average age and main home language

Name (pseudonym)	Year group (average age in brackets)	Main home language (self-reported and teacher reported)
Primary school A (group a)		
Rabia	1 (age 5yr 6mth)	Malay
May	1 (age 5yr 6mth)	Malay
Primary school A school (group b)		
Samira	2 (age 6yr 6mth)	Hindi
Abdul	2 (age 6yr 6mth)	Bengali
Fahad	2 (age 6yr 6mth)	Bengali
Mariam	2 (age 6yr 6mth)	Arabic
Primary school A (group c)		
Rita	2 (age 6yr 6mth)	Chinese
Anil	2 (age 6yr 6mth)	Hindi
Jasmine	2 (age 6yr 6mth)	Hindi
Primary school A (group d)		
Tilly	3 (age 7yr 6mth)	Panjabi
Nahila	3 (age 7yr 6mth)	Bengali
Maria	3 (age 7yr 6mth)	Croatian
Emily	3 (age 7yr 6mth)	Chinese
Khalid	3 (age 7yr 6mth)	Somali

Table 8.2 below provides background data on children who participated in group work set up to address research question 2 (noted below).

The small group conversations were elicited from an invitation to draw, which was expressed as 'draw something about you and your languages that you'd like to share with us'. This research approach was designed to be flexible and the children were reassured they could draw what they

Table 8.2 Drawing task design participant background data

Primary school B

Name (pseudonym)	Year group (average age in brackets)	Main home language (self-reported and teacher reported)
Abdullah	1 (age 5yr 6mth)	Somali
Khalid	3 (age 7yr 6mth)	Somali
Salma	3 (age 7yr 6mth)	Somali
Ahmed	4 (age 8yr 6 mth)	Somali

wished and what they wanted to share and they could keep their drawings after the activity. This offer was taken up by many of the children, which could be seen as a measure of children's willing participation in the activity and their care and investment in it. As part of my flexible research approach I had a list of guiding questions which I sought to explore with the children but I did not work through each question rigidly with each group but rather I bore them in mind as children shared their drawings and talked about their languages and interests. Given that the drawings were all personal and different, the conversations naturally took off in different directions and the children initiated questions with each other as well as responding to my questions. The guiding questions were as follows:

(1) Which languages do you speak at home?
(2) Who do you speak with in those languages?
(3) Who decides which languages you use together?
(4) What about at school?
(5) What about in the future – would you like to use your different languages at school? Why, or why not?
(6) Would using your different languages at school help you in your learning?

Discussion in heritage language task

A second research activity was used in order to explore research question 2. The activity was designed to provide children with an experience of engaging in a classroom-type of activity using their heritage language, for example Somali. The children were grouped in a way that they would be able to engage in a shared language other than English. The children were asked to work with Dawes and Sams' (2004) 'talk box' materials designed to promote talk in primary classrooms and based wholly on visual materials. Each activity involved an open-ended task which required interaction and decision-making in order to be completed. The activity was then open to being completed in a shared language without any prompting or framing in English. One of the activities chosen for use in the research involved sorting through a series of line drawings and discussing how they could be grouped and how the agreed rationale for the grouping could be explained/justified. A second activity was to report the story conveyed in a set of images which contained no written text. My intention, as a researcher, was to audio record these interactions and to then translate and transcribe the data ready for analysis, however, as is shown later, this activity did not go as planned.

The findings of the study are outlined in brief in this chapter rather than in full detail. Their purpose here is essentially to provide context for the vignettes discussed later in the chapter while the focus of the vignettes is on ethical issues, in line with the purpose of this volume.

The data from the conversations conducted in relation to research question 1 were transcribed and then grouped for analysis into themes (Braun & Clarke, 2016), a process intended to be inclusive of the full data set to avoid the criticism of cherry-picking data to fit a pre-determined agenda (Mann, 2011). The themes were derived from the data generated from the researcher's conversations with the groups of children. The themes reflected a wide ranging set of ways in which children engaged in everyday life using their languages in particular contexts and also translanguaging; that is, making use of different linguistic resources in a single interaction (see, e.g. García & Li Wei, 2014). The data were analysed and themes were derived inductively from the data as follows:

(1) children's demonstration of metalinguistic awareness;
(2) children's appreciation of their multilingualism as a 'private language';
(3) children's experiences of using languages with family and at home;
(4) children's associations of languages with religious practices;
(5) children's awareness of their language choices in contexts.

As stated above, the data discussed in the remaining sections of the chapter are not directly based on the findings grouped into themes 1–5 above, instead, the four vignettes presented are based on my researcher reflections on the processes of the research which were written after each day of data gathering. The vignettes were composed for their capacity to highlight wider issues of methodological choices and ethical realities in research with children at the time of researching, hence their inclusion in my research diary.

Review of Studies Exploring Children's Perspectives on their Multilingual Lives

This section acknowledges previous research into children's perspectives on their multilingualism and learning as opposed to the wider set of studies which explore the phenomenon of multilingualism or linguistic practices per se through, for example, interactional analysis. In particular, the selected studies reviewed are considered from the standpoint of the research and ethical practices used in eliciting children's perspectives on their linguistic practices. The rationale for this specific focus is guided by the main concerns of this chapter.

Ethical practices: Choosing where to talk and with whom

Studies of languages use and interaction with/ involving children can be challenging to researchers in that they are using language to elicit the focus of their research which is also language and as such it is easily influenced by contextual factors such as place and people present at the time of data collection. Mills (2001) used semi-structured interviews to explore with third generation, British Asian young people their experiences of language, culture and identity as they grew up in the West Midlands, England. In the paper Mills offered detailed insights into her own methodological and ethical research practices so that readers would appreciate the conditions in which the data were gathered. Mills suggested that this group of young people were under-researched which signalled the ethical issue of whose voices are represented in research and whose are omitted (see chapters by Ibrahim and Mathew & Pinter in this volume). In the paper Mills gave particular methodological and ethical attention to the conditions in which she engaged in semi-structured interviews with the young people, who were defined as school-aged, ranging from 5 to 19 years old. Steps she took to ensure the children were comfortable within the research encounter included offering the opportunity for families' choices of when and where the interviews took place and avoiding interrupting the young people's school experiences. Also, Mills was flexible in her approach so that some interviews took place with the child's mother present if the young person showed a preference for this. The ways in which children's data was to be used was explained and the author (2001: 385) reported that 'all children agreed that their mothers could read their transcripts later and were aware of this additional audience.' Issues of place and people involved and present in the research encounters were important to Mills. These dimensions of her research practice open up, for other researchers, valuable ethical and methodological questions which merit consideration.

Children's linguistic repertoires and endangered languages

Pietikäinen (2012) also researched children's perspectives on multilingualism in the Sámpi area which stretches across northern Norway, Sweden, Finland and north-western Russia. As the author explains that children in this region may speak one of the nine Sami languages which have an endangered status. The ethical challenges of exploring linguistic practices and repertoires of endangered languages with children are fully discussed in the work. This includes issues of linguistic competence whether it assessed by the individual or by others, perhaps of different generations, within the same community, as well as identity issues as revealed through language use. Pietikäinen (2012) offers reflections on how different methodological solutions can facilitate rather than exacerbate sensitivities surrounding linguistic competence, or lack of competence, and identity. The use of a multimodal research approach, such as eliciting children's drawings, allows the researcher to maintain their research focus while also perhaps making it less likely that researcher assumptions will be made about the phenomenon, in this case, children's multilingual practices or preference (see also chapters by Ibrahim,

Zandian and Prasad in this volume). Pietikäinen showed how she protected children from any possible harm to self-esteem if a child's lack of fluency in a language became apparent during the research.

Researchers' linguistic choices in research with children

Martin and Stuart-Smith (1998: 239) sought to understand the 'feelings about being bilingual and becoming biliterate' of 50 children aged 6 and 7 who all shared Sikh heritage and the Panjabi language, and were living in the West Midlands in England. As part of their research practice the researchers designed a bilingual research approach so that children were interviewed firstly in Panjabi by a Panjabi-speaking researcher and then a second interview was carried out in English by the authors of the paper. In their words this was an important, methodological choice 'if we were to investigate the notion that children construct their knowledge, meaning and identity through language' Martin and Stuart-Smith (1998: 240). The authors opened their study to the possibility that children may express themselves differently in their different languages and that by accessing children's wider linguistic repertoires a more 'enriched' data set may, potentially, be created.

Child-centred techniques for researching children's languages

Yaacob and Gardner (2012) reported on their research using role-play as a technique to elicit children's language and also explored the classroom experiences of young learners aged between six and eight. Role-play was evaluated as being age appropriate as a research technique by the researchers in that it was highly authentic for the children who spontaneously engaged in socio-dramatic play regularly. Role-plays therefore provided a more authentic medium of communication in their research and they saw the possibility for authentic responses, which might take the form of a kinaesthetic or verbal response such as posing a new question to the researcher. This is in contrast to more traditional research methods such as interviews which tend to demand responses involving self-analysis or reflexivity. Their approach to research with children was informed by the work of mainstream educators Clark and Moss' (2001) Mosaic Approach, explored earlier.

As stated earlier, the practical implications of these research principles, together with issues raised in this short, selected review of published studies, will be revisited in the concluding discussion in this chapter.

In summary, this short, selected review of previous studies exploring children's perspectives on their multilingualism has raised issues such as how methodologies can be crafted or selected to ensure they are age appropriate and engaging for children and young people as research participants (e.g. use of visual methods). Further, researchers have elaborated on how they set up ethical research encounters responsive to specific circumstances of the lives of children and their families and communities (e.g. respecting linguistic competence) as well as their preferences for engaging here and now (e.g. with parents present or not). Finally, the rights of children as participants have been respected through clear communication about how their engagement in the research will be used. These factors in research with children in relation to their languages provide me with a valuable background against which I can explore my own research practices and experiences in the following sections of this chapter.

Vignettes of Researcher and Research Participant Engagement and Interaction

This section presents four vignettes representing four dimensions of ethical dilemmas in researching with children. As already set out, each vignette is composed from elements of both my research diary and the audio recorded conversations.

Vignette 1: Throwing hats in the air

The first vignette below can be characterized as being concerned with issues of voluntary informed consent with children as participants. Gaining informed consent is a central concern of ethical research practice (see introductory chapter by Kuchah & Pinter in this volume) which has been extensively discussed by academic and professional associations, for example the British Educational Research Association (2018) and the National Children's Bureau (2003). The nature of informed consent when researching with children is problematized, by Edwards and Alldred (2001), who question whether the location of research in an institution in which children have only limited choices and opportunities to exercise their agency in itself works in opposition to the concept of informed consent. The authors' consideration of this tension leads them to conclude that a more nuanced concept of 'educated consent' would be more valid when considering how children are introduced to the possibility of participating in a research project when in school (see also García Mayo as well as Mourão in this volume). The term 'educated consent' seeks to acknowledge the unavoidable power imbalance at play in a school context between teachers and pupils or adults and children, whereby, in the main, children are required to do as adults tell them. Educated consent would offer children in research studies an opportunity to learn about what is being asked of them prior to their assent or consent to participate, and of course emphasise that not participating is possible. The researcher would, of course, need to manage the situation where some children may wish to participate and others may not. The challenge of this proposition for my research was about how I could present myself and my research interests to potential research participants and reassure myself that the information I was offering was clear and relevant to children's understanding of the world.

Vignette 1

To begin the group activity (drawing and talking) I explained who I was and what my research was about to a group of four children aged 6 and 7, including two girls and two boys. We were all sitting around the same table with drawing paper and pens available. I felt it was important not to make assumptions about children's understanding of my job and my research. To start off I said I worked in a university and asked the children who knew what a university was. At this point one of the children enthusiastically shared a response, speaking and using gestures to explain that his aunt went to the local university. He gestured his understanding of what happened at a university by saying that he knew that at a university everyone had a hat and threw them up in the air 'like this' at which point he mimed throwing a cap up in the air in delight, as he must have seen in real life or in moving or still images from a graduation day. Other children nodded or showed recognition of this brief comment and mime. I felt relieved, based on the children's responses, that I had provided a recognisable start to my introduction and that one child had felt confident to share their understanding and co-construct the event with me.

My reflections on Vignette 1 are that in seeking informed consent it may help the researcher to conceptualize the process as a dialogue rather than as a researcher-monologue. The dialogue seems to be effective if it involves a sharing of understandings on the part of both researcher and research participants and such dialogues also naturally invite questions from the children, which is valuable practice in terms of establishing common ground. I felt reassured to know that the context I was sharing with the children was one that at least one child recognized and had their own family connections with.

Vignette 2: 'I don't want to talk any more'

Children's continued willingness, in the moment, to engage with research is a challenge which researchers have noted in their work. In their research into the experiences of being involved in research involving children with speech, language and communication needs, Press *et al.* (2011) report on using a process of 'monitoring' to identify any signs of the child's distress during research. Such signs would be taken as a withdrawal of assent to participate in the research at that time and the researchers would act accordingly. Similar monitoring was used in the research discussed in this chapter.

As noted earlier, my approach to interacting with children about their languages and everyday concerns was framed in small groups around the drawing of an aspect of children's personal interests which then was the starting point for a conversation about the interest itself and languages used in connection to it. In the majority of groups children appeared to be content to both draw and talk about their pictures and associated matters. It was important for me as a researcher, and an adult in the school context, however, to monitor children's levels of comfort and continued willingness to engage in the research activity. An example of monitoring in practice is provided in Vignette 2 recounted below.

Vignette 2

A pair of year 1 children (aged 5 and 6, named here as Rabia and May), began the drawing activity and started the conversations about the drawing, moving on to connected topics arising from the pictures. From the beginning of the speaking part of the activity Rabia seemed more impatient and less willing to talk than May. This was demonstrated at first by shorter answers and by her answers only adding her confirmation to what May had said for example saying 'I'm like her', rather than adding a personal contribution. As the conversation progressed, mainly with May, Rabia joined in stating emphatically 'I don't want to talk any more' and at the same time she turned her back at me. I made a gentle comment along the lines of that was fine and continued the conversation with May who still seemed willing to talk. As the conversation with May progressed through different topics, I kept an eye on Rabia and wondered if I should offer to take her back to her classroom. I was conflicted as to whether this was a good idea – would it draw attention to her discomfort or would it empower her decision not to continue with the conversation? With these conflicting thoughts in mind I continued talking with May for a short while. During this time, Rabia moved away from our table and appeared comfortable browsing some displays and books elsewhere in the room. Shortly after, and when May had engaged me with some new topics about her hobbies, Rabia returned to our table and rejoined the conversation about her own hobbies.

This vignette illustrates how researchers need to maintain an ethical awareness of how the research encounter is developing moment by moment during its execution. A researcher cannot rely on the knowledge that consent or assent has been given by children themselves and their gatekeepers (parents or guardians and teachers) and therefore they have continued permission to carry out their research plan in full. As noted above, Press *et al.* (2011) comment that for adult researchers it is important to notice continued or withdrawn enjoyment or comfort on the part of the participants to maintain an ethical stance. This needs to be honoured by the researcher even when the completion of the research is put at risk. However, the researcher also needs to remember that sometimes the unexpected happens in interactions and in the case of Vignette 2 the feelings of discomfort and withdrawal were temporary and shortly afterwards Rabia rejoined the dialogue demonstrating her preference and agency to manage her participation.

Vignette 3: 'I speak Italian'

All researchers need to be aware of the risk that participants may seek to please them with the answers given in research interactions rather than those interactions being a reflection of actual thoughts, feelings or experiences. A different angle on this phenomenon is explored by Yaacob and Gardner (2012) who discussed young children's innate playfulness. The researchers capitalized on this by using role play as a research technique to explore children's perspectives which, they hoped, would be a familiar experience for the children. They also, however, suggested that this playfulness may extend to the point that in engaging with the researchers children may also be inventive in what they say to the researchers, which may mean the research data elicited is characterized by playful invention, instead of being an account of first-hand experience. This possibility illustrates how researchers may find themselves balancing between wanting to engage children in motivating and familiar activities for their research while also generating data with the children which can answer their research questions and be used in research reports. Vignette 3 below, outlines an incident within my research which raises similar questions about the potentially playful nature of children's engagement in research.

Vignette 3

As I introduced myself to the group of four children I was conscious of sharing what might be relevant to the children in relation to what I was asking them to talk with me about. As part of this process, I explained my interest in the many languages people can speak and I offered some examples of the languages I knew or was learning. One of my examples was that 'I can speak Italian'. This language was not one of the languages which tended to be used in the school. When I finished my short introduction the children each said something about themselves which included, in the case of Samira, a pupil aged 6, that she spoke Hindi and Italian. None of the other three children mentioned knowing Italian, but rather, the languages noted were Bengali and Arabic.

Samira's comment that she spoke Italian put me in an uncomfortable position in that I felt unsure of whether she did in fact speak Italian or was she mirroring my statement? Her response may have been reflecting the tension, discussed by Edwards and Alldred (2001) about whether or not children really do have agency to express themselves and their preferences in school-based research. My conflicted feelings originated in questions such as, was Samira trying to please me, an adult, by aligning herself with my stated languages, or was I being disingenuous in not expecting one of the children to be able to speak Italian because I was being overly guided by the class-teachers' lead and she had not noted that any of the children spoke Italian? By engaging in research which has been shaped by an adult researcher it is at moments like this that I question if I followed Brooker's (2011) call to take children seriously. Taking children seriously would perhaps be more effectively achieved if children were engaging with issues of importance to them, shaped by them and with them taking a leading role. Researchers need to be aware that the way in which they introduce themselves and present the research may, inadvertently, shape the responses of the children, whose voices the researcher is seeking to elicit and listen to. To achieve an ethos of respectful engagement with children may require adult researchers to review when and how they introduce themselves in a research encounter.

Vignette 4: Whispering in groups

This vignette concerns authentic language use within the activity used to elicit language used in context for the research. The challenge for any researcher focusing on language in their research and using language to explore language has been discussed, for example, by Grosjean (1998), Holmes *et al.* (2013) and, as mentioned earlier in this chapter, Martin and Stuart-Smith (1998). Grosjean introduced a set of methodological and conceptual challenges for bilingualism researchers, to describe how variables such as the context and task in which research data are elicited, for example, can have an influence on the nature of the language used and whether or not code-switching is present on that particular occasion. Holmes *et al.* (2013) make a call for researchers to share their choices and practices in a transparent way when engaging in research which involves moving between different languages at all stages of the research. Martin and Stuart-Smith (1998), as noted earlier, conducted their research in children's two languages in order to study how their responses differed in these two conditions. These issues show us that eliciting language use that is authentic for the research participants is not necessarily straightforward, and Vignette 4 below illustrates the many factors which may have an influence on research participants' communication style and the potential impact of a researcher and the context on the chosen communication style.

Vignette 4

The activity I set up to explore research question 2 (what is the potential for children's learning if they access all of their languages?) was based on some picture-based sorting activities from the Talk Box book (Dawes & Sams, 2004). I was in the school library with a group of 8 Somali speaking children who had agreed to work with me in the research. I set up the activity with the task explained and the pictures shared out and explained that I would record them completing the activity. I wanted to ensure that I continued to have their informed consent. I gave the instruction that the group could complete the activity in the language that they preferred, which could be English or it could be Somali. I left the children to complete the task and went to browse some of the books further away from them so that they did not feel uncomfortable by being observed by me. As I moved around the library I could hear the children's voices so that I knew they were engaging with each other, even if it was very quiet. When I felt they had had enough time I returned to the table and asked if they would explain to me how they sorted the pictures and what their rationale was, which they willingly did. Later in the day when I listened to my recording I could not hear the children's utterances as they had appeared to whisper to each other to complete the task. The whispering could have been in Somali or English but it was too quiet to be heard.

My experience in Vignette 4 brought home to me the artificial nature of what I as a researcher felt would be a straightforward activity on this occasion. Various ways of interpreting what happened can be proposed. The children could be interpreted as having used their agency to, politely, engage to some extent with the activity but to withdraw their full participation by whispering and not making their voices available to me as the researcher. Group work always had to be conducted quietly in the school so as not to disturb others, and this concern may have been reflected in the children's very quiet responses. Or, maybe the request of a non-Somali speaking adult in the school context to use their Somali language, a language usually associated with home, family and life outside of school, may have been intrusive or unwelcome in some way. Possibly I had not explained fully enough the purpose of my recording and the children had not had time to become familiar with speaking together in Somali while being recorded.

As in the discussion of Vignette 3 above, my reflection is that researchers' agendas would benefit more from being shaped by children's concerns and interests which would perhaps result in children's more active engagement and their confident voices being heard, in both the literal and metaphorical senses. Concrete changes to my research approach could have involved approaching the activities with a Somali-speaking co-researcher who could have initiated some speaking activities with the children as practice prior to the beginning of the recording. Alternatively, more time becoming familiar with the goal of the research, being recorded and listening to the practice recordings could have broken down any barriers children may have felt.

Concluding Reflections

Children's languages in research

To begin this concluding set of reflections on my experiences of researching children's perspectives on being multilingual and the unexpected aspects of the research process, I present this quotation from Meena, the young character-narrator in Meera Syal's novel *Anita and Me*:

> It felt so strange to hear Punjabi under the stars. It was an indoor language to me, an almost guilty secret which the elders would only share away from prying English eyes and ears. On the street in shops on buses in parks I noticed how the volume would go up when they spoke English telling us kids not to wander off asking the price of something intimate, personal, about feelings as opposed to acquisitions, they switched to Punjabi and the volume became a conspiratorial whisper. (Syal, 1996: 203)

A novel offers a fictional account of lives and experiences and is therefore different from a research study. However, this extract offers some possible pointers for the researcher into children's perspectives on their multilingualism in terms of how children learn not just the languages themselves but *about* their family and community languages through the practices they encounter in everyday life. This could encourage researchers to re-interrogate their methodological approach and question whether it is consistent with their research aims, values and the phenomenon at the heart of the research. So, if, in the UK at the current time, languages other than English are most naturally occurring in communities and homes then aiming to elicit them, as I did (see Vignette 4) in school may sound and feel unusual, in the same way Meena reports in the novel *Anita and Me*. An alternative research methodology may be more appropriate such as linguistic ethnography (as advocated by e.g. Martin & Martin-Jones, 2016) in the naturalistic setting of the home or the community.

As Pietikäinen (2012) noted in her research into the Sami languages, which are characterized as endangered, researchers need to take care that their research practices do not cause harm by exposing competences in different languages which may be viewed or judged in particular ways by different community members. Pietikäinen's response to this challenge was to make use of visual methods to engage with children and young people. This point leads to a second concluding thought which relates to the need for flexible, in the moment, review of ethical practice on the part of the researcher. Kubanyiova (2008) uses the term micro-ethics to refer to this type of research practice. In this case, it could refer to how researchers need to maintain their commitment to respecting children's rights in the research and managing risk of any kind throughout the research process.

Flexibility in research

Vignette 2 illustrated how, even after expected and standard informed consent processes have been used, it is not guaranteed that research participants will maintain the same level of willingness to engage in a study throughout. This issue applies equally when adults are research participants as well. With reference to Press *et al.*'s (2011) concept of monitoring it seems essential for researchers to maintain an alert and flexible mindset during their research practice. If a researcher practises monitoring during their data collection, it will bring them closer to maintaining their ethical duty to their research participants. In the case of researching with children this could mean being attentive to children's engagement and flexible to children's changes in demeanour. When children's rights are respected then the right not to participate needs to be a feasible option for children. If a child does show signs of no longer wishing to participate a question about why this might be can be asked, which leads to the final, broad, reflection in the form of a question about who, in fact, has set the research agenda.

Whose agenda shapes the research? A possible way forward

Children's levels of engagement in my research varied according to the individuals involved and many factors including perhaps their level of commitment to what was being asked of them. This led me back to considering Brooker's (2011) demand that we as a society and as a community of researchers continue to work on how we can take children's views and rights seriously. As a researcher I am left with the recognition that although my research study sought research with children and to learn about their perspectives, the agenda had been shaped by my adult view of the world. An alternative to the model of research I worked with would have been a stronger model of researching with children where the research would have been conceptualized as a collaborative process from the outset. An incident in my research also pointed the way to this approach. It happened when one child was describing, with enthusiasm, how in her family they all wore new, special clothes to celebrate Eid. At that moment, another child joined in and asked her a question about this, matching the enthusiasm of the first speaker. A model of research into children's multilingualism in which children interview or find out from each other about questions they themselves have designed would be a promising, if challenging, prospect which, it could be hoped, would be engaging for children as participants and enlightening for adults.

References

Auer, P. (1998) The monolingual bias in bilingualism research, or: Why bilingual talk is (still) a challenge for linguistics. In M. Heller (ed.) *Bilingualism: A Social Approach* Basingstoke: Palgrave.

Braun, V. and Clarke, V. (2006) Using thematic analysis in psychology. *Qualitative Research in Psychology* 3 (2), 77–101.

Babayigit, S. (2014) Contributions of word-level and verbal skills to written expression: Comparison of learners who speak English as a first (L1) and second language (L2). *Reading and Writing* 14 (7), 1207–1229.

Blodgett, A.T., Schinke, R.J., Smith, B., Peltier, D. and Pheasant, C. (2011) In indigenous words: Exploring vignettes as a narrative strategy for presenting the research voices of Aboriginal community members. *Qualitative Inquiry* 17 (6), 522–533.

British Educational Research Association (2018) See https://www.bera.ac.uk/publication/ethical-guidelines-for-educational-research-2018

Brooker, L. (2011) Taking children seriously: An alternative agenda for research? *Journal of Early Childhood Research* 9 (2), 137–149.

Clark, A. and Moss, P. (2001) *Listening to Young Children: The Mosaic Approach.* London: National Children's Bureau.

Dawes, L. and Sams, C. (2004) *Talk Box: Speaking and Listening Activities for Learning at Key Stage 1.* Abingdon: David Fulton Publishers.

Edwards, A. and Alldred, P. (2001) Children and school-based research: 'informed consent' or 'educated consent'? *British Educational Research Journal* 27 (3), 347–365.

García, O. and Li Wei (2014) *Translanguaging: Language, Bilingualism and Education.* Cham: Springer.

Grosjean, F. (1998) Studying bilinguals: Methodological and conceptual issues in *Bilingualism: Language and Cognition* 1 (1998), 131–149.

Holmes, P., Fay, R., Andrews, J. and Attia, M. (2013) Researching multilingually: New theoretical and methodological directions. *International Journal of Applied Linguistics* 23 (3), 285–299.

Kabadayi, A. (2008) Analysis of the socio-demographic structure and thoughts of the Turkish bilingual children on 'bilingualism' in Germany. *Education 3–13* 36 (1), 15–26.

Kubanyiova, M. (2008) Rethinking research ethics in contemporary applied linguistics: The tension between macroethical and microethical perspectives in situated research. *The Modern Language Journal* 92 (4), 503–518.

Mann, S. (2011) A critical review of qualitative interviews in applied linguistics. *Applied Linguistics* 32 (1), 6–24.

Martin, D. and Stuart-Smith, J. (1998) Exploring bilingual children's perceptions of being bilingual and biliterate: Implications for educational provision. *British Journal of Sociology of Education* 19 (2), 237–254.

Martin, D. and Martin-Jones, M. (2016) (eds) *Researching Multilingualism: Critical and Ethnographic Perspectives.* London: Routledge.

Mills, J. (2001) Being bilingual: Perspectives of third generation Asian children on language, culture and identity. *International Journal of Bilingual Education and Bilingualism* 4 (6), 383–402.

Painter, C. (1998) *Learning Through Language in Early Childhood.* London: Cassell.

Pietikäinen, S. (2012) Experiences and expressions of multilingualism: Visual ethnography and discourse analysis in research with Sami children. In S. Gardner and M.

Martin-Jones (eds) *Multilingualism, Discourse and Ethnography*. London: Routledge.

Press, F., Bradley, B.S., Goodfellow, J., Harrison, L.J., McLeod, S., Sumsion, J., Elwick, S. and Stratigos, T. (2011) Listening to infants about what life is like in childcare: A mosaic approach. In S. Roulstone and S. McLeod (eds) *Listening to Children and Young People with Speech, Language and Communication Needs*. Guidlford: J. and R. Press Ltd.

Syal, M. (1996) *Anita and Me*. London: Fourth Estate.

The National Children's Bureau (2003) See https://www.ncb.org.uk/resources-publications/guidelines-research-children-and-young-people

UN (1989) Convention on the rights of the child. See https://downloads.unicef.org.uk/wp-content/uploads/2010/05/UNCRC_united_nations_convention_on_the_rights_of_the_child.pdf (accessed on 28 June 2018).

Vertovec, S. (2007) Super-diversity and its implications. *Ethnic and Racial Studies* 29 (6), 1024–1054.

Yaacob, S. and Gardner, S. (2012) Young learner perspectives through researcher-initiated role-play. In S. Gardner and M. Martin-Jones (eds) *Multilingualism, Discourse and Ethnography*. London: Routledge.

9 Navigating Cultural and Methodological Complexities in Research with Children in a Sub-Saharan African Context

Kuchah Kuchah and Lizzi O. Milligan

Different forms of English language education (ELE) including English as a second/Foreign language (ESL/EFL) and English as a medium of instruction (EMI) continue to expand across Sub-Saharan Africa, despite significant concerns about their impact on educational quality and inequalities (Kuchah, 2016; Milligan & Tikly, 2016). This trend requires more careful and inclusive approaches to research in order to better understand and address the variety of issues that ELE might pose for multilingual children, especially from socioeconomically lower backgrounds. In this chapter, we argue for the importance of child-focused research while highlighting the ethical and methodological complexities in this type of research through examples from research about ELE with young learners in school contexts in Cameroon. We suggest that such complexities can be heightened in research in many contexts in Sub-Saharan Africa and elsewhere where child-focused research is shaped by a constant interplay of forces between indigenous and imported sociocultural and linguistic norms, for example, through policies that promote learner-centred pedagogies.

Despite the ever-growing and sometimes pervasive impact of English language on the education and future aspirations of children in Sub-Saharan Africa, research about young learner ELE is still scarce. This paucity means that the discourses that define what counts as quality ELE can often be driven by northern conceptions of 'best practice' (Altinyelken, 2010; Nsamenang, 2008; Smith, 2011). Such practices have generally been considered in terms of their alignment with the rhetoric of learner-centredness – 'its potential for cognitive development, respect for human rights and goals of emancipation, and possibilities for future-oriented skills development' (Schweisfurth, 2013a: 6) – rather than with the contexts within which children in underprivileged state school contexts learn.

In this scant literature, there is very little research on ELE in multilingual Sub-Saharan African contexts in which the perspectives of young learners have been prioritized. In this regard, our research has sought to include children's voices as a gateway into understanding their lived experiences of schooling in order to bring these to bear on ELE policy and practice. We have argued (e.g. in Kuchah *et al.*, forthcoming) that this is particularly important given the need for greater and more contextualized understandings of how learning (in) English impacts on the learning processes and outcomes advocated by United Nations Sustainable Development Goal 4, namely, to 'ensure inclusive and equitable quality education and promote lifelong learning opportunities for all' by 2030. As Scott (2008: 88) has argued, 'the best people to provide information on the child's perspectives, actions and attitudes are children themselves.'

While we are advocates of conducting research with children, we have frequently reflected on the disjuncture between the learner-centred pedagogies promoted in national educational policies and the cultural and ecological realities of Sub-Saharan African classrooms (Schweisfurth, 2011; Serbessa, 2006) and the implications of this for conducting meaningful child-focused research in this and similar contexts globally. In this chapter we share these reflections, drawing from our individual and shared research experiences in Cameroon. Although the examples from which we draw our conclusions are based on our research in Cameroon, we believe that some of the issues raised, for example, about the 'top-down' pedagogic and cultural context and the potential impact on relationships with the researcher would apply beyond Cameroon and not only in Sub-Saharan Africa but to many contexts also included in the book (see, for example, Zandian in this volume)

Learner-centred Education, Participatory Research and the Cultural Context of SSA

Learner-centred education has emerged as the preferred approach to education over the last three decades following the United Nations Convention of the Rights of the Child (UNCRC, 1989) but its roots can be traced as far back as to the work of Socrates (400 BC) which emphasized self-reflection, critical thinking, reasoning and logic (Vlastos, 1983). In the last century, various philosophical and psychological underpinnings of learner-centredness have linked it to progressive pedagogy and the development of democratic skills in learners (Dewey, 1916), social transformation and emancipation (Freire, 1972) and the value of personal experiences (Piaget, 1928) and interpersonal interaction (Bruner, 1966; Vygotsky, 1978) in constructing knowledge. More recently, learner-centred education has been promoted as part of global and national agenda for achieving universal quality and inclusive basic education particularly in the global south where teacher-centred pedagogic approaches have been known to dominate classroom practices (Pontefract & Hardman, 2005). Learner-centred education is often contrasted with traditional forms of teacher-dominated practices such as lecturing, drilling and rote learning and embraced for its potential to give learners, and demand from them, 'a relatively high level of active control over the contents and processes of learning. What is learned, and how, are therefore shaped by learners' needs, capacities and interests' (Schweisfurth, 2013b: 20). Policy discourses have drawn from evidence in the field of cognitive psychology to suggest that deep and meaningful learning can only be achieved through learner engagement with, and co-construction of, knowledge with teachers and peers. With the enactment of the UNCRC (see Kuchah & Pinter in this volume), learner-centredness has also been seen from a rights-based perspective (UNICEF, 2007) as a way of recognizing children's voices in decision making in and about their education. Underlying these discourses is the intention to create child-friendly democratic learning environments (Sriprakash, 2010) based on the assumption that learner-centred education provides a 'foundation for the building of democratic citizens and societies and therefore national development capacity' (Schweisfurth, 2011: 425).

Despite the positive policy discourses around learner-centred education (LCE), research in Sub-Saharan Africa shows very little success with its implementation (e.g. Farrell, 2002). A large part of the literature shows that the implementation of LCE 'is riddled with stories of failures grand and small' (Schweisfurth, 2011: 425). Accounts of challenges and failures in the implementation of LCE have been recorded across the continent, for example in Botswana (Koosimile, 2005), Kenya (Sawamura & Sifuna, 2008), Niger (Goza et al., 2008) and Tanzania (Komba & Nkumbi, 2008). These studies, like studies elsewhere in the Global South, suggest that classroom practice remains teacher dominated, with learners' participation limited to answering teacher questions. While studies suggest some practical obstacles to implementation, for example, inadequate teacher training and large class sizes, there is also significant evidence that suggests that implementation could be hampered by sociocultural factors (e.g. Altinyenken, 2010; Muthwii, 2001; Schweisfurth, 2011). This literature offers some important reflections for child-focused researchers about the ways that good practice conceptualized elsewhere can encounter challenges in practice.

Of particular relevance here is the consideration of the ways in which cultural forces influence adult–child relationships in this context; in fact, culture 'interacts profoundly with teacher-learner relationships and classroom behavioural norms' (Schweisfurth, 2013a: 4) and the power distances within such relationships are often an extension of the child's home experiences. Altinyelken (2010: 167) explains that in traditional African cultures,

> ...children are brought up to respect adults and those in authority. Questioning or challenging them are not often considered appropriate behaviour. Indeed, in many African societies, the relationship between adult and child is one of respect and authority. Children are not encouraged to question; they are expected to be respectful, charming and smiling in the company of elders.

In a study that examined the embodiment of stranger–child interactions with 22 one-year old children in the cultural contexts of German and Cameroonian families of different socioeconomic backgrounds (Otto et al., 2014), significant behavioural differences were observed not only between the children, but also between the adult strangers from both contexts. The study found that German children took initiatives during interaction with the adult stranger while Cameroonian children simply followed the stranger's suggestions. In their interactions with children from the opposite culture, the German adult stranger displayed a much more responsive-sensitive approach when interacting with Cameroonian children while the Cameroonian stranger was directive. These differences, while not conclusive or generalizable, suggest that there might be cultural forms of adult–child interactions and knowledge transmission which tend to promote adult dominance over child agency.

The philosophical ideas around learner-centred education discussed above have also been translated into child-centred research in recent years, particularly thanks to the work of researchers within the 'New Sociology of Childhood' movement (e.g. Christensen & Prout, 2002; Maybin, 2006). These researchers have pushed the boundaries of traditional research which involves children as unknowing objects, or adult-controlled subjects, of research (e.g. Piaget, 1963; Wu, 2003) towards a more democratic and inclusive involvement of children as active participants and agents with some control over the research agenda (Alderson, 2005; Pinter, 2019). Such research has been conceptualized as research *with* and/or *by* children (Kellett, 2010) and recognizes children's right to express their views freely in all matters affecting their lives (UNCRC Art 12) and their 'freedom to seek, receive and impart information and ideas of all kinds regardless of frontiers, either orally, in writing or in print, in the form of art, or through any other media of the child's choice' (UNCRC Art 13). An important innovative component of this research therefore is the use of participatory methods and activities (O'Kane, 2008; Pinter et al., 2013) which are consistent with the pedagogical and ecological experiences of young learners (Turek, 2013). However, this final point re-affirms assumptions of a universal familiarity with participatory and learner-centred pedagogies.

Central to the methodological choice to engage participatory methods is often a conscious decision by the researcher to not only give children a voice but to challenge the power relations between the researcher and the researched (Packard, 2008). Milligan (2016), for example, explains how the use of visual narrative interviews with secondary school learners in Western Kenya allowed for a shift in how participants viewed her as an adult, teacher and outsider. However, this type of research can encounter similar challenges to those described above for the implementation of LCE policies and it is important that the limitations of this type of research for re-presenting the child's voice are acknowledged (Spyrou, 2011). Breaking existing cultural norms in research with children in this kind of context requires a paradigm shift which in turn creates methodological challenges that need to be acknowledged. Because methodological issues are closely linked to ethical issues in child research (Pinter, 2011) such a paradigm shift cannot be without its own methodological and ethical complexities. Given the circumstances we have discussed above, it is not unusual that research approaches which seek to engage children as active participants and decision makers in the research process might be impeded by children's own cultural experiences, realities and expectations (see also Zandian in this volume). In what follows, we discuss three illustrative research experiences in which we have had to navigate the complex methodological and ethical dilemmas of engaging with children as active participants in research in Cameroon.

Of Confidentiality, Children's Silence, Voices and the Influence of Adults

In a study that sought to investigate appropriate English language pedagogy in a Cameroonian context (Kuchah, 2013) the first author of this chapter designed a methodological procedure that included participatory activities for eliciting 10–11-year-old children's perspectives of what counted as good teaching. The main study collected data from classroom observations and stimulated recall interviews with observed teachers as well as participatory child-group interviews with children from the teachers' classes. Preliminary findings from the different data sets formed the basis of focus group discussions with a larger group of teachers from the two research sites covered in the study.

Child-group interviews mainly sought to elicit children's accounts of instances of good teaching by their teachers and children's explanations of how these instances were useful to their language learning. Children also had the liberty to talk about instances of bad teaching and to make suggestions about how language teachers could organize teaching to better support their learning. Because this was a context where decisions on pedagogic matters have never taken learners' perspectives into consideration and where, as we have shown above, children are most often perceived as recipients, not generators of knowledge (Kuchah & Pinter, 2012) it was important for the researcher to invest in identity and relationship building with the children over a considerable period of time, in order to create an enabling environment for children's voices and perspectives to emerge. The extent to which the children in this study were involved as active participants has been documented in the literature (see Kuchah & Pinter, 2012; Pinter *et al.*, 2013). Here, we examine possible understandings of the children's 'choice' to be silent, or to express themselves verbally during the research encounter and discuss how this choice and what they say might be a legitimate expression of their thoughts, opinions and feelings or influenced by the adults, institutions and communities within which they are growing up.

At the start of each child-group interview, the researcher engaged children in a collaborative reconstruction of the purpose and process of the interactive encounter based on previous conversations during the weeks of socialization and reminded them of basic ethical principles such as confidentiality and anonymity as in the following excerpt:

> Kuchah: Now, I want you to understand clearly what we will be doing here today, ok? I will get your ideas, I will listen to you, but everything is between you and me. I am not going to share what we say here with anybody in your school. I will do my analysis alone and I will try to use your ideas when I write a book and when I am working with teachers, but I am not going to use any of your names. So be as honest as possible, tell me everything and don't be afraid that I am going to tell your teachers. I told you I will not show them your drawings, nobody will listen to this conversation between you and me, but I will use it in the future to work with your teachers and other teachers in Cameroon.

Despite these assurances, their verbal consent obtained over three weeks of socialization, and their enthusiasm during the interview, there were still instances where some hitherto vocal children were reticent to speak particularly when this had to do with negative comments about their teacher. Prior to the interview, children were asked to draw their teacher (Mr T) and write something memorable he usually says as a stimulus for further discussions. The following excerpt comes after one of the children (Lydia) has explained why her picture of their teacher looks like a monster and this unexpected direction causes unease in another child (Jemia) who had, a few moments before this episode, been called out to see her mother (we return to this below):

> Kuchah: Well Jemia, tell me what you think. Lydia says it is difficult to talk about your teacher. What do you think, Jemia?
> Jemia: (Silent)
> Kuchah: What is the matter Jemia? Are you afraid to speak?
> Jemia: Yes
> Kuchah: Wait a minute, are you ashamed or afraid?

Jemia: Afraid
Kuchah: Afraid of what? That I will tell him?
Jemia: (nods reluctantly)
Kuchah: Why? (speaking to all) Do you remember what I told you last
           week and even today about our discussion?

At this point, the researcher might have moved on to another child willing to speak and saved Jemia the trouble of having to speak about a subject she was clearly uncomfortable about, but he chose, with the help of the group of children, to reconstruct the confidentiality promise. It is only when the children themselves reconstruct this that Jemia is reassured and goes on to explain why she did not like the teacher. Further interactions lead to Jemia identifying another teacher as her best teacher (Mr I), a suggestion which was overwhelmingly supported by the other group members and as has been explained elsewhere (Kuchah & Pinter, 2012) led to the inclusion of a seventh teacher to the initial list of six teachers recommended by adult stakeholders. From this point on in the conversation, Jemia's focus is on the positive practices of her chosen teacher (Mr I) avoiding most of the conversation related to Mr T.

Jemia's reaction above shows just how difficult it might be to gain the trust of children especially in relation to discussions that involve negative evaluations of other adults, when these are teachers they have been nurtured to respect and obey. While rapport building through socialization activities with children is an important part of gaining their trust, researchers in contexts such as this one, where local and pedagogic cultures are often top-down, need to bear in mind that obtaining critical information about adults from what children say might not always be straightforward. Listening to children's silence and observing their avoidance of certain parts of a conversation might, in the case of Jemia, be a more reliable source of legitimate data, especially as observing a child's rights includes their right *not* to say anything or everything.

Another ethical issue that arises from the example above is the extent to which researchers can be certain that what children in this context, or other contexts where the prevailing culture is 'top-down', choose to say or not in adult–child encounters is a reflection of their own ideas and opinions rather than a reproduction of adult or societal discourses. Much later after this child-group interview, the school head teacher revealed to Kuchah that despite giving consent for Jemia to be part of the research, the mother was worried that her daughter might reveal to Kuchah some unpleasant things about her teacher which she did not want a 'stranger' researcher to hear about. It would seem that she had, in giving her consent, asked her daughter what her thoughts about her teacher were and had received some very negative comments from Jemia, which she did not think appropriate for a child to be saying about her teacher. The fact that Jemia's initial enthusiasm dropped just after she was called out to see her mother and the fact that the head teacher tried to convince the researcher to tell her some of the things he had heard about the teacher suggest that Jemia might have been grappling with torn loyalties to her mother and herself, or simply representing her mother's fears rather than her own.

A further example where children's voice might actually be a representation of family discourses comes from our recent British Council funded English Language Teaching Research Award (ELTRA) research study (Kuchah *et al.*, forthcoming) discussed in detail below. As part of the process of involving students in decision making about at least some aspects of the research process (Pinter, 2019) the researchers asked children to choose the language they were most comfortable with for the group and individual interviews. All children insisted that English was the language of choice but in the actual interactions, French was clearly the predominant language. Their 'choice' of language reflected not only predominant institutional and policy discourses – which proscribed French language in English medium schools (*informal conversation with Head Teachers*) except during the French language lesson – but also socio-political discourses which have produced two macro-ethnic identities in Cameroon (Anchimbe, 2006; Wolf, 2001). In one of the individual child interviews a child, who was clearly struggling to express herself in English and therefore was encouraged by the researcher to speak in French, expressed the view that her learning will be better facilitated if her teacher could explain complex concepts to her in French. Yet when asked whether if she had the option to choose which school she would like to attend, between an Anglophone and a Francophone school, she insisted that she would prefer an Anglophone school. Although the reasons for her 'choice' were related to socio-affective factors like her friendships, it is also likely that she was aligning with a discourse from home that had imposed on her an Anglophone identity which she needed to sustain. In the following excerpt, she clearly sees herself as an Anglophone:

Kuchah: Et toi, tu t'identifies comme une anglophone ou Francophone? (*Do you identify yourself as an Anglophone or as a Francophone ?*)
S: Anglophone
Kuchah: Pourquoi ? (*why ?*)
S: Parce que je suis dans une école anglophone; j'apprends en anglais (*Because I am in an Anglophone school ; I am learning in English*)
Kuchah: Mais tu viens de me dire que tu préfères que ta maitresse t'explique les leçons an français non ? (*But you just told me you prefer when your teacher explains lessons to you in French.*)
S: Oui, parce que je vais comprendre mieux. Je suis anglophone mais je suis aussi bilingue; donc parfois j'ai des difficultés avec l'anglais. (*Yes, because I will understand better. I am Anglophone but I am also bilingual ; sometimes I have difficulties with English*)

This excerpt brings to the fore a wider issue with data generated through interviews, particularly in relation to what Block (2000) refers to as the many 'voices' in which interviewees speak and the complexities involved in analysing and interpreting interviews even with adult participants. In relation to child-focused research, Spyrou (2011: 151) argues that 'researchers need to reflect on the processes which produce children's voices in research, the power imbalances that shape them and the ideological contexts which inform their production.' The two examples above illustrate the complexity of interpreting children's voices and silence as representative of their perspectives, rather than the enactment of adult discourses within their environment. The multi-layered and messy nature of children's voices especially in contexts such as Cameroon where children are nurtured to be submissive and receptive to adult guidance and control (Otto & Keller, 2015) requires child-focused researchers to be constantly reflective and self-critical about the conduct and interpretation of research involving children as it might be possible that children's voices could indeed be a reproduction of adult voices (see also Andrews, this volume).

Informed Consent, Due Diligence and the Insider-Outsider Conundrum in Child-focused Research

In a recent British Council funded ELTRA research project (Kuchah et al., forthcoming) we set out to document and understand the range of learning resources, and strategies that multilingual children from predominantly French-speaking homes draw upon in order to access and navigate the curriculum in English medium primary schools in Cameroon. Research in Cameroon has shown that the rush for EMI is often based on parents' perceptions of the economic advantages of English language locally and internationally (Anchimbe, 2007; Kuchah, 2018) and their dissatisfaction with the quality of English language provision in French-medium state schools (Kouega, 2003) rather than on their ability to support their children through education in a language that is not familiar to them. Our study therefore aimed to focus mainly on children from French-speaking (Francophone) homes and to gain insights into their lived experiences of learning in the medium of English.

In the initial proposal, submitted in April 2017 we committed to following ethical procedures laid down in the British Educational Research Association (BERA, 2011) as well as the ethical review process at a UK University. Following these meant that we needed to be very transparent in the information we gave parents and other gatekeepers to ensure that their consent was sufficiently informed. Transparency in this case meant, letting parents, school authorities and even the children know that our focus was on Francophone children and excluded children from

Anglophone homes. The opening paragraph of our consent request form read as follows:

> Dear Parents/guardian, we are a team of researchers from the University of Bath, UK, the University of Yaounde 1, Cameroon and the Ministry of Basic Education. We are conducting a research study on the learning strategies and resources of Francophone children in Anglophone schools and we would like to invite your child to participate in the study. We would like to seek your consent for him/her to take part in the study which, we hope, will help us improve the quality of English medium education in Cameroon.

However, on arrival in the selected schools, the research team, which, by the way, was made up of three Cameroonians (including a former and a current policymaker in the Cameroonian Ministry of Basic Education and an academic in the University of Yaoundé 1) and a British Academic, learned that it had become literally dangerous to explicitly conduct a study targeting Francophone children especially when the entire research team was made up of Anglophones. This was because a long-standing historical and political crisis encapsulated in the 'Anglophone problem' (Fon, 2019; Fonchingong, 2013; Konings & Nyamnjoh, 1997) had degenerated into an armed conflict generating anti Francophone and Anglophone discourses on both sides and school boycott in the English speaking regions of the country. According to Human Rights Watch (2019) the conflict led to the killing of 420 civilians in the Anglophone regions in 2017 and an estimated 437,500 people were displaced from the Anglophone regions. Because of the conflict, a majority of schools in the two Anglophone regions of the country had shut down in the 2016–2017 academic year; in May 2018, an estimated 42,500 children were still out of school in that part of the country. While the research team had assumed that this had no impact on the lives of the selected schools or schools in Francophone parts of the country in general and in the selected schools in Yaoundé, in particular, we were advised by head teachers and teachers that it would be safer to avoid direct mention of Francophone children in talking about the study to parents. As a result, the final consent request sent to parents was adjusted to include the head teachers as authors and read as follows:

> Dear Parents/guardian, a team of researchers from the University of Bath, UK, the University of Yaounde 1, Cameroon and the Ministry of Basic Education are conducting a research study on children's learning strategies and resources in our school. Your child has been selected as one of those who will participate in the study. The findings of this study will help us improve the quality of education we give your children.

This example illustrates how a classroom-based research project with young learners can be easily assimilated into broader adult-led sociopolitical debates in contexts of conflict. Despite the multilingual and multicultural nature of Cameroon, ethnicity has most often been defined in terms of two colonial relationships with France and England, and as Wolf (2001: 223) explains 'the feeling of unity is so strong that "being Anglophone" [or Francophone] denotes a new ethnicity, transcending older ethnicities'. It has also been suggested that 'although multicultural- ism in terms of ethnic diversity is unexpectedly not yet a problem for national unity [in Cameroon], ethnicity along the Francophone- Anglophone dichotomy is, and has drawn such attention that it threatens national unity more than anything else in the country' (Ayafor, 2005: 124). Sensibility to historical and situational variables, such as the sociopolitical situation in Cameroon is important even to local researchers who might not be aware of how schools deal with apparently broader conflicts. In being transparent to school head teachers and teachers, we benefitted from their local wisdom and modified our approach to the study.

The example cited above raises a number of ethical issues which need to be critically considered by academic researchers involved in school- based research. The advice from these school stakeholders raises the important issue of due diligence within a research site before field work, particularly for researchers coming in from 'outside'. The research team, had assumed that, by virtue of our familiarity with, and in some sense authority within, the educational system, obtaining informed consent from parents was going to be straight forward, but our assumptions of 'insider' understandings were challenged by the real insiders – head teachers and their staff – who interacted with parents on a day-to-day basis and were therefore better placed to identify potential subtleties in the interpretation of our consent document. This example highlights how loose the boundaries between being an insider and an outsider in school- based research can be; how quickly even local researchers can become 'outsiders' in a research setting they are familiar with and might raise even more complex issues, in other settings, to the University-based researcher who has little or no contact with schools and the reality of the school context within which they are conducting research. What is more, our line of action raises a critical ethical question in relation to require- ments for honesty, transparency and avoidance of deception or subter- fuge in obtaining informed consent (BERA, 2011, 2018) which could, arguably be justified by the intentions of the study and the welfare of the researchers as their being Anglophone could have easily led to the research being construed as divisive at a time when the country is desper- ate for national unity.

Rethinking Child Control in Research

The actual data collection for the ELTRA study consisted of class- room observations, group and art-based individual interviews with chil- dren and interactive group tasks. The interactive group tasks were designed to record student verbal interactions while they performed a maths and English task, jointly designed by their teachers, in order to gain insights into the linguistic resources they drew upon to access and develop learning in an EMI context. The main study included 22 students from four classrooms across two schools but the trial of our data collection instruments was conducted with four students each randomly selected from the four classrooms studied. For example, the four children were presented with the interactive tasks in order to verify their suitability to the children's interests. Here, we were also guided by recommendations in the literature for research involving young learners to consider learner agency in the negotiation of important aspects of the research process (Pinter, 2014, 2019) to avoid possible adult (mis)representations. The English language task designed by teachers required students to write a letter to a potential pupil of their school convincing them to come to their school rather than to another school in the capital city, Yaoundé. Feedback on this activity from the four students led to a change in the initial English language task from a letter to a story about 'an old woman who lived in the forest'. More importantly, it also emerged from the discussions with the four students that children preferred to perform the tasks unsupervised, a proposal which the research team had equally considered as the best way of eliciting valid data about the range of linguistic resources Francophone multilingual children actually use to construct knowledge and understanding.

Agreeing to an unsupervised task, while consistent with the paradigmatic position of our study did not seem to reflect the reality of their learning culture. All 12 lessons observed were teacher fronted with lengthy explanations by the teacher and occasional questions requiring choral responses from students. Children's interaction in English was mainly limited to 'safe talk' (Rubagumya, 2003) as very often they were only required to show understanding through completing teacher statements using one or two words (see Kuchah *et al.*, forthcoming). Their preference for an unsupervised task, as we shall show below, might therefore have been a desire for freedom to play while performing a task as their most important collaborative activities in school seemed to be their playtime activities. In the following example from the main study, the researcher and children co-constructed the first sentence of the story – 'Once upon a time there was an old woman who lived in a forest...' – and they were then required to complete the story and give it a title in the absence of the researcher. The title they chose for their story was *The Magic Forest* and the co-construction of the story, which was mostly mediated by the use of French, took much longer time than usual and was dominated by off-task interactions. In the following example, the children's interactions early into their text construction activity shows some evidence of negotiation, establishing rules and procedures to ensure democratic cooperation but also includes instances of personality clashes and ownership issues:

S1: Dit, ce que je vais écrire. (*Say what I should write*)
S2: Non, dit ce que on va écrire. (*No, say what we should write*)
S3: S1 aime trop se faire voir. Tu n'es que notre secrétaire, ne fait pas comme si c'est toi qui écris tout (*S1 likes to show off. You are only our secretary, don't behave as if it's you who is doing all the writing*)

Further, into the task interactions, one of the students (S5) returns from a comfort break and offers to take over writing for the group from another student but, as the interaction below shows, the collaborative experience easily transforms into chaos:

S5: Thank you! Donne moi je continue à écrire. (*Give me let me continue writing*)
S3: Saw avec (*with*) 'A' the past tense of see. Saw.
S4: Echo! Echo!
S1: A lake and she saw...
S5: Vous êtes revenus à quel point? (*To which part [of the story] have you returned ?*)
S4: Nous somme au ciel. (*We are in the sky*)
S2: On te demande une question calme toi tu réponds mal. Après tu me donne aussi moi j'écris non? (*She asked you a question calmly but you respond poorly. Later, you hand [the paper] over to me let me write, right?*)
S4: Moi je n'aime pas écrire. (*I don't like writing*)
S5: Bon celui-ci est clair. On continue alors. (*Okay, this [sentence] is clear. Let's continue then*)
S4: Je n'en peux plus, je suis foiré. (*I can't do any more, I am poor*)
S1: Drink water.
S4: Les poissons sentent dans l'eau... (*The fish smell in the water*)

The two excerpts above, though emanating from children's group interactions in relation to the task, did not quite focus on the task objective. What this seems to illustrate is that the new-found freedom to work together in the absence of an adult observer meant that a huge amount of time was spent on off-task conversations (see also García Mayo in this volume). The total recorded transcript of a story-writing task in this group for example, amounted to 40,477 words with the actual written story consisting of only 308 words. Engaging children in an unsupervised group work task, though they wanted it, was a pedagogically unfamiliar experience for them, which they were unable to manage within the given time-frame of 30 mins and therefore required additional time to achieve 308 words. While the outcome of the interactive process provided useful data for the study, it does raise the question about how researchers can better mediate between children's decisions and child-controlled activities and adult researchers' control in a context where children might be unfamiliar with the types of learner-centred and participatory approaches that research *with* children requires.

Conclusion

In this chapter, we have argued that conducting child-focused research is not straightforward especially when the researcher is external to the sociopolitical and cultural realities of learners. We have shown that ethical and methodological complexities with child-focused, school-based research can be a result of disconnections between participatory approaches for researching with children and the ecological and pedagogic realities of learning cultures in contexts such as Cameroon. In this context, children are not used to being asked about things that matter to them either at home or in school as decisions are often taken by adults, based on their conceptions of childhood, as subordinates (see also Ellis & Ibrahim in this volume). Even where student leadership bodies are in place (e.g. class or school prefects), the members are often appointed by teachers – rather than voted via democratic processes amongst students – with the expectation to help teachers maintain discipline with the classroom and school environment. As a result, child-focused researchers may sometimes need to reconsider how they mediate between child-controlled and adult-controlled components of a research process as well as how they understand and interpret what children say or refuse to say in a research encounter.

In the examples we have discussed here, our roles, as researchers were mainly etic and this meant that we needed to negotiate our relationship with the children and try to understand the context within which they encounter learning. Despite this, there are indications that building trust with children as well as getting to understand their lived experiences and how these might affect their participation in research could take more than the life-cycle of a research project.

Our recommendations for researchers is that additional effort therefore needs to be put into understanding the micro (home), meso (school) and macro (national) forces that influence children's experiences and discourses. In Cameroon, as in other contexts in Sub-Saharan Africa, education still depends largely on adults and the teacher as the main sources of knowledge and this dependence promotes a paradigmatic view of teaching as knowledge transmission with children seen as passive recipients, rather than active co-constructors of knowledge. Tabulawa (1997: 192) describes this as a 'banking education pedagogical paradigm' which may hamper children's ability to question and challenge adults. Therefore, it is important to bear in mind the possibility that what children tell us might actually represent a complex web of ideologies and discourses within the home and school environment rather than their own formed opinions. Engaging children as active participants in research requires a careful and critical deconstruction of their social experiences and realities while at the same time creating an enabling environment for their views, ideas and opinions to emerge and be nurtured. This may take time but is worth it for the insights that children can bring about their learning; 'the omission of these perspectives can easily lead to researchers making interpretations and representations that are very short-sighted and which miss the point' (Thomson, 2008: 1).

References

Alderson, P. (2005) Designing ethical research with children. In A. Farrell (ed.) *Ethical Research with Children* (pp. 27–36). Maidenhead: Open University Press.

Altinyelken, H.K. (2010) Pedagogical renewal in sub-Saharan Africa: The case of Uganda. *Comparative Education* 46 (2), 151–171.

Anchimbe, E. (2006) Functional seclusion and the future of indigenous languages in Africa: The case of Cameroon. In J. Mugane, P. Hutchison and D.A. Worman (eds) *Selected Proceedings of the 35th Annual Conference on African Linguistics* (pp. 94–103). Somerville, MA: Cascadilla Proceedings Project.

Anchimbe, E.A. (2007) Linguabridity: Redefining linguistic identities among children in urban areas. In E.A. Anchimbe (ed.) *Linguistic Identity in Postcolonial Multilingual Spaces* (pp. 66–86). Newcastle: Cambridge Scholars Publishing.

Ayafor, I.M. (2005) Official bilingualism in Cameroon: Instrumental or integrative policy? In J. Cohen, K.T. McAlister, K. Rolstad and J. MacSwan (eds) *Proceedings of the 4th International Symposium on Bilingualism* (pp. 123–142). Somerville, MA: Cascadilla Press.

BERA (British Educational Research Association) (2011) *Ethical Guidelines for Educational Research*. London: BERA.

BERA (British Educational Research Association) (2018) *Ethical Guidelines for Educational Research* (4th edn). London: BERA.

Block, D. (2000) Problematizing interview data: Voices in the mind's machine? *TESOL Quarterly* 34 (4), 757–763.

Bruner, J. (1966) *Toward a Theory of Instruction*. London: Harvard University Press.

Christensen, P. and James, A. (eds) (2008) *Research with Children: Perspectives and Practices*. London: Routledge.

Christensen, P. and Prout, A. (2002) Working with ethical symmetry in social research with children. *Childhood* 9 (4), 477–497.

Dewey, J. (1916) *Democracy and Education*. New York: MacMillan.

Farrell, J.P. (2002) The Aga Khan Foundation experience compared with emerging alternatives to formal schooling. In S.E. Anderson (ed.) *School Improvement through Teacher Development: Case Studies of the Aga Khan Foundation Projects in East Africa* (pp. 247–270). Lisse: Swets and Zeitlinger Publishers.

Fon, N.N.A. (2019) Official bilingualism in Cameroon: An endangered policy? *African Studies Quarterly* 18 (2), 55–66.

Fonchingong, T. (2013) The quest for autonomy: The case of Anglophone Cameroon. *African Journal of Political Science and International Relations* 7 (5), 224–236.

Freire, P. (1972) *Pedagogy of the Oppressed*. London: Writers and Readers Pub Cooperatives.

Goza, N.A., Kallekoye, Z.I. and Mounkaila, H. (2008) Training of supervisors of primary school teacher training institutions and quality of basic education in Niger: An analysis of problems, motivation and working conditions. *Journal of International Cooperation in Education* 11 (3), 55–66.

Human Rights Watch (2019) World Report 2019: Cameroon Events of 2018. See https://www.hrw.org/world-report/2019/country-chapters/cameroon (accessed 24 July 2019).

Kellett, M. (2010) *Rethinking Children and Research: Attitudes in Contemporary Society.* London: Continuum.

Komba, W.L. and Nkumbi, E. (2008) Teacher professional development in Tanzania: Perceptions and practices. *Journal of International Cooperation in Education* 11 (3), 67–83.

Konings, P. and Nyamnjoh, F.B. (1997) The anglophone problem in Cameroon. *Journal of Modern African Studies* 35 (2), 207–229.

Koosimile, A.T. (2005) Teachers' experiences with an adapted IGCSE physics syllabus in Botswana. *International Journal of Education and Development* 25, 209–219.

Kouega, J.P. (2003) English in Francophone elementary grades in Cameroon. *Language and Education* 17 (6), 408–420.

Kuchah, H.K. (2013) Context-Appropriate ELT pedagogy: An investigation in cameroonian primary schools. Unpublished PhD Thesis, Centre for Applied Linguistics, University of Warwick, UK.

Kuchah, K. (2016) English medium instruction in an English-French bilingual setting: Issues of quality and equity in Cameroon. *Comparative Education* 52 (3), 311–327.

Kuchah, K. (2018) Early English medium instruction in Francophone Cameroon: The injustice of equal opportunity. *System* 72, 37–47.

Kuchah, K., Milligan, L.O., Ubanako, V.N. and Njika, J. (forthcoming) English Medium Instruction (EMI) in a multilingual Francophone context: An investigation of the learning resources and strategies of primary school children in Cameroon. London: British Council.

Kuchah, K. and Pinter, A. (2012) 'Was this an interview?' Breaking the power barrier in adult-child interviews in an African context. *Issues in Educational Research* 22 (3), 283–297.

Maybin, J. (2006) *Children's Voices: Talk, Knowledge and Identity.* Basingstoke: Palgrave Macmillan.

Milligan, L. (2016) Insider-outsider-inbetweener? Researcher positioning, participative methods and cross-cultural educational research. *Compare: A Journal of Comparative and International Education* 46 (2), 235–250.

Milligan, L.O. and Tikly, L. (2016) English as a medium of instruction in postcolonial contexts: Issues of quality, equity and social justice. *Comparative Education* 52 (3), 277–280.

Muthwii, M. (2001) *Language Policy and Practices in Kenya and Uganda: Perceptions of Parents, Pupils and Teachers on the Use of Mother Tongue, Kiswahili and English in Primary Schools.* Nairobi: Phoenix Publishers.

Nsamenang, A.B. (2008) Agency in early childhood learning and development in Cameroon. *Contemporary Issues in Early Childhood* 9 (3), 211–223.

O'Kane, C. (2008) The development of participatory techniques: Facilitating children's views about decisions which affect them. In P. Christensen and A. James (eds) *Research with Children: Perspectives and Practices* (pp. 125–155). London: Routledge.

Otto, H. and Keller, H. (2015) A good child is a calm child: How maternal conceptions of proper demeanor impact the development of stranger anxiety in Cameroonian Nso children. *Psychological Topics* 24 (1), 1–25.

Otto, H., Potinius, I. and Keller, H. (2014) Cultural differences in stranger–child interactions: A comparison between German middle-class and Cameroonian Nso stranger–infant dyads. *Journal of Cross-Cultural Psychology* 45 (2), 322–334.

Packard, J. (2008) 'I'm gonna show you what it's really like out here': The power and limitation of participatory visual methods. *Visual Studies* 23 (1), 63–77.

Piaget, J. (1928) *Judgement and Reasoning in the Child.* London: Kegan Paul.

Piaget, J. (1963) *The Language and the Thought of the Child.* London: Routledge and Kegan Paul.

Pinter, A. (2011) *Children Learning Second Languages*. Basingstoke: Palgrave Macmillan.

Pinter, A. (2014) Child participant roles in applied linguistics research. *Applied Linguistics* 35 (2), 168–183.

Pinter, A. (2019) Research issues with young learners. In S. Garton and F. Copland (eds) *The Routledge Handbook of Teaching English to Young Learners* (pp. 411–424). New York: Routledge.

Pinter, A., Kuchah, K. and Smith, R. (2013) Online forum report – researching with children. *ELT Journal* 67 (4), 484–487.

Pontefract, C. and Hardman, F. (2005) The discourse of classroom interaction in Kenyan primary schools. *Comparative Education* 41 (1), 87–106.

Rubagumya, C.M. (2003) English medium primary schools in Tanzania: A new 'linguistic market' in education. In M. Qorro *et al.* (eds) *Language of Instruction in Tanzania and South Africa*. Dar es Salaam: E & D Publishers.

Sawamura, N. and Sifuna, D.N. (2008) Universalizing primary education in Kenya: Is it beneficial and sustainable? *Journal of International Cooperation in Education* 11 (3), 103–118.

Schweisfurth, M. (2011) Learner-centred education in developing country contexts: From solution to problem? *International Journal of Educational Development* 31, 425–432.

Schweisfurth, M. (2013a) Learner-centred education in international perspective. *Journal of International and Comparative Education* 2 (1), 1–8.

Schweisfurth, M. (2013b) *Learner-Centred Education in International Perspective: Whose Pedagogy for Whose Development?* London: Routledge.

Scott, J. (2008) Children as respondents: The challenge for quantitative methods. In P. Christensen and A. James (eds) *Research with Children: Perspectives and Practices* (pp. 87–108). London: Routledge.

Serbessa, D.D. (2006) Tension between traditional and modern teaching-learning approaches in Ethiopian primary schools. *Journal of International Cooperation in Education* 9 (1), 123–140.

Smith, R. (2011) Teaching English in difficult circumstances: A new research agenda. In T. Pattison (ed.) *IATEFL 2010 Harrogate Conference Selections* (pp. 78–80). Canterbury: IATEFL.

Spyrou, S. (2011) The limits of children's voices: From authenticity to critical, reflexive representation. *Childhood* 18 (2), 151–165.

Sriprakash, A. (2010) Child-centred education and the promise of democratic learning: Pedagogic messages in rural Indian primary schools. *International Journal of Educational Development* 30, 297–304.

Tabulawa, R. (1997) Pedagogical classroom practice and the social context: The case of Botswana. *International Journal of Educational Development* 17 (2), 189–204.

Thomson, P. (2008) *Doing Visual Research with Children and Young People*. Oxford: Routledge.

Turek, A. (2013) Engaging young learners in L2 research. *University of Reading Language Studies Working Papers* 5, 32–40.

UNICEF (2007) *A Human Rights-Based Approach to Education for All*. New York: UNICEF.

United Nations (1989) *United Nations Conventions of the Rights of the Child*. New York: United Nations.

Vlastos, G. (1983) The Socratic Elenchus. *Oxford Studies in Ancient Philosophy* 1, 27–58.

Vygotsky, L. (1978) *Mind and Society: The Development of Higher Mental Processes*. Cambridge, MA: Harvard University Press.

Wolf, H.G. (2001) *English in Cameroon*. Berlin: Mouton de Gruyter.

Wu, X. (2003) Intrinsic motivation and young language learners: The impact of the classroom environment. *System* 31 (4), 501–517.

Part 3

Teacher Education and Research with Children

10 Teachers' Image of the Child in an ELT Context

Gail Ellis and Nayr Ibrahim

Introduction

In the course of the 20th century the concepts of the child and childhood have evolved dramatically. Children were traditionally treated as invisible objects, vulnerable and dependent, devoid of a voice and excluded from social structures and processes. Towards the end of the century, a paradigm shift altered the discourse around the child: children became rights-bearing subjects, they are capable human beings with their own opinions and perspectives and can participate fully in society (Clark, 2017; Jones & Walker, 2011). These rights have now been recognized in national policy, for example, the UK Children Act (1989), and international conventions, such as, the United Nations Convention on the Rights of the Child (UNCRC, 1989).

The shift in paradigm from being denied participation to being accepted as competent, contributing social actors has had a significant impact on the educational world. According to Woodhead and Montgomery (2003) childhood is socially situated and constructed. As a result, children are social actors and negotiate multiple positionings in the social and cultural world they inhabit. This implies that children have the right to exercise agency in the social context of the school, where educational decision-making depends on the interdependent and reciprocal (O'Neill, 1994) relationships between the child and the adult. It also implies listening actively to the child as a pre-requisite for acting on what the child says. However, there is little evidence that listening to and acting on what the child says is common practice in classrooms (Lundy, 2007).

The English Language Teaching (ELT) profession is largely based on adult perspectives of language teaching, learning, teacher education and how materials are conceptualized. The unprecedented expansion of teaching English to children (Enever, 2011, 2019) now raises the issues of, not only age-appropriate methodologies and materials (Cameron, 2003), but also the status of the child. Only recently have attempts been made to integrate a rights perspective to TEYL (Teaching English to Young Learners) by researchers, such as, Pinter (2011), Pinter and Zandian (2012), Pinter *et al.* (2013) looking at research *with* children rather than *on* children, and Ellis and Ibrahim (2015) focusing on giving children a voice in the EFL classroom by developing learning to learn strategies with children. In April 2018, the IATEFL Young Learners and Teenagers SIG Pre-Conference Event in Brighton dedicated a full day to exploring children's rights in ELT, *Children's rights, children's future: practical applications in TEYLs,* giving it visibility and prominence at an international ELT conference. Although the theme of children's rights may appear 'beyond the remit of the English language teacher' (Davies, 2018), an event dedicated to this subject recognized its importance both in the ELT classroom as well as in teacher education and as part of the teacher's wider professional role.

Background to the Study

The impetus for this study came from a one-day induction workshop we held in Paris for 30 teachers of pre-primary children some years ago. The teachers in this induction session were working for a private organization in a fee-paying, out-of-school context in different countries across Europe. The training aimed to support the teachers in implementing a new pre-primary programme promoted by the British Council.

The teachers

All the teachers had English as their first language or were highly proficient speakers of English. Their experience of teaching English in pre-primary ranged from one to five or more years. Most had followed a typical English as a foreign language training route and had a CELTA (Certificate in Teaching English to Speakers of Other Languages) qualification for teaching adults. Some had also completed a young learner extension course such as the Cambridge Young Learner (YL) Extension to CELTA or the Trinity TYLEC (Teaching Young Learners Extension Certificate). However, extension courses focus on a wide range of ages (6–17 age span), and often make broad generalizations about 'young learners'. These courses often lack a focus on the 'specific requirements with regard to teaching methodology, course structure, materials and learning environment' (Ellis, 2014: 76) for the life stages which fall within the umbrella term 'young learners', in other words, pre-primary, primary and secondary. Furthermore, they do not usually include a pre-primary focus and do not include the study of children's rights or encourage teachers to reflect on their own theories and constructions of children and childhood.

The new pre-primary programme

Although children's rights and agency have only recently been highlighted, many historically well-established approaches to the education of young children such as Froebel (Tovey, 2016), Steiner (Nicol & Taplin, 2017) and Montessori (Isaacs, 2012) have also focused on young children's capacities as agents in their own learning. This tradition has continued amongst more recent approaches, such as Reggio Emilia (Edwards & Rinaldi, 2012; Rinaldi, 2001; Thornton & Brunton, 2015), and the HighScope approach (Hohmann *et al.*, 2008; Wiltshire, 2012), which have played, and are playing, an important role in early childhood education settings internationally. The latter two approaches appeared in the UK in the 1980s and have influenced the Early Years Foundation Stage framework (EYFS, Department of Education, 2017), which was first introduced in England in 2008, and outlines the standards for learning, development and care for children from birth to five.

The new pre-primary programme is underpinned by the philosophy of the EYFS and the HighScope approach (Hohmann *et al.*, 2008) to early childhood education. The EYFS expresses concern for the child as a social agent and active learner, as exemplified by the three characteristics of effective teaching and learning (Department of Education, 2017: 10) which are:

- playing and exploring
- active learning
- creating and thinking critically

and its four overarching principles which should shape practice in early years settings (2017: 6):

- a unique child: observing how a child is learning,
- positive relationships: what adults could do,
- enabling environments: what adults could provide,
- children develop and learn in different ways and at different rates: respecting individual differences.

The HighScope approach provides a flexible structure and routine via the 'plan-do-review' cycle of activities which emphasizes shared control and active learning and focuses children's attention on what they are doing and how they are doing it. It shows faith that pre-primary children can reflect on and express their views about their own learning, given appropriate support and scaffolding. It also recognizes children as active learners with agency who are capable of reflection and decision-making from an early age (Nisbet & Shucksmith, 1986; Whitebread, 2012). For many teachers, this pedagogical approach requires a rethinking of the power dynamics in the adult–child relationship moving to one of more shared control.

The induction session

We began the induction by asking teachers to explore and to discuss with others in the group their own views of the child and of childhood.

We wanted to encourage the teachers to re-examine their beliefs and attitudes because these impact on the type of relationships they establish with children in the classroom. This discussion activity therefore aimed to help teachers

- establish their own theories and constructions of the child and of childhood,
- recognize children's reflective capacities given appropriate support and scaffolding,
- recognize children as rights holders.

When asked about own theories and constructions of childhood, the teachers' responses ranged from

- adjectives describing children's characteristics – these were often emotive, for example, 'innocent, pure, cute, fragile, sweet, kind, funny', and designated the child as passive and dependent,
- phrases that reflected their view of the child as an object to which they do things,
- phrases which showed some awareness of the child as an individual with rights and their own perspectives.

Overall, responses from the induction session showed that the teachers held views of the child as mostly passive and had limited awareness of children's rights. These views prompted us to question whether they were typical of EFL teachers of children working in other contexts. We therefore conducted an online survey in January 2017 to elicit a wider range of views of the child and of childhood, which is discussed in this chapter.

Theoretical Background to the Online Survey Study

In this section, we give an overview of the three main areas which provide the theoretical background to the study:

- a children's rights perspective;
- operationalizing Article 12 of the UNCRC according to Lundy's (2007) model of child participation;
- the new sociological approach to conceptualizing childhood

These areas provide theoretical perspectives that conceptualize the child as an individual and as a social actor in his/her own right.

A children's rights perspective

Our study is embedded in a children's rights perspective which was enshrined in the UNCRC in 1989 (see the introductory chapter to this volume). However, most classrooms are rigid and highly structured spaces and many teachers may feel it is not possible to move to a relationship of more shared control. We nevertheless believe the classroom should provide a conducive space for children to exercise their participation rights, if the teacher is equipped with the values, attitudes, skills, knowledge and critical understanding of children's rights to enable this.

The UNCRC is the first international human rights agreement to bring together a universal set of standards concerning children. It is also the first to present children's rights as a legally binding imperative. The convention defines childhood as a separate space from adulthood and recognizes that children are the holders of their own rights. They are not passive recipients of adult intervention but empowered actors in their own development. In particular, Article 12 (UNCRC) states that

(1) 'Parties shall assure to the child who is capable of forming his or her own views the right to express those views freely in all matters affecting the child, the views of the child being given due weight in accordance with the age and maturity of the child'.

(2) 'For this purpose, the child shall in particular be provided the opportunity to be heard in any judicial and administrative proceedings affecting the child, either directly, or through a representative or an appropriate body, in a manner consistent with the procedural rules of national law'.

The document recognizes the child as a full human being with integrity and personality and the ability to participate freely in society. According to UNICEF, childhood is not just the space between birth and adulthood; it refers to the state and condition of a child's life and to the quality of those years. It is a separate and safe space where children are 'resourceful citizens, capable of helping to build a better future for all' (UNICEF, 2002: 16). Furthermore, in order for children's voices to be heard, we need to employ 'a pedagogy of listening', where we 'listen' to the child, accompany the child in discovering their world and not just speak for the child. According to Rinaldi (2001: 4) 'listening is an active verb, which involves giving an interpretation, giving meaning to the message and value to those who are being listened to'. Within an educational context 'listening is central to responsive and reciprocal relationships when the object is teaching and learning' (Clark & Moss, 2011: Preface by Carr).

The UNCRC has, however, been criticized especially around the threefold categorization of protection, provision and participation rights, known as the '3Ps' (Dillen, 2006: 238; Qvortrup et al., 1994: 36). Furthermore, the Convention contains a number of inconsistencies and is open to various interpretations. Alderson (2000: 439) summarizes the common criticisms which include a fear that the convention gives children too much liberty and not enough protection, that this liberty could undermine respect for adults, including parents and teachers, and that children could become greedy, selfish and irresponsible. The convention is also criticized for being based on an idealistic western vision of childhood, and as being unrealistic as it fails to take into account differences which exist between countries and cultures (Garnier, 2012). Alderson (2000: 440) responds to these criticisms by affirming that, for example, Article 12 is about 'taking part and not taking charge'. For example, in a democratic classroom children and the teacher will together negotiate responsibilities, learning activities, learning partners or groups, topics and resources and so on. This decision-making process is about participating collaboratively, not about taking over control. The convention is also about necessities not luxuries, and it does not endorse selfish individualism, as 'rights are collective not individual' (Alderson, 2000: 442). She concludes that the convention is an effective tool for monitoring the rights of children and can be used as a tool for change.

While we can see that implementing children's rights is a teacher's ethical duty as it is not just 'a model of good pedagogical practice (or policymaking) but a legally binding obligation' (Lundy, 2007: 930), schools are traditionally highly structured, hierarchical organizations. Teachers are confined by organizational constraints such as restrictive curricula, prescribed methods and pre-defined outcomes, rigid assessment systems and rules and regulations. These constraints can make it seem challenging for the teacher to 'give over' some agency and to 'give' their pupils a voice. Consequently, they may underplay, ignore or even deny children their rights. Teachers may also fear that their authority may be undermined, or they may believe that children are too young and not capable of expressing their opinions or views, or of participating in making decisions and choices about their learning. Furthermore, as children's rights rarely form part of ELT training programmes, many teachers lack an awareness of these and do not have the skills or strategies to enable children to exercise their rights. We are, therefore, faced with an ethical dilemma as these organizational constraints, fears, beliefs and lack of training conflict with the ethos of creating a democratic classroom.

The Lundy model of child participation

According to Alderson (2000: 440) Article 12 'grants to children a share in making decisions which affect them'. This sharing has four levels, but the UNCRC only deals with the first three: 'to express a view, to be informed about the details and opinions within a decision and to have their view taken into account, according to the child's age and ability, by adults who are making the decision' (Alderson, 2000). The fourth level is 'the right to be the main decider in matters which affect the child'. This right is 'only for children who are able to make an informed decision in their own best interests' (Alderson, 2000). Lundy (2007) acknowledges this complexity and considers that Article 12 falls short of its initial purpose, as children's views are not given due weight in education and the scope of the Article is not fully understood. Obstacles to the successful implementation of the Article include a lack of informed understanding thereof, the extent to which children and adults should be involved, and the concept of 'pupil voice' (Lundy, 2007: 930) which camouflages and detracts from the need to act on children's opinions. She focuses on a reinterpretation of Article 12 and expands the second part 'the child's right to have the view given due weight' (Lundy, 2007: 933), so that children's views are not just listened to but also acted upon and that they are informed of any action taken.

Lundy proposes a model (Figure 10.1) for conceptualizing Article 12, which attempts to capture more fully the true extent of these legal obligations to children including educational decision-making. Her model resulted from a research study across Northern Ireland (Kilkelly *et al.*, 2005), which involved 1064 school children from 27 schools including mainstream schools, special schools and Irish medium schools. The main aim of this research was to identify areas where children's rights were ignored or underplayed in all areas of their lives, including education. Lundy employed a range of data collection methods and children contributed to the research through drawing pictures, writing stories, designing posters or undertaking tasks that were appropriate to their level of understanding. Her research showed that when children were consulted their views were often not acted upon which revealed that the message of Article 12 often remained at a tokenistic level in school contexts. For example, teachers often asked their classes which activities they preferred but did not use this feedback to inform their practice and plan next steps.

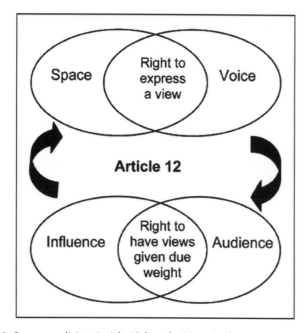

Figure 10.1 Conceptualizing Article 12 (Lundy, 2007: 932)

Lundy's model consists of four distinct interrelated elements, which show that Article 12 has an explicit chronology:

- Space: Children must be given the opportunity to express a view;
- Voice: Children must be facilitated to express their views;
- Audience: The view must be listened to;
- Influence: The view must be acted upon, as appropriate.

Lundy's model goes beyond the popular notion of 'pupil voice' (Lundy, 2007) which often results in only tokenistic opportunities for children to participate in decision-making. For example, if children are consulted, the issues they get to discuss are often predetermined by teachers and are often about more superficial aspects of school life such as the colour of uniforms or canteen menus rather than teaching techniques and subject matter. We wanted to find out to what extent teachers implemented any of the four elements of the model.

New sociology of childhood

A new sociological approach to conceptualizing childhood aimed to find ways of accessing the child's world, where children are seen as a social group and as contributing social actors (Mayall, 2002: 247). This approach focuses on the child as an individual in their own right, the child as *being* in the present, in other words, the here and now of childhood, and their everyday lives as children rather than the child as *becoming;* that is, citizens and adults of the future (James *et al.*, 1998; Qvortrup, 1985). This focus on the future overlooks the child as *being* in the present and ignores their opinions and perspectives as relevant to their own lives.

Christensen and Prout (2002: 480) refer to four ways of viewing childhood and children in research: the child as object, the child as subject, the child as social actor and the child as participant and co-researcher.

(1) *Child as object*, that is, a person acted upon by others. This view of the child neglects the understanding of children as social persons in their own right and is based on the assumption of children's dependency. For example, in schools children are usually controlled by the systems in place. They are often told what to do and when, for example, when they can sit down or stand up, when it is their turn to answer a question, when they can take a break, what colour pen to use and many other things.

(2) *Child as subject* recognizes the child as a person with subjectivity but it is the adult who decides whether the child can or cannot participate in a particular event. This is usually dependent on age-based criteria, for example, a child's stage of development and maturity. For example, the following comment from a research project conducted in 2000 (Ellis, 2000: 78) in France shows that the teacher considers the

children are too young to be given explanations about what they are going to learn: 'To tell a class of 8 year olds what the aims of a lesson are, is, in my opinion, pointless.'

(3) *Child as social actor* recognizes children as having their own experiences and understandings. Children are seen to act, take part in, change and become changed by the social and cultural world they live in. For example, research carried out in Indian primary English classrooms by Pinter *et al.* (2016: 21) revealed that children were capable of sharing their views about what type of English language learning they wanted and enjoyed. The researchers noticed that when children were invited to discover knowledge for themselves, they started to participate fully, made decisions for themselves and worked in collaboration with each other (see also Mathew & Pinter in this volume). Ellis and Ibrahim (2015: 96) when eliciting evidence from primary-aged children learning English in a private out-of-school context about the impact of learning to learn on the teaching and learning process, also found that children were capable of expressing their opinions on how they learn: 'I like talking about my activity with my partner. We can share each other's ideas and help each other.'

(4) *Child as participant and co-researcher* views children as active participants which emphasises children's participation rights and promotes the idea that children be involved, informed, consulted and heard on issues relating to their lives. For example, Modugala (2018) collected data via a questionnaire and participatory techniques to better understand her pupils' preferences about the ways they wanted to learn and about the materials they would like to use.

Data Collection and Analysis

For the purpose of the present study we collected data from an online survey generated by Survey Monkey in January 2017. We sent it to colleagues, associates and acquaintances in teacher training colleges, universities, teacher associations and educational institutions around the world, to be shared with teachers. The survey was also posted on some social media sites in order to allow for greater access and visibility. The survey consisted of eight questions. Questions 1–4 were closed questions about the teachers and their teaching context.

Questions 5–8 elicited teacher's views of children and of childhood and were open questions to avoid influencing responses. Each question elicited comments that highlighted a different focus of the view of childhood. This provided both quantitative and qualitative data. Teachers' comments from questions 5–8 were analysed and sorted based on the categories per question in Table 10.1. Analysis of responses to questions 5 and 6 centre on the child and the place of childhood in society and

Table 10.1 Categories of analysis per question

Q5: What is your perspective of childhood?	the being and becoming of childhood	Child focus
Q6: What is your view/image of the child?	child as object, subject, social actor, participant/co-researcher	Child focus
Q7: How would you describe your relationship with children?	teacher as partner vs teacher as authority	Adult focus
Q8: How do your responses to questions 5, 6 and 7 influence your teaching practice?	teacher as authority, facilitator, partner	Adult focus

questions 7 and 8 shift the focus to the adult or the teacher and how they perceive their relationship with the child.

Data were exported from the survey to Excel to enable us to analyse the language respondents used to express their views. In addition, we entered recurring words from questions 5 and 7 into a word cloud creator, WordItOut, in order to visualize the highest number of recurring words and to indicate how the majority of respondents viewed the child in the EFL classroom.

Findings

Questions 1–4. The respondents and their teaching context

We received 226 responses from teachers working in 38 countries, with the highest number of responses coming from Algeria, Croatia, France, Italy, Poland, Spain and Ukraine. Fifty percent of respondents worked in extra-curricular, out-of-school settings, that is, private, fee-paying language institutes or language schools. Thirty-six percent of teachers worked in mainstream state schools, and some worked in both private and state settings (Figure 10.2).

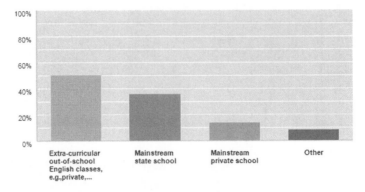

Figure 10.2 Question 2. Which educational setting do you work in?

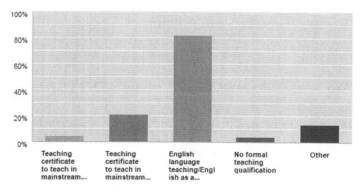

Figure 10.3 Question 4. What teaching qualifications do you have?

Ninety-five percent of all teachers taught primary aged children while 22% taught pre-primary children and some taught both age groups. Eighty-two percent of the respondents had an ELT/English as a foreign language qualification and 20% of teachers had a teaching certificate to teach in mainstream education at primary level, and some had both of these. A few respondents had no teaching qualifications (Figure 10.3).

Question 5. What is your perspective of childhood?

In response to question 5, we categorized the responses into two themes, child as *being* or *becoming* (James *et al.*, 1998; Qvortrup, 1985), which provided evidence that the majority of respondents saw the child as an adult in the making or a future citizen. A few comments reflected both *being* and *becoming* (Figure 10.4), which indicates that these are not always polarized or mutually exclusive concepts, and that there are multiple perspectives of how some teachers might view the child.

We identified some key words relating to the adult playing a role in 'shaping, forming, moulding' the child into a future citizen; that is, the

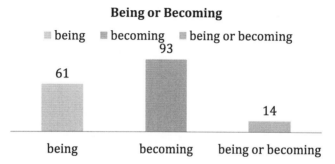

Figure 10.4 Responses* categorized into *being* or *becoming*
*Numbers refer to number of respondents.

Figure 10.5 Word cloud for *becoming*

child as *becoming*. We then counted the number of times these words recurred and entered them into the word cloud creator. This generated a word cloud showing the words most frequently used by respondents (Figure 10.5). We can see that the most frequently used words, for example, 'preparation, base, formation' indicate respondents' views that childhood is learning to become a functioning adult. Some words are also linked to the perceived vulnerability of childhood 'delicate, fragility, protect'

In comparison, the respondents emphasising *being* used terms that reflected children as active participants capable of making choices about their own lives, as well as in the classroom about their own learning. Figure 10.6 highlights words that reflect the 'here and now of childhood' (Mayall, 2002), the child as a meaning-maker with agency and competence.

When comparing the *becoming* and the *being* related terms from the word clouds we identified often contradictory, complex beliefs as reflected by the language employed by the teachers in the study (see Table 10.2).

In addition to the responses above, one respondent used a metaphor by referring to the child as 'a little person under construction... and we [teachers] are the language engineers'. This response clearly illustrates that the child is viewed as an adult in the making. While it is acknowledged that children are growing and developing and that part of childhood is learning to become a functioning adult , responses overall indicate that teachers focus more on the child as *becoming* and less on the child as *being* (see Figure 10.4). From a language learning perspective, responses to question 5 accord the active or principal role to the teacher. Based on these findings, we conclude that the child's role in the inherently dynamic language learning process is most probably underplayed and overlooked.

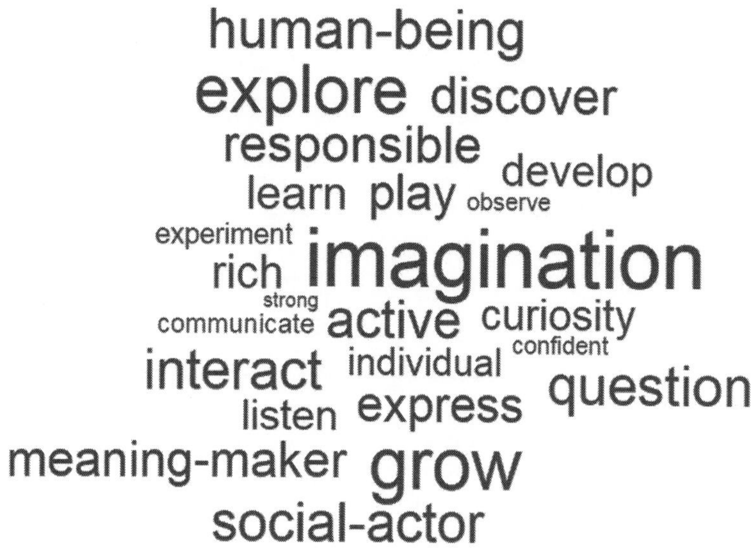

Figure 10.6 Word cloud for *being*

Table 10.2 Contrasting themes in the *becoming* and *being* categories

Becoming	Being
Vulnerable, dependent child	**Strong, independent child**
innocent, fragility, ephemeral, guileless, delicate, naive, easily-hurt, protect, help, supervision, innocent	confident, social actor, responsible communicate
Passive child	**Active child**
absorb, unconscious, acceptance, depend	explore, curiosity, discover, experiment, play, meaning-maker, interact, express, imagination, observe, question
Child as future individual, adult in the making, an educational outcome	**Child as an individual now**
	human being, rich, listen, individual
shaped, create, later life, adult, preparation, mould, influence, form, spring, dawn, step, base, early, foundation	

Question 6. What is your view/image of the child?

We sorted responses from question 6, into the four categories of the view of the child as discussed by Christensen and Prout (2002): child as object, child as subject, child as social actor, and child as participant and co-researcher. We were unable to categorize quite a large number of the responses (59) as they were purely descriptive statements about the child, such as they are 'curious, intuitive, happy, emotional, energetic, inspiring, innocent, lively, fragile, spontaneous, carefree, naïve, sweet, cute,

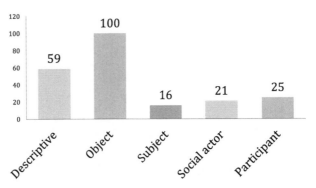

Figure 10.7 Question 6. What is your view/image of the child*?
*Numbers refer to number of respondents.

vulnerable.' These adjectives attest to society's vision of children as innocent and needing protection and match our first experience of eliciting
teachers' views of the child in the induction session in Paris. As the
descriptive statement category was our second largest category (59 out of
221), we decided to include this as an additional category in Figure 10.7.

Child as object

Responses indicated that there was a tendency for teachers to view
the child as an object (100 out of 221 responses). Several respondents
used metaphors which referred to a range of different objects, often
empty or blank, such as an empty vessel. The objects named are loaded
with significance and have cultural references (Jin & Cortazzi, 2008).
Some are inanimate which reflect teacher's view of the child as inert and
passive in need of the adult to teach them, 'A white page we fill in', 'a
blank page', 'a blank sheet of paper', 'a blank slate', 'a clean slate', 'an
empty/blank canvas', 'a tiny growing vessel ready to be filled'. Some
objects also denote size thereby relegating children to a position of infe-
riority in relation to the dominant adult, 'a small plant', 'a child is like a
bud', 'just a bulb…a very nice bulb', 'a little sun'. Furthermore, metaphors of light, although positive, still reflect the need for adult intervention, 'They are like stars, and we need to help them shine brighter, or a
light needing to turn on'.

The metaphor of 'a sponge', with one respondent referring to a child
as 'an impulsive sponge' denotes an unthinking child, a child who simply
reacts to a context created by the adult without reflecting on their own
role and rights in the adult world. We speculate that the numerous uses of
the noun 'sponge' when referring to how children learn, may originate
from a widespread common misconception of Montessori's classic work,
The Absorbent Mind. The metaphor of 'a sponge' as used by our respondents, views children as passive in their learning. However, Montessori

(2007: 5) writes, 'the child has a type of mind that absorbs knowledge and instructs himself' which indicates the active and thoughtful processes involved in learning.

This passive view of children by respondents is also reflected by the use of the passive voice (in italics in Figure 10.8) when referring to children. This relegates them to passive objects, even though they were saying positive things about them.

Child as subject

In the child as subject category, the 16 responses show that children were recognized as children and individuals in their own right (Figure 10.9).

Child as social actor

We classified 21 responses into 'child as social actor'. These responses, for example, 'a natural scientist', 'understands the world around him', 'knows exactly what they want', reflect children who understand and construct the social, cultural and educational situations they experience and actively influence them.

> 'Young and (mostly) innocent young mind *to be shaped and developed*, pointed in right direction.'
>
> 'They have *to be 'handled'* with high care and respect.'
>
> 'An individual with their own set of wants, needs and opinions, but one which *needs to be made aware of* functioning within a group.'
>
> 'Every child *should be dealt with* individually as we deal with our own children.'

Figure 10.8 Child as object – use of the passive voice

> I see them as actual children and not miniature adults.
>
> Each child possesses a different personality and a different level of maturity.
>
> The child is a central figure in the classroom, so my lessons are very child-centred.
>
> A human being who should be treated with respect.
>
> A child is a person with his own character and expectations of life.

Figure 10.9 Child as subject: Example of responses identifying children as children and individuals

responsible for own actions

make decisions

have their own ideas

we learn from them

a complete human being

have their own unique way

can do things on their own

make choices

a contributor of own ideas

Figure 10.10 Child as an active participant

Child as participant and co-researcher

Twenty-five respondents viewed the child as an active participant (Figure 10.10).

These responses depict children as active, responsible, independent beings who are involved in their own construction of meaning and are acting on their choices.

Question 7. How would you describe your relationship with children?

The responses to question 7, show the power dynamics in the adult–child relationship which is transposed into the teacher-pupil relationship in the classroom. The data fell into three categories 'teacher-as-partner', 'teacher as authority' and some which fell into both categories. 'Teacher-as-partner' has an equal relationship with the child and 'teacher-as-authority' thereby placing the child in a more subordinate and passive role. It was interesting to see that the balance tilts towards the teacher as partner (Figure 10.11).

However, again, we were unable to categorize 95 responses because the question was replied to very literally and included comments like, 'excellent, fine, very good, friendly'. This highlighted the limitation of surveys as a data collection method both in terms of formulating questions and in interpreting questions and responses. We would need to review the formulation of this question for further research or use a different method to gain further data.

We created word clouds (Figure 10.12) to highlight the terms that were used by respondents in each category. Words on the left reflect control and discipline, while the words on the right reflect respect, collaboration and togetherness.

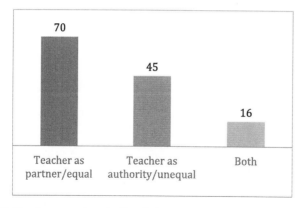

Figure 10.11 Teacher as partner/authority*
*Numbers refer to number of respondents.

Figure 10.12 Word clouds teacher as authority and teacher as partner, respectively

Question 8. How do your responses to questions 5, 6 and 7 influence your teaching practice?

The final question asked teachers to reflect on the impact their view of the child has on their teaching practices. Responses focused on their relationship with the child, which influences their teaching practices depending on the role they adopt in the classroom. Responses were classified according to the following roles: Teacher as authority or facilitator /partner, which represent a continuum from teacher control to shared control between teacher and child (Figure 10.13).

In the role of 'teacher as facilitator', which is the largest category, teachers are aware of the need to give children space to participate and voice their opinions. However, only 39 respondents categorized as 'teacher as partner' described a more democratic approach to working with children in an ELT context. For example, a British teacher working in an out-of-school context in Thailand who had completed a training course in Childhood Studies explains her development along the continuum from

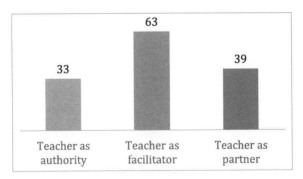

Figure 10.13 Teacher as authority/facilitator/partner*
*Numbers refer to number of respondents.

'teacher as authority' to 'teacher as partner', 'I've greatly changed my teaching practice from one where the teacher does most of the talking based on a pre-planned agenda to a flexible one that demands and allows more participation from the children and their imaginations.'

Returning to Lundy's model of child participation, the majority of teachers' comments reflect that they give children space and voice, while some go as far as mentioning that children's views should be listened to, they see them as contributors and responsible for their own learning. Yet we found no evidence of the fourth element; that is, influence. Teachers' comments did not reveal that they were acting upon children's views and perspectives as appropriate. This may be because of the limitations of this research tool and what it managed to elicit, or because teachers are simply not used to acting in this way.

Discussion and Recommendations

The findings from this study highlight the complexity of teachers' perceptions of children and childhood. Although overall teachers' responses reflect a more traditional view of childhood, some teachers nonetheless show that they have, or are in the process of developing, a view of the child as a competent and active member of the classroom. In some cases, teachers show awareness of both traditional and more active roles of children in their responses.

When we compared teachers' qualifications with the categories in question 8, we expected the teachers with a teaching certificate to teach in mainstream education would express their relationship with the child as more participative and facilitative, as a result of their comprehensive training which includes age-appropriate classroom and behaviour management and input on how to use routines to establish a structured and positive classroom climate of mutual confidence and respect. In some cases, training may also include Childhood Studies or Early Years training and an understanding of children's rights. However, in contrast to our expectations, the data showed that the teachers with less formal qualifications (English language teaching/English as a foreign language qualification) expressed their relationship with the child more as partner and facilitator, while the mainstream teachers fell almost equally into both the authority and facilitator categories and very few in the partner category.

We postulate that the reason why teachers with ELT/English as a foreign language qualification seem to describe their role as a facilitator and partner is a result of their training in communicative methodology as covered extensively on courses like the CELTA. A communicative approach encourages more learner participation, involvement and collaboration, increases 'student talking time', puts a greater focus on fluency and less on accuracy. It therefore seems to take a less authoritative stance to teaching and learning. Teachers with this qualification for teaching adults may have transferred this approach to their classrooms when teaching children.

Lundy's research has shown that consulting with children improves teaching and learning; it builds children's self-esteem, develops their autonomy and their self-expression and fosters a more democratic school ethos. In order for this to happen, we recommend a whole-school approach to respecting children's rights and to implementing a participative philosophy where there is shared control in the adult–child relationship. Given the traditional structures of most schools, ethical guidelines for the implementation of an effective whole-school approach are recommended, so that all staff understand their obligations vis à vis the UNCRC. For example, where teachers are concerned, to help them understand the implications of the UNCRC and its confirmation of the equal status of children as the subjects of rights, we recommend that initial training and continuous professional development should increase knowledge and understanding of the UNCRC. Furthermore, training should also focus on practical concerns by providing teachers with guidelines on how to implement Article 12 in the ELT classroom in collaboration with the children.

Conclusion

In conclusion, training should help teachers construct their own theories of children and childhood in order to appreciate a possible status for children as genuine partners in education and in the ELT classroom. For this to happen, teachers need to move along the continuum from a 'technician applying prescribed methods to produce pre-defined outcomes, to a reflective democratic and 'rich' professional' (Moss, 2010) who uses a pedagogy of relationship and of listening, and who creates possibilities for all children. Even small steps such as building in opportunities for choice can make a difference and can begin the teacher's task to fulfil their ethical duty and contribute to the creation of a democratic ELT classroom and a children's rights culture.

References

Alderson, P. (2000) UN convention on the rights of the child: Some common criticisms and suggested responses. *Child Abuse Review* 9, 439–443.

Cameron, L. (2003) Challenges for ELT from the expansion in teaching children. *ELT Journal* 57 (2), 105–112.

Christensen, P. and James, A. (eds) (2000) *Research with Children*. London: Falmer.

Christensen, P. and Prout, A. (2002) Working with ethical symmetry in social research with children. *Childhood* 9 (4), 477–497.

Clark, A. (2017) *Listening to Young Children* (3rd edn). London: Jessica Kingsley Publishers.

Clark, A. and Moss, P. (2011) *Listening to Young Children: The Mosaic Approach*. London: NCB.

Davies, A. (2018) IATEFL 2018 YLTSIG PCE Review: Children's Rights, Children's Future: Practical Applications in TEYLs. *YLTSIG Blog 2 May*. See https://yltsig. iatefl.org/2018/05/02/iatefl-2018-yltsig-pce-review-childrens-rights-childrens-fut ure-practical-applications-in-teyls

Department for Education (2017) *Statutory Framework for the Early Years Foundation Stage: Setting the Standards for Learning, Development and Care for Children from Birth to Five*. London: Crown Copyright. See https://assets.publishing.service.gov.uk/ government/uploads/system/uploads/attachment_data/file/596629/EYFS_STATUTO RY_FRAMEWORK_2017.pdf

Dillen, A. (2006) Children between liberation and care: Ethical perspectives on the rights of children and parent-child relationships. *International Journal of Children's Spirituality* 11 (2), 237–250.

Edwards, C. and Rinaldi, C. (eds) (2012) *The Diary of Laura: Perspectives on a Reggio Emilia Diary*. St. Paul, MN: Redleaf.

Ellis, G. (2000) Is it worth it? Convincing teachers of the value of developing metacognitive awareness in children. In B. Sinclair, I. McGrath and T. Lamb (eds) *Learner Autonomy, Teacher Autonomy: Future Directions*. Harlow: Longman in association with the British Council.

Ellis, G. (2014) Young learners': Clarifying our terms. *ELT Journal* 68 (1), 75–78.

Ellis, G. and Ibrahim, N. (2015) *Teaching Children How to Learn*. Peaslake: Delta Publishing.

Enever, J. (2011) (ed.) *ELLiE: Early Language Learning in Europe*. London: The British Council.

Enever, J. (2019) *Policy and Politic of Global Primary English*. Oxford: Oxford University Press.

Garnier, A. (2012) Criticisms of Children's Rights. See https://www.humanium.org/en/ criticisms-of-childrens-rights/

Hohmann, M., Epstein, A.S. and Weikart, D. (2008) *Educating Young Children: Active Learning Practices for Preschool and Child Care Programs* (3rd edn). High/Scope Educational Research Foundation.

Isaacs, B. (2012) *Understanding the Montessori Approach*. Oxon: Routledge.

James, A., Jenks, C. and Prout, A. (1998) *Theorising Childhood*. Cambridge: Polity Press.

Jin, L. and Cortazzi, M. (2008) Images of teachers, learning and questioning in Chinese cultures of learning. In E. Berendt (ed.) *Metaphors of Learning, Cross-Cultural Perspectives* (pp. 177–202). Amsterdam: John Benjamins Publishing Company.

Jones, P. and Walker, G. (2011) *Children's Rights in Practice*. London: Sage Publications.

Kilkelly, U., Kilpatrick, R., Lundy, L., Moore, L., Scraton, P., Davey, C., Dwyer, C. and McAlister, S. (2005) *Children's Rights in Northern Ireland*. Belfast: Northern Ireland Commissioner for Children and Young People.

Lundy, L. (2007) 'Voice' is not enough: Conceptualising Article 12 of the United Nations Convention on the Rights of the Child. *British Educational Research Journal* 33 (6), 927–942.

Mayall, B. (2002) *Towards A Sociology for Childhood: Thinking from Children's Lives*. London: Open University Press.

Modugala, M. (2018) Listening to children's perceptions and experiences of English language teaching material. In B. Tomlinon and A. Keedwel (eds) *Explorations: Teaching and Learning English in India. Issue 11 Understanding Learners – Researching Learners' Perceptions*. British Council India.

Montessori, M. (2007) *The Absorbent Mind*. Radford: Wilder Publications LLC.

Moss, P. (2010) What is Your Image of the Child? *UNESCO Policy Brief on Early Childhood*. N° 47.

Nicol, J. and Taplin, T.J. (2017) *Understanding the Steiner Waldorf Approach: Early Years Education in Practice* (2nd edn). London: Routledge.

Nisbet, J. and Shucksmith, J. (1986) *Learning Strategies*. London: Routledge.

O'Neill, J. (1994) *The Missing Child in Liberal Theory*. Toronto/London: University of Toronto Press.

Pinter, A. (2011) *Children Learning Second Languages: Research and Practice in Applied Linguistics*. Basingstoke: Palgrave Macmillan.

Pinter, A., Kuchah, K. and Smith, R. (2013) Researching with children. *ELT Journal* 67 (4), 484–487.

Pinter, A., Mathew, R. and Smith, R. (2016) Children and teachers as co-researchers in Indian primary English classrooms. *ELT Research Papers 16.03*. London: British Council.

Pinter, A. and Zandian, S. (2012) 'I thought it would be tiny little one phrase that we said, in a huge big pile of papers': (cf. Kuchah and Pinter, and Pinter and Zandian) Children's reactions on their involvement in participatory research. *Qualitative Research* 15 (2), 235–250.

Qvortrup, J. (1985) Placing children in the division of labour. In P. Close and P. Collins (eds) *Family and Economy in Modern Society*. London: Macmillan.

Qvortrup, J. (1996) Monitoring childhood: Its social, economic and political features. In E. Verhellen (ed.) *Monitoring Children's Rights*. The Hague: Martin Nijhoff Publishers.

Qvortrup, J., Bardy, M., Sgritta, G. and Wintersberger, H. (eds) (1994) *Childhood Matters: Social Theory, Practice and Politics*. Aldershot: Avebury.

Rinaldi, C. (2001) A pedagogy of listening: A perspective of listening from Reggio Emilia. *Children in Europe* 2–5.

Thornton, L. and Brunton, P. (2015) *Understanding the Reggio Approach* (3rd edn). Oxon: Routledge.

Tovey, H. (2016) *Bringing the Froebel Approach to Your Early Years Practice* (2nd edn). London: Routledge.

UK Children Act (1989) Available at http://www.legislation.gov.uk/ukpga/1989/41/contents

UNICEF (1989) *The United Nations Convention on the Rights of the Child*. See https://www.unicef.org.uk/wp-content/uploads/2010/05/UNCRC_united_nations_convention_on_the_rights_of_the_child.pdf

UNICEF (2002) *A world fit for children*. United Nations.

Whitebread, D. (2012) *Developmental Psychology and Early Childhood Education*. London: Sage Publications.

Wiltshire, M. (2012) *Understanding the HighScope Approach*. Oxon: Routledge.

Woodhead, M. and Montgomery, H. (2003) *Understanding Childhood: An Interdisciplinary Approach*. Chichester: The Open University.

11 Children and Teachers as Co-researchers in Indian Classrooms: Some Ethical Issues

Rama Mathew and Annamaria Pinter

Introduction

This paper discusses some ethical issues in a British Council (BC) funded study (English Language Teaching Research Partnerships Award 2015) which involved children and teachers working collaboratively on classroom research projects in India. This chapter will first of all provide an overview of the project entitled 'Children and teachers as co-researchers in Indian primary English classrooms' explaining its structure, its main aims, methods and the outcomes. Then we focus on the ethical challenges that we faced especially in relation to the complexities of undertaking action research projects with children as active participants/co-researchers in the Indian context. While the main focus of this chapter is intended to be on ethical issues relating to working with children, it is inevitable that a project such as the one described here, which involved a close collaboration between teachers and children as partners in classroom action research, would be embedded within a broader ethical lens. This is especially so because the project itself was new to the educational context of the teachers and children and any sustainable development and implementation of the project processes would inextricably impact on the overall dynamics of the existing school institutional cultures (Fullan, 2007). The broader ethical dilemmas discussed in this chapter are therefore complex in nature and though we cannot give categorical answers to all the questions that arose during and after the project, we nevertheless highlight them and share our reflections about aspects of our work from an ethical point of view.

The British Council Project

Our project (Pinter et al., 2016) was focused on previously unchartered territory within English language teaching (ELT). The main aim was to find out how both learners and teachers made sense of the concept of 'children as co-researchers'. There is a growing literature that documents children's experiences as co-researchers and even researchers in their own right outside our field (e.g. Coppock, 2011; Kellett, 2010b; Kellett *et al.*, 2004; O'Reilly *et al.*, 2013; Thomas, 2017) as well as in our field (Pinter, 2014; Pinter *et al.*, 2013; Pinter & Zandian, 2014; Pinter & Mathew, 2017) but our BC project was unique in its intent to explore what the actual practice of working with learners as co-researchers in classrooms would look like and how such a concept could be implemented in ordinary classrooms.

Kellett (2010a) proposed a framework that explains the types of roles children can take on in research. These include either being simply objects of adult research or participating in research in taking on more active subject roles. Kellett further divides these roles into research 'on, about, with and by' children. Research 'on' children refers to studies where children are unknowing passive recipients of adult research and have no real understanding of what is going on. Research 'about' children covers studies where children are acknowledged as subjects and individuals with unique experiences, and are prompted to contribute, but the perspectives that emerge overall are still only from adults since it is the adults who make all the decisions in the research. The last two roles or categories of research involving children are described as research 'with' and 'by' children. Research 'with' children considers them as partners in inquiry, with various possibilities whereby children may be asking questions, adding new perspectives and/or taking on active roles during data collection, for example, interviewing each other. It was this particular role, research *'with'* children; that is, inviting children to be co-researchers or partners alongside teachers in classroom action research that we were interested in exploring in this project. Research by children is rare but it refers to studies where children are in control of the whole project and are being assisted by adults only from the background.

Our project focused on Indian classrooms (with children aged 6–14) with volunteer teachers who came together from different parts of India. It involved 25 teachers (five of whom started a few months earlier than the rest of the group and thus acted as mentors) who explored their own English classrooms in cycles of action research by involving children as co-researchers.

The first author of this chapter is a senior teacher educator from India, who is fully conversant with the Indian school system and had worked with many school teachers on various classroom research projects prior to this project in 2015. In this role, relying on her existing network, she was able to invite experienced teachers who were likely to be interested in participating. The volunteer teachers were enthusiastic and keen to experiment with new ideas and joined the project to satisfy their own professional interests. They all worked in different types of schools (including government schools as well as private schools) and since they were individual volunteers, they came with varying degrees of school involvement.

This initial arrangement, a consequence of the recruitment strategy of individuals rather than whole schools, presented an ethical dilemma in itself because while all school principals were consulted at the beginning and were happy with the project initially, over time, their involvement, interest and support fluctuated a great deal and this put some of the participating teachers under pressure. It turned out, for example, that some school principals only really took state-organized professional development or research seriously and over time grew skeptical about the benefit of a project like ours. Given that this was not a project that embraced professional development opportunities for the whole school, inevitably, all individual teachers were constantly navigating a balance between the project and their school's pressures and established routines and practices. At one end of the cline, there were some school authorities who remained very enthusiastic about the idea of teachers and children researching together, as they saw this as a progressive step, and something that could eventually be cascaded across the whole school. At the other end, there were those principals who simply 'allowed' the teachers to conduct their studies, as an optional extra, as long as the set syllabus was completed and children were prepared for the summative exams. Accordingly, some teachers enjoyed more collegiality and support whereas others chose to take on the project as an intellectual and professional challenge, and approached it as an additional layer on top of their normal work.

The overarching ethical concern about the extent to which an individual teacher's involvement in a project can be smoothly embedded into the everyday running of the school, therefore, has been a key ethical issue that we have had to grapple with throughout and will return to discussing further in this chapter.

The structure of the project workshops

As mentioned above, the group of 25 teachers came from different types of schools from across the whole of India. Given that many teachers worked with large classes and taught across year groups, overall more than 800 children were involved. As the project was a collaborative effort between two universities in the UK and in India, two academic facilitators (the two authors of this chapter) collaborated on leading the project. We, the two academic facilitators, were involved in writing the original proposal for the project and were responsible for managing the data collection and the analysis as well as the publications arising from the project. We also organized a series of workshop events in India to bring the 25 teachers together. These three workshops were the backbone of the project where we attempted to make sense of what it means to work with children as co-researchers and how this work might take shape in the classroom. Throughout the project we shared insights and reflected on the teachers' ongoing efforts of implementing a research partnership with the children in their classrooms.

At the initial workshop we first of all explored and negotiated our individual and joint understandings of this special type of action research and discussed possible ways of involving children as co-researchers. This was a new idea and new perspective for many, and our initial discussions were based on our reading of some published academic articles (such as Pinter & Zandian, 2014) as well as hands-on experiences of those five mentor teachers who started the process earlier. By the end of the first workshop all teachers planned some ideas for potential mini-projects which were related to the theme of children as co-researchers to be implemented in their own classrooms before they returned to their context.

In the second workshop, which happened about four months later, all teachers came together and shared their experiences by presenting both successes and challenges that arose from their ongoing work in their classrooms. Children from local schools in Delhi, who had been working with the teachers as co-researchers, attended the workshop as active participants sharing their experiences and views. After this workshop teachers again went back to their classrooms to continue with their projects and/or start new projects based on fresh inspirations from their colleagues' work and our ongoing discussions.

Finally, in the last workshop, again, about four months later, all teachers gave a presentation about their journey since the very beginning, and shared both their learners' work and research as well as their own reflections as action researchers working in collaboration with the children.

The empirical data in this study came from a variety of sources, including recorded discussions and focus group interviews with teachers during the workshops, teachers' and learner presentations in the workshops, shared classroom materials and teachers' as well as learners' reflective journals. The data we collected and analyzed overall suggested that the children reported overwhelmingly positive experiences and the project also led to significant gains in professional development for teachers. Both the learners and the teachers enjoyed working in partnership with each other, and the teachers were surprised about the level of responsibility and maturity exhibited by their learners (see Pinter *et al.* (2016) and Pinter & Mathew (2017) for further details).

The project clearly demonstrated that learners liked the freedom to choose their own tasks, materials and strategies in the classroom. They performed better, they became more vocal and creative, and could take a stand when something was thrust upon them. School work became more fun, children worked collaboratively, made rules which they followed, unlike when teachers prescribed these for them. The teachers reflected on the impact of the project on their learners towards the end:

> *My children now will not accept anything ready-made: they want to do things for themselves;*

> *In my class the children themselves will not let me stop after this project; they have gained confidence and they have also become more proficient in English;*

> *The children have more choice and voice, and they listen to me much better and the quality of learning has got better in my class, they really inspire me with their ideas;*

> *The confidence levels have increased. Some can do a bilingual text, some only Hindi and some can only draw. But they are all eager to participate and progress according to their levels.*

Rights-based ethics and children

The focus of our BC project was on children first and foremost and our desire to give children more space, more choice and voice in classrooms. Such a decision in itself is strongly motivated by ethical principles relating to the main tenets of UNCRC (the Declaration of the Rights of the Child, United Nations, 1989). Based on this international initiative the idea that children are rights-bearing citizens has been gaining ground and many researchers working with children advocate a need to listen to and act on the views of children in all areas of their lives (see the introductory chapter to this volume). Respecting children's rights and listening to children in order to understand them from their own perspectives are principles advocated by the 'New Childhood Studies' (James & Prout, 1997; Kehily, 2004). Accordingly, ethical research with children takes their voices seriously, focuses on their agenda and allows for more democratic and more inclusive research methods (e.g. Clark & Moss, 2005; O' Kane, 2008; Punch, 2002). In essence, our project was designed to bring children's views and perspectives to the fore in the classroom action research projects. We viewed the children as active, capable subjects, rather than passive objects of adult research.

The challenge for us as a group was to explore how children could be positioned as 'knowers' and 'experts' in the classrooms. At the beginning, naturally, this was an abstract idea for the teachers, and they were quite skeptical about the feasibility of implementing it in concrete terms. In many classrooms therefore teachers simply decided to discuss with the children the aims of the BC project and opted to explore together how to implement it. Inevitably, the process of making sense of *children as co-researchers*, was different in different classrooms and teachers' new relationships with their learners were also different. However, in all cases the children initiated ideas, designed learning materials and suggested activities to implement. Teachers and learners experimented with a range of ideas but underneath all experiences seemed to be a process of 'democratizing' the classrooms, offering choice and responsibility to the children.

In one classroom, for example, the children and the teacher decided that they wanted to focus their classroom action research on the impact of reading storybooks selected by learners. Children were invited to choose a storybook to read from a large selection/ cupboard full of books. They were given complete autonomy in their choices, which meant that they were allowed to not only select whatever they wanted but to put back any book in the cupboard if they did not like it. In this way, everyone ended up reading books they were happy with and became fully engaged. Some children volunteered to tell their stories in class and this led to a sense of accomplishment, which was contagious, and in turn, more and more learners became motivated to do this. In the end, the class prepared a short questionnaire to explore the impact of stories on learning English. The results of the questionnaire were analysed and presented, which led to deep reflections about the learning process and also public presentations about their research work.

Overall, the underlying ethical call relating to the UNCRC (1989) of needing to listen to the children and give them an opportunity to contribute actively to the action research projects was certainly observed in this project. However, this did not help to eliminate ethical dilemmas, but instead, if anything, complicated matters further as we shall see later in this chapter.

Ethics in action research: Informal versus formal research

The relationship between classroom action research and formal ethics is an uneasy match. Boundaries between what is just normal everyday practice with a critical/ research stance and what is formalized action research is a grey area. The idea of a teacher researching her/his own classroom is in a sense closely linked to (good) teaching: when teachers, in their everyday practice take a critical or research stance, they are experimenting with ideas, tried and tested or quite new, with a tentativeness that in research parlance are called hypotheses. These teachers are looking for evidence, to see what works and what does not and why. All this can be regarded as 'good' teaching, also known as the 'zone of accepted practice' (Zeni, 1998: 13). This is in contrast to the transmission model of teaching where a pre-decided curriculum is 'covered' under strict time constraints, unquestioningly or even under protest, both of which happen quite often in the Indian context. In any context, the critical/ research stance, which brings with it systematic questioning of one's own teaching and constant experimentation, has been seen as an important dimension of professionalism (see Stenhouse, 1975: 144).

The concept of a reflective practitioner is also relevant to this research stance. Stenhouse (1975: 89) referred to Dewey's reflective theory of teaching as 'the active, careful and persistent examination of any belief, or purported form of knowledge, in the light of the grounds that support it and the further conclusions toward which it tends'. Reflective educators are constantly testing the assumptions and inferences they have made about their work as teachers. Reflective practice is, in essence, a kind of 'reflective conversation' (Schön, 1983, 1987) involving the educator, students, parents and other teachers. Reflective educators experiment and approach their classrooms with a research stance. Cochran-Smith and Lytle (2009: 121) similarly claim that 'working from and with an inquiry stance, then, involves a continual process of making current arrangements problematic; questioning the ways knowledge and practice are constructed, evaluated and used.' This again suggests that 'good' teachers may be undertaking informal investigations in their classrooms as part of their normal practice all the time. In fact such practice is highly ethical in the sense that broadly speaking an inquiry stance ultimately supports best possible learning outcomes and always prioritises learners.

Where the boundaries lie between an everyday inquiry stance and a more formal research stance seems unclear, and in fact, often an activity that starts as informal experimenting may evolve into a more formal research undertaking. Dikilitaş (2015) discusses teacher engagement with research and suggests that if it involves a systematic approach from planning the research design to writing up the research and presenting it at a conference, then these formalized outcomes will necessitate more formal ethical procedures and they can no longer be considered just informal experimentation in the classroom. Anderson (1996) asserts that a teacher's experimentation with innovative methods 'might be considered research if she or he intends to write a manuscript about it for publication' (1996: 279). Zeni (1998, citing Smith, 1990) recommends that the golden rule is for classroom action researchers to ask the question: 'What are the likely consequences of this research? (1998: 17).

The teachers we worked with in the project were all highly enthusiastic volunteers who were eager to develop their professional skills and were open to trying out different ideas in their classrooms, and indeed had already been experimenting in their classrooms routinely. Yet, on top of these informal layers, we, as a group, also needed to acknowledge that the project represented a more formal inquiry with the intention that we would write up and disseminate our findings. Prior to the start of the project, following generic UK institutional ethical principles, information leaflets and consent forms had been drafted for all prospective participants (teachers, children and parents) but in the actual context of the study we became less sure about the appropriateness of these. As Kubanyiova (2008) suggests, ethical principles cannot be applied uniformly to all situations but instead each situation will require a balanced ethical decision making process that will be unique to that context.

Consent issues

When the project began, the initial invitation letter sent out to the teachers explained the aims of the project and gave a good indication of the time needed and the kind of commitment the project was likely to demand. The letter also stressed the need to discuss the project with the school principal and request permission/approval from the teachers' local education authorities. All teachers except one had a positive initial reaction to the project from their school authorities. The teacher who couldn't get her principal to agree to any research of any kind felt very strongly that she was perfectly within her rights to carry on with the project as she was convinced that her new knowledge and experience would feed into improving learning outcomes for her students. She also felt strongly that her principal's stance to reject the project was unreasonable. She decided to compromise by carrying out the project work in addition to her normal classes. Even though we were aware of the broader ethical issue, we had to let the teacher decide what was best for her. She clearly disagreed with her principal and felt that in fact the principal's actions were unethical in trying to deny her this experience of working in the project.

The example of this teacher illustrates here that our primary concern was to explore the notion of children and teachers as co-researchers and as such, we perhaps had not given full thought to the wider ethical issues that might arise within the school culture, where there may not be continued backing from the leadership. The varying degrees of involvement and support from school principals and other teachers suggests that researchers setting out to do any school based research involving change in teaching approaches, such as the one in this project, need to consider the institutional obligations which the school principal may be under (to ensure curriculum is delivered, or that satisfactory results are obtained on external exams), and to consider the functioning of the school as a whole community.

In the first workshop all teacher participants were invited to fill in and sign a version of a standard consent form where they formally volunteered to become participants in the project and thus gave their permission to us, the facilitators, to record discussions, presentations in the workshops and focus group interviews. Still in the first workshop, we also discussed the need to ask for children's and parents' consent in order for the children to participate in the study in a more formal way.

Before completing the necessary ethics paperwork for the UK university ethics board we had already been aware of some of the challenges of negotiating children's consent/assent. The literature discussing issues around working with children as active research participants clearly problematizes the conflicting issues of vulnerability on the one hand and agency on the other (e.g. Christensen & Prout, 2002). Indeed in this project the children were going to participate not just in object roles, but in active subject roles as co-researchers. We were aware that the children had to be carefully prepared for this active role. They needed to understand what the project was about and what their roles were going to be. Ideally, in addition to their parents' permissions, we also intended to confirm their own willingness to participate in these active roles. This complex task was further complicated by sociocultural/ local constraints such as for example the fact that in India no local guidelines exist at all when it comes to school-based research involving children as ordinary participants, let alone as co-researchers.

While we, the whole team, including the teachers, were confident from the start that the work in their English classrooms would be of benefit to the children rather than affecting them in a negative way, and that acting as co-researchers was not going to interfere in a negative way with their work and their assessment at school, it was nonetheless important to formalize the process of negotiating their consent in their roles as participants/co-researchers. Formalizing this process also has the potential to further legitimize the project from the perspectives of school principals.

The following draft consent form (Figure 11.1) and a child information leaflet had been prepared in advance of the workshops with the intention that teachers could adapt this in their classrooms and think about implementing it taking local needs and restrictions into account.

When we discussed the questions in this form, many teaches felt that it was better to present these issues to the children *verbally only* rather than ask them to sign a form. Nonetheless all teachers took a copy of this form back home with them to consider the practicalities of implementation.

With regard to parents, separate information leaflets and draft consent forms had been prepared in advance and these were also discussed alongside the children's forms. Immediately, there was uncertainty in the group regarding the usefulness of consent forms and information leaflets for parents. Teachers were convinced that it was going to be better to negotiate consent with parents verbally too, rather than 'put them off' with these forms. It turned out that in many state schools parents could not be reached easily or indeed not at all, and even those who could be reached were not used to getting written communication from the schools. Other parents simply did not have the required literacy skills to read and respond to the leaflets. Given that many of the children came from very challenging backgrounds as first generation learners, teachers were sometimes uncertain as to who to approach in the absence of any parent/ guardian contact details. Many teachers therefore faced a dilemma about what was more ethical, to exclude children who did not have a signed consent form from parents or to include them in what they ultimately considered to be, first and foremost, a pedagogical activity or intervention

This project is about children like you doing some research in their own classrooms. If you are interested in this, please read the leaflet and talk to your teacher.

- Have you read the leaflet?

Yes/ No (boxes to tick)

- Have you talked to the teacher?

Yes/No (boxes to tick)

- Would you like to take part?

Yes/No (boxes to tick)

Your teacher might sometimes tape-record you talking about the project or working on the project. This helps her remember exactly what happened. This data will be stored and analysed by a team of researchers in the UK and will only be used to illustrate what happens in your classroom. No individuals will be identified or recognised.

- Are you ok with this?

Yes/No (boxes to tick)

- If you are not enjoying the project any more or for some reason you do not want to participate, you can tell the teacher and he/she will give you a different task. It is ok for you to stop participating at any time. You understand you have a choice about participating in the project.

Yes/ No (boxes to tick)

- There may be a chance to take an active role in helping the teacher in this project in a different way, such as by giving advice, designing questions, interviewing other children, and/or discussing how to investigate something. Do you think you might be interested in this?

Yes/No (boxes to tick)

- If you have read the leaflet and talked to your teacher, and you are happy to participate, please sign:

Signed:

Name:

Date:

Figure 11.1 Sample child consent form to be administered to the children in their L1

in their own classrooms rather than a more formal research project. Many teachers felt that the formal aspects of the project with its demands on formal procedures was secondary to the pedagogical benefits. We had long discussions about these dilemmas and eventually we agreed that the teachers would each handle their own dilemmas locally, striking a compromise that felt right and fair in their own micro-context.

Tensions within the whole school contexts

Working in the project meant that children and teachers got comfortable and familiar with this new way of collaborating and the question arose: 'What next?' Learners constantly asked, 'Why aren't we doing these things in other classes in the school?' When some children from their primary school moved to a high school and decided to keep in touch with their previous teacher, they were quite surprised that their new teacher didn't give them any 'choice and a voice'.

Teachers reported that children put in a plea for continuation: *I want this project to be continued*. Children also expressed a desire not to go back to what they experienced before such as rote learning: *We stopped feeling the need to learn by memory only. We have now become capable of answering questions all by ourselves.*

On the one hand, offering children greater responsibilities and choices in their learning is in line with the rights-based approach to research ethics, on the other hand children wanting to carry on with the project when it comes to an end, and children wanting to make changes to other classes clearly brings a new concern. Is it ethical to introduce learners to approaches and ways of working that they cannot continue with beyond the project? This concern relates back to the teachers' involvement as individuals rather than as whole school communities and suggests that, however well-meant classroom-based action research involving children as co-researchers is in theory, its sustainability is certainly questionable. Without situating the research in a wider context and seeking more formal institutional approval rather than just the consent of individual teachers and the initial verbal consent of the principal, the teacher(s) involved may burnout with the stresses the change introduces, potentially jeopardize their jobs if the changes are viewed as systemically disruptive and undesirable, or may become isolated from other members of staff, or ostracized by them for being a 'troublemaker'. The impact for the children could be de-motivation with school or disruptive behavior in other lessons. These are all important ethical issues which researchers investigating the possibility of involving children and teachers as co-researchers need to consider and seek ways of addressing from an institutional level so that sustainability could be guaranteed. One way of implementing sustainability is to engage children as co-researchers in after school clubs rather than in mainstream classrooms.

Despite the broader ethical issue raised here, overall the majority of the teachers have reported very positive experiences. In some schools it was possible for teachers to share their experience, and colleagues in these schools were eager to implement similar approaches in their classes. Evidence from some teachers and students that we have observed is heartwarming and reassuring as to the lasting effects of the project. One teacher suggests that it has all been worthwhile as she is now inspiring others: *Teachers in my school started approaching me, can you tell me, can you take circle time, can you help. This is my greatest achievement.*

Roles and representation-related dilemmas

We, the project team including the teachers' students, developed a bond over the year through various forms of dialogue. In this way our identity as belonging to a community of practice was well established. Each one of us cherished this and looked forward to the next face-to-face workshop, which helped us to consolidate the work done and plan the next steps. However, while we managed to invite some children, this could happen only in Delhi where the workshops took place. Children from other parts of the country could not be physically present, except through their work, or audio and video recordings. The funding did not allow travel for all children, nor would this have been practically possible. This raises another important ethical issue regarding who is selected to participate to represent the 800 children in the larger project. When children are invited to participate actively in research as partners, it is almost always the case that children with superior social skills and those who are high achievers and communicate effectively get selected. This raises important questions about shy, quiet children and those who are less communicative. These children are almost always left out with the consequence that their views and insights are marginalized. In any one research project who gets selected to participate and who does not is an ethical dilemma. Some children have opportunities to work alongside teachers in project that may be beneficial in terms of developing important skills and some do not. Is this ethical? Just how selection processes work in any project involving children must also be given serious thought especially if the experiences of the selected few are positive and potentially transformative.

In Indian schools there is a culture of respecting authority – for example, teachers, parents and others in positions of power – rather than ever questioning what they do, at least overtly. As one teacher observes: *I think in our school system hierarchy is not only appreciated, but it is celebrated by some. And it is quietly tolerated by others.* In our project we wanted true collaboration. Two of us from different universities in two countries and the teachers representing different kinds of schools from different states – public/private, rural/semi-urban/urban, primary/upper primary, English/mother tongue medium – and their students, participated in it collaboratively. Throughout we, the facilitators, attempted to create an atmosphere of no hierarchy at all. The children were not just informants or subjects but were invited to be equal partners and they were reminded all along that we were trying to learn from them. Each of us brought different perspectives from our own teacher training and teaching-learning contexts to bear on the project that enriched our discussions and our learning. Although the idea for the whole project came initially from the second author, and the funding from British Council, UK, the work that happened in the form of three workshops, presentations by teachers and even participation of some students from the local project schools, could be seen as mutually negotiated, and not hierarchical, with expertise flowing from us to teachers but also from children to teachers and teachers to us and in other non-linear ways.

Even though we all had different roles as insiders and outsiders we attempted to create an atmosphere where all knowledge was equally appreciated. Insider researchers in this case were the teachers who interrogated their own teaching-learning processes alongside their co-researchers, the children, to 'understand' it better, as Allwright (2015) would argue, while outsiders were the university 'academic' researchers who were much removed from the classrooms in question. However, knowledge and experience from all sides was appreciated and an emphasis throughout was put firmly on the children's knowledge construction processes.

The teachers all read relevant and interesting articles together and made sense of these in their own ways and spent time discussing successes but also dilemmas and challenges emphasising all along that there were no clear-cut answers and none of us were experts. The teachers inspired each other with examples of work from their own contexts. We celebrated all efforts and achievements and advised teachers to take steps that were feasible and felt right for them. Working in this way did not create any 'power differentials separating the researchers from the researched', as Wolf (1992) cautions us about this. In fact teachers unequivocally acknowledged and appreciated the non-hierarchical nature of our project as one of them comments here:

> In this project and during the workshops there are so many participants from different fields and status: principals, teachers, professors but in the workshop we all came together; the comfort which I found here, that gave me the motivation to speak out and participate wholeheartedly.

And yet, the question arises, as to whether it is possible to achieve a true balance of power and shared ownership. Moreover, every now and then teachers subtly made us aware of the fact that we, the academic coordinators, were after all the 'experts' so we had to accept this responsibility when it came to major decisions. Ultimately, writing about the project, interpreting the data and representing the children's as well as the teachers' voices is mediated by our own lens, which is the lens of the academic facilitators. The reporting can never be complete, free of bias or guarantee to represent the 'truth'. This remains a major criticism of child research as well. Children's voices are messy and multi-layered and are ultimately (re)-represented by adults even in projects like ours where they were intentionally given space, choice and voice (Komulainen, 2007). Misrepresentation of children's views, although not intentional, seems nonetheless an inevitable possibility. So, what is the most ethical way of reporting research like this? How can the children's, the teachers' and the academic researchers' voices all be represented fairly? How can the children's voices be represented in an authentic way and for what audiences?

Goldstein (2000) argues that as university-based researchers it seems the best we could hope for would be a research relationship 'that approaches a state of symbiosis: research that is mutually beneficial to both the researcher and the researched and hurts no one in the process' (Goldstein, 2000: 524). Goldstein adds further: 'provided the research relationship is mutually satisfactory and mutually understood, unequal partnerships are not necessarily a problem' (Goldstein, 2000: 524). Similar parallel processes apply in classroom action research where children are co-researchers. It is only through mutual respect and shifting roles (teachers becoming learners and learners taking on teaching roles) that the integrity of such partnership can be sustained.

Conclusion

While research in general aims to question the *status quo* of any existing practice, in the case of classroom action research that enables children to take on a bigger responsibility for their learning, ethical considerations will become even more complicated. Formal codes of conduct must work as useful reference points and reminders of important principles to consider but on another level the messy everyday 'in-situ' dilemmas of the local context should always be negotiated with what we consider the most important principles of ethics, which are honesty/integrity, professional commitment and listening to one's conscience. Groundwater-Smith and Mockler (2007) also comment as follows: '...if there is not some fidelity to the stories that matter to the practitioner but may not be of great account to the state, then there has been a serious omission in ethical terms' (2007: 201). Ethical processes, not just guidelines, will follow for each specific teacher research exercise when one is mindful of their own integrity.

Since this was a one-year project, we couldn't put in a scheme for sustainability at the school level. It was a modest effort at experimenting with the concept of children as co-researchers in ordinary classrooms. A bigger project would have to plan for involving other teachers in the school as well as principals and parents, and take into account considerations and restrictions specific to each school context. A competitive (as opposed to a collaborative) climate is a widespread phenomenon in Indian schools (see Mathew, 2005, 2015 for some details), given that teachers have to train children to face fierce competition, and that they personally get credit for children's achievements. This results in teachers working in isolation and becoming silent innovators. The next step needs to be to explore possibilities of whole school approaches involving the teachers and children more holistically. This will not only minimize the broader ethical issues we have discussed in this chapter but would hopefully go some way towards a more harmonious school-based transformation and sustainability.

References

Allwright, D. (2015) Putting 'understanding' first in practitioner research. In K. Dikilitaş, R. Smith and W. Trotman (eds) *Teacher-Researchers in Action*. IATEFL Research Special Interest Group (pp. 19–36). IATEFL.

Anderson, P.V. (1996) Ethics, institutional review boards, and the involvement of human participants in composition research. In P. Mortensen and G.E. Kirsch (eds) *Ethics and Representation in Qualitative Studies of Literacy*, (pp. 260–286). Urbana, IL: National Council of Teachers of English.

Christensen, P. and Prout, A. (2002) Working with ethical symmetry in social research with children. *Childhood* 9 (4), 477–497.

Clark, A. and Moss, P. (2005) *Listening to Children: The Mosaic Approach*. London: National Children's Bureau Enterprises.

Cochran-Smith, M. and Lytle, S. (2009) *Inquiry as Stance: Practitioner Research for the Next Generation* NY: Teachers College Press.

Coppock, V. (2011) Children as peer researchers: Reflections on a journey of mutual discovery. *Children and Society* 25 (6), 435–466.

Dikilitaş, K. (2015) Professional development through teacher-research. In K. Dikilitaş, R. Smith and W. Trotman (eds) *Teacher-Researchers in Action*. IATEFL Research Special Interest Group (pp. 47–55). IATEFL.

Fullan, M. (2007) *The Meaning of Educational Change*. London: Routledge.

Goldstein, L.S. (2000) Ethical dilemmas in designing collaborative research: Lessons learned the hard way. *International Journal of Qualitative Studies in Education* 13 (5), 517–530, doi: 10.1080/09518390050156431.

Groundwater-Smith, S. and Mockler, N. (2007) Ethics in practitioner research: An issue of quality. *Research Papers in Education* 22, 199–211.

James, A. and Prout, A. (eds) (1997) *Constructing and Re-constructing Childhood*. Basingstoke: Falmer Press.

Kehily, M.J. (2004) *Childhood Studies: An Introduction*. Open University Press.

Kellett, M. (2010a) *Rethinking Children and Research: Attitudes in Contemporary Society*. London: Continuum.

Kellett, M. (2010b) Small shoes, big steps! Empowering children as active researchers. *American Journal of Community Psychology* 46, 195–203.

Kellett, M., Forrest, R., Dent, N. and Ward, S. (2004) Just teach us the skills, please, we'll do the rest! Empowering ten-year-olds as active researchers. *Children and Society* 18, 329–343.

Komulainen, S. (2007) The ambiguity of the child's 'voice' in social research. *Childhood* 14 (1), 11–28.

Kubanyiova, M. (2008) Rethinking research ethics in contemporary applied linguistics: The tension between macroethical and microethical perspectives in situated research. *The Modern Language Journal* 92 (4), 503–518.

Mathew, R. (2005) How do teachers learn and grow? In A. Pulverness (ed.) *IATEFL 2004: Liverpool Conference: Selections*. IATEFL Publication.

Mathew, R. (2015) Teacher development as the future of teacher education. In G. Pickering and P. Gunashekar (eds) *Innovation in English Language Teacher Education* (pp.29–37). British Council.

O'Kane, C. (2008) The development of participatory techniques: Facilitating children's views about decisions which affect them. In P. Christensen and A. James (eds) *Research with Children: Perspectives and Practices* (pp. 125–155). London: Routledge

O'Reilly, M., Ronzoni, P. and Dogra, N. (2013) *Research with Children: Theory and Practice*. London: Sage.

Pinter, A. (2014) Child participant roles in applied linguistics research. *Applied Linguistics* 35 (2), 168–183.

Pinter, A., Kuchah, K. and Smith, R. (2013) Research with children *ELT Journal* 67 (4), 484–487.

Pinter, A. and Mathew, R. (2017) Links between teacher development and working with children as co-researchers. In E. Wilden and R. Porsch (eds) *The Professional Development of In-service and Pre-service Primary EFL Teachers. National and international research* (pp. 141–152). Münster: Waxmann.

Pinter, A., Mathew, R. and Smith, R. (2016) *Children and Teachers as Co-researchers in Indian Primary English Classrooms: ELT Research Paper 16.03*. London: British Council.

Pinter, A. and Zandian, S. (2014) I don't ever want to leave this room; benefits of researching 'with' children. *ELT Journal* 68 (1), 64–74.

Punch, S. (2002) Research with children: The same or different from research with adults? *Childhood* 9 (3), 321–41.

Schön, D.A. (1983) *The Reflective Practitioner*. New York: Basic Books.

Schön, D.A. (1987) *Educating the Reflective Practitioner: Toward a New Design for Teaching and Learning in the Professions*. San Francisco: Jossey-Bass.

Stenhouse, L. (1975) *An Introduction to Curriculum Research and Development*. London: Heinemann.

Thomas, N. (2017) Turning the tables: Children as researchers. In P. Christensen and A. James (eds) *Research with Children: Perspectives and Practices* (pp. 160–179). London: Routledge.

United Nations (1989) *United Nations Conventions on the Rights of the Child*. New York: United Nations.

Wolf, D.L. (1992) Situating feminist dilemmas in fieldwork. In D.L. Wolf (ed.) *Feminist Dilemmas in Fieldwork* (pp. 1–55). New York: Westview Press.

Zeni, J. (1998) A guide to ethical issues and action research. *Educational Action Research* 6 (1), 9–19.

12 The Ethical Practices of Collecting Informed Consent from Child Participants in Action Research Projects

Sandie Mourão

Action Research in Teacher Education

The inclusion of action research, or teacher research, is common in teacher education, in pre-service and in-service training. Burns (2010) highlights the relevance of action research for promoting and supporting 'a self-reflective, critical and systematic approach to exploring teaching practice' (2010: 2). Action research is said to lead student teachers (STs) to experience autonomy 'as learners of teaching and teachers of learning' (Jiménez Raya *et al.*, 2017: 107), and, as such, action research can foster the development of understanding and transformation, and reinforces the role of teachers as agents of change (Vieira, 2017: 87). Action research is also about understanding the multiple perspectives of teaching and learning, but if seen as an experiential pedagogy, it focuses on 'self-directed professional learning' for individuals or for groups (i.e. learners, peers and mentors) (Jiménez Raya *et al.*, 2017: 109). Although action research is considered participatory; that is, involving others (e.g. the learners) when included in pre-service teacher education, it tends to result in the ST trying to understand something about their practice on their own. This usually means the children are involved, but as participants with no particular expectations rather than active and involved participants, with a voice in the research activities.

Research Ethics and Informed Consent

Ethical scrutiny in research is usually, though not always, a legal and institutional requirement, and following research ethics guidelines is meant to ensure that research is conducted in a moral and responsible way. However, action research undertaken by STs is not always as stringently planned as it should be and there may be a 'relaxing of some of the restrictions' (Phillips & Carr, 2010: 96). Phillips and Carr justify this by stating the following: 'as action research is embedded into the teaching and learning process and, as a teacher you would not need to gain permission if the research was not formal and you did not plan on making the research public' (Phillips & Carr, 2010: 96). Nevertheless, they reiterate that if the research is going to be published in any form, or if the children are going to be filmed, audio recorded or photographed, permission must be sought (see also Mathew & Pinter in this volume).

One of the issues associated with research ethics is whose permission is needed for the research to take place (Burns, 2010: 34). Permission, or informed consent, requires that researchers provide everyone who is involved in their research with sufficient information so that each can decide whether they want to take part or not. With regard to whose permission is needed for the research in a classroom of children, this includes (but is not restricted to) obtaining informed consent from the school authorities, the children and their parents or legal representatives, as they are legally minors.

Burns suggests that '(I)n primary school situations in particular, participants may be too young to understand the implications of giving permission' (2010: 36). This is typical of publications within English language teaching (ELT), which tend to view children as voiceless, perceiving them as incompetent and lacking in ability to consent to, or contribute in any way to the design, implementation or interpretation of the research. Nevertheless, Alderson (2005: 29) outlines three ways in which children can become involved in research:

(1) as unknowing objects, not asked to give consent and unaware of the research focus;
(2) as aware subjects, asked for their informed consent but within adult-designed research projects;
(3) as active participants, participating in research which uses flexible methods suited to children, and where they may also be involved in planning, directing, conducting and reporting research.

Traditionally, children have been conceptualized as 'unknowing objects' where they are seen as voiceless, incompetent and lacking in ability to consent to, or contribute in any way to the design, implementation or interpretation of the research (Lundy, 2007). Views have changed over recent decades, and Christensen and Prout (2002) suggest that when a more child-centred approach is taken, children are seen as 'social actor[s] with their own experiences and understandings' (2002: 481). They are 'aware subjects' and their opinions are respected, or they are 'active participants' and involved in the research on multiple levels (see Chapter 1 of this volume).

Within the more child-centred approach to research with children, the distinction between child and adult is not taken for granted and whatever research methods are employed, these are seen to 'suit the persons involved in the study' (Christensen & Prout, 2002: 481). An 'ethical symmetry' is recommended, that is the 'ethical relationship between researcher and informant is the same' (2002: 482). Children are respected and given an opportunity to have an opinion and have this opinion listened to and acted on, as would be expected if the research involved adults.

The British Educational Research Association provides a very clear set of guidelines for researchers with sections, though brief, on working with children. These guidelines highlight the 'structural inequalities' (BERA, 2018: 6) which emerge from 'the perceived authority of adults' resulting in children either finding it difficult or feeling intimidated by researchers' questions, or finding it difficult to say 'no' (Harcourt & Conroy, 2011: 43). With ethical standards being the same for children as for adults, 'equality is [the] starting point' and the adult researcher needs to recognize and 'consider their actions, responsibilities, use of appropriate methods and ways of communication throughout the research process' (Christensen & Prout, 2002: 484). As such, the adult researcher should be able to work consciously towards listening to and respecting children's views. This is not only good pedagogical practice but 'a legally binding obligation' (Lundy, 2007: 931), for Article 12 of the United Nations Convention on the Rights of the Child (UNCRC) declares:

> Parties shall assure to the child who is capable of forming his or her own views the right to express those views freely in all matters affecting the child, the views of the child being given due weight in accordance with the age and maturity of the child. (United Nations, 1989)

Alderson (2008: 91–2) suggests children's participation in research should be seen on multiple levels.

(1) Being informed
(2) Expressing a view
(3) Influencing the decision-making
(4) Being the main decider

Often participation is defined by the last level only; that is, 'being the main decider' (Alderson, 2008: 92). However, the first three levels are also important in the decision-making process. These levels suggest that first, children have understood; second, can form a view based on their understanding; and third, are considered able to form a view. This culminates in children making informed decisions and their decisions being accepted and respected. The first three levels are evident in the UNCRC – children have the right to participate in decisions affecting their lives and as such to communicate their views and opinions. When children are part of a research project, they should be informed participants and the informing needs to be done in a way which provides them with the means to truly understand what is being done and for what reasons, so they genuinely can give *informed consent*. This is in contrast to obtaining *assent*, which merely implies that the child(ren), without knowing the details, have agreed to take part in the study once their parents or legal representatives have given permission.

Collecting Informed Consent

Informed consent is approval given by research participants, in written or verbal form, once they have been told about the nature and implications of their involvement in a study (Bogdan & Biklen, 2007: 272). According to Burns:

> Participants have a right to know about the purpose, the procedures, possible effects of the research on them, and how the research will be used, and should not be deceived or tricked about the aims of the research. (Burns, 2010: 35)

Phillips and Carr (2010: 98) consider the following to be the most important points to include when informing parents of an action research project planned to take place in the classroom their child is a participant of:

- the topic of the project;
- the objective of the project;
- strategies that will be implemented;
- data to be collected;
- a timeline of the project;
- how the project will be made public;
- why videotaping or picture-taking will occur (if applicable);
- why any pictures or videos might be produced for presentations (if applicable);
- how confidentiality will be maintained;
- what the potential risk to students are (if any).

Regarding what to tell the children who are in the STs' classroom, Phillips and Carr advise that (student)teachers should explain to the children that they are 'doing this study to become a better teacher' (2010: 98). The information should be shared in such a way that children can at least understand that their teacher is doing a small piece of research to contribute to their (the children's and the teacher's) learning, how it may involve them and what the implications are. Children should be given the opportunity to ask questions and to further understand their roles through their questions and the adult researcher's answers.

Fine and Sandstrom (1988) suggest that 'children [as young as 3 years old] should be told as much as possible' (1988: 46), and in addition to the above information, children also need to be informed of their rights (Shaw *et al.*, 2011). These include:

(1) that their identities will not be revealed;
(2) that they do not have to participate;
(3) that they can withdraw from the research activities at any time;
(4) that they can ask questions about the research at any time.

Of extreme importance is the removal of any form of coercion. Finally, children should be told that they can also ask about the results if they wish. All this can be undertaken through verbal explanations, showing pictures or artefacts or in writing or a combination of these (Einarsdóttir, 2007).

Flewitt (2005: 4) refers to ongoing consent in research with young children, as consent which is repeatedly 'negotiated in situated contexts'. Consent is thus seen as a social process, an ongoing dialogue, which is revisited at regular intervals during a study (Kuchah & Pinter, 2012).The implications of this are that even though a teacher has obtained informed consent from a child at the beginning of a study, it is appropriate to remind the child of what is happening as the project progresses, and that they can opt-out if they wish at any time. This might be equally relevant when a child is being recorded, observed, or a piece of their work is being collected as data.

The remaining sections of this chapter show how a group of STs on a Masters in Education programme at Nova University Lisbon, Portugal attempted to ensure that children really were informed, given a voice and listened to regarding their wish to be part of an action research project in their classrooms.

Background

Education in Portugal

Formal compulsory education in Portugal is referred to as basic education and made up of three sequential cycles followed by secondary education:

- first cycle (grades 1 to 4, ages 6 to 9)
- second cycle (grades 5 to 6, ages 10 to 11)
- third cycle (grades 7 to 9, ages 12 to 14)
- secondary education (grades 10 to 12, ages 15 to 17).

Foreign language (FL) education (English or French) was made compulsory in the second cycle during the education reforms of the late 1980s; however, in 2012 English became the only FL to be taught in this cycle and then in 2015 English was introduced into the first cycle, at grade 3 (age 8).

Until the recent changes in the English curriculum, there were two routes to becoming a teacher of English: to obtain a degree in English at a university and complete a period of professionalization to teach English in the third cycle or secondary education, or to obtain a degree in basic education at a polytechnic institute with a specialization in English for the second cycle. With the inclusion of English as a curricular subject in the first cycle (grades 3 and 4), a new teacher recruitment group emerged, and this prompted the creation of a pre-service Masters in Education programme for Teaching English in the first Cycle of Basic Education, provided by 12 higher education institutions (HEIs) in Portugal. This is a three-semester professional Masters programme, which incorporates a two-semester practicum placement in schools. To apply to this programme students must be graduates (or equivalent) and have a C1 level of English.

The Masters in Education in Teaching English in the first Cycle of Basic Education at Nova University Lisbon

The Masters programme at Nova University Lisbon, as with the majority of other HEI Master's courses for primary English teachers in Portugal, incorporates a practicum placement in Semesters 2 and 3, involving STs in observations, co-teaching, solo-teaching and a small action research project. A short final report is also required by all STs, describing the action research project and reflecting on its relevance for their professional development and the benefits brought to the learners. This report is discussed and defended in a public viva.

The action research project begins to take shape during the STs' visits to a school in Semester 2, where they observe a group of children and teach alongside their school-based mentor. At the same time as the practicum, the STs attend a Supervision Seminar at the university, which focuses on supporting their development as reflective and autonomous practitioners. Here they are supported in their teacher research, which includes understanding the ethics of conducting research, in particular with children.

To my knowledge very little has been written about the practicalities of how to go about obtaining informed consent from children during action research projects in the field of primary ELT. This is restricted to Pinter (2011), who mentions obtaining consent, and suggests that children can be asked to describe what they have understood about a particular research project (2011: 209). As such, when I began to teach research ethics and the implications for classroom practice in the Supervision Seminar, there were no concrete examples available to show the STs. I challenged them to come up with an approach they felt was aligned with the recommendations for respecting ethical symmetry while undertaking their action research projects.

Undertaking the Challenge

This section of the chapter describes my analysis of the different approaches taken by STs to obtaining informed consent from children during their practicum action research projects. These STs were from two cohorts, conducting their action research projects between September and December of 2016 and 2017 – a total of 15 STs. To further contribute to my analysis, and for the purposes of this chapter, I obtained data from three other sources:

- notes of STs' comments during their Supervision Seminar;
- a short email survey sent to the STs, with a view to obtaining more specific details about the number of children who did not wish to participate in their action research, as well as the STs' personal opinion about asking children's consent and a justification of this opinion;
- The final reports for relevant references to the complexities of handling informed consent during their action research projects.

Approaches to collecting informed consent

The STs collected informed consent from the school directors, the parents or legal representatives and the children, in accordance with educational research ethics guidelines (BERA, 2018; Phillips & Carr, 2010). Generally, when research involves adults, a short description of the research procedures is given in writing and the adult signs a form, acknowledging full understanding of the procedures and implications. It is assumed that adults are intellectually mature enough to understand the explanation they have read. Making their action research projects comprehensible to children caused the STs a fair bit of deliberation, in particular around how they could be sure the children had genuinely understood the explanations. Although it appears to be the norm when researching in classrooms with children (Einarsdóttir, 2007), the STs decided that giving a verbal explanation and receiving oral consent was not enough. It did not really indicate that the children had understood enough to make an informed decision about their participation, and it did not take into account the principles outlined above, which enable children's active participation. The STs also decided that children might like to sign a piece of paper indicating whether they were giving consent or not, so this became a generalized approach undertaken by all STs but in a variety of ways.

Verbal explanations

All verbal explanations were given in Portuguese so that the children were provided every opportunity to understand what they were being asked to do. These explanations were always accompanied by a written document. In their reports STs described how they explained their research to the children, highlighting the relevance of conversing with them about different aspects of the project and clarifying with them specific details like who might read the report or whether a child could still stay in the class even if they didn't want to participate in the study. Several

STs outlined their concern about ensuring children really understood what was happening by giving them an opportunity to ask questions.

> I felt [it was] important that learners could understand ... that they were free to decide if they wanted to take part or to decline. Learners were given an opportunity to ask questions and I answered their doubts and reaffirmed that their participation was voluntary, and they could stop to participate at any time. If that was the case, I would not include their answers in my study. (Nobre, 2017: 9)

In her report, Santana (2017) shared unease about her status during the verbal explanations, 'I also had to adopt an attitude in class where students did not feel obliged to participate' (2017: 8). This was the only mention of being aware of overcoming coercion, and this may have occurred because Santana's action research project looked at teacher action and attitude and its effects on learners.

Cravo (2017) outlined in her report how she used visual support, a PowerPoint presentation (see Figure 12.1), to help children understand her study: 'I used a mind map that included the image of Homer Simpson, which is familiar and appealing to children, and child friendly words as visual aids to explain my study' (2017: 9). From Figure 12.1 it is possible to see the 'child-friendly words' Cravo is referring to. She has rephrased the more formal 'Self-awareness' and labelled it 'Who am I?' as well as translating it into Portuguese. In her survey response to me she wrote,

> By showing them what my study was I intended children to get to know my aims before they would or not give me their consent. I felt that children's 'yes' or 'no' should follow their understanding of my study, so as to avoid [asking for] their consent to be [seen] as something simply done to abide by [the rules]. (Survey response, November, 2017).

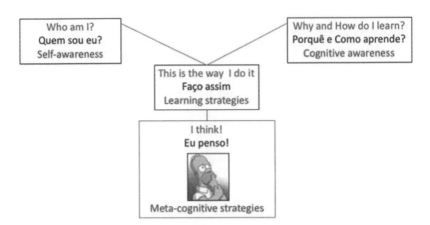

Figure 12.1 Mind map to explain the ST's action research study (Cravo, 2017)

Cravo's action research project investigated the teacher's role in fostering reflection and how this in turn supported the children's learning, so using this approach to explain her study contributed to not only helping children understand her study, but also to introduce her research topic.

Written explanations

The written documents used to obtain informed consent usually summarized the points that had been explained orally by the STs. Several of the STs' reports mentioned using special language for these written documents: 'All letters were written in Portuguese and the one given to the children had child friendly and very accessible language' (Alexandre, 2018: 11), or the language was 'written in a more informal and playful manner' (Santos, 2018: 12).

Admitting to being a student was a typical strategy in attempting to bring the children closer to the ST's experience and several STs used this to help children understand what they were doing. Florença relates children's response to this strategy in her report: 'When asked if they had any questions the children mainly were curious that I was still studying and one of the students asked me until what age one studies' (Florença, 2017: 18).

Another way of making the request for consent more informal was to turn it into an invitation. Militec (2017) gave her request for a consent document the title 'An invitation to participate in my project' (2017: 30, my translation) and the word 'invitation' was used in several of the written documents. Colaço (2017), researching awareness of cultural diversity in her class, decided to invite children to join her on a journey, with the request for consent document showing a plane flying across the page with a banner that read in Portuguese: 'Do you want to make this journey with me?' It continued like this:

> For this journey, and to discover what is different, we don't need to leave the classroom or take a lot of baggage with us. What we need for this journey is just an open mind, to use our imagination and, of course, to really want to learn English. (Colaço, 2017: 34, my translation)

Taking the idea of discovery and openness to acceptance, Colaço is not only asking for consent, but introducing her children to the topic of the research, much as Cravo did earlier in her PowerPoint slide.

Santana's (2017) action research involved asking children's opinions about the qualities of a good teacher, as well as what they particularly enjoyed doing when learning English. Their opinions fed into the creation of an innovative Primary Teacher Confirmation Scale – a questionnaire, which measured whether students felt confirmed; that is, valued, significant individuals (Ellis, 2000: 265) – as such enabling children's participation by respecting their opinions and preferences. To highlight the importance of their involvement, the request for a consent document was aimed directly at the child reader, 'Me and Xana's study' ['*Eu e o estudo da Xana*'] (Santana, 2017: 35). Here Santana not only implies the children are involved in her study, but she places them in the leading position, '*Me and Xana's study*', rather than 'Xana's study and *me*'.

Helping children to understand

As already described, embracing a student identity was a typical approach to bringing the children closer to the ST's experience, and several STs used this to help children understand what they were doing. Using child-friendly analogies were also fairly common. In her report, Cunha (2017) explained how she used a 'class newsletter' as an analogy to help children visualize what would happen to the data she collects: 'In the end I will analyze all the questionnaires, the reports and the tables I will be making during the activities, like they were a class 'newsletter' and include them in my final project' (2017: 32, my translation). Some STs used more formal wording, but provided carefully rephrased explanations, for example, 'Your participation is voluntary, this means, you decide if you participate or not' (Militic, 2017: 30, my translation).

Anonymity and pseudonyms were sometimes referred to, following up the verbal explanations in writing, for example 'Your name will never be revealed. Your participation will be anonymous. Nobody will know your name because you will have a number, or a code name instead of your real name' (Militec, 2017: 30, my translation). Or, 'Your name or picture will never appear in my project. You can invent a name for yourself (a pseudonym) and if you don't do this, I will use a code number so I can identify you' (Alexandre, 2018: 36 my translation).

All but one ST insisted that the children completed the consent form in the classroom. Florença, on the other hand, explained everything orally and then gave the form to the children suggesting they take it home, which was another approach to helping the children understand through sharing concerns with parents. The request for consent opened with: 'Read this document with care. You can talk to your parents about it. If you have any doubts you can ask me' (2017: 36, my translation). This request for consent continued in a fairly formal manner, clearly outlining what was going to happen. Figure 12.2 shows an excerpt.

The balance between formality and informality was not an easy dilemma to overcome, but Florença managed this in the original document by combining the more formal written description within a surrounding frame of small yellow stars.

Anonymity

As has been mentioned, the process of remaining anonymous was explained to the children and to help them understand this, many STs

(...) I would like you to be part of my study. But before this it is important you know what will happen.

If you decide to participate, and your parents give you permission, I will ask you to:

- Fill in a questionnaire
- Complete some worksheets related to my study
- Talk about the results of the questionnaires and give your opinions

I will also take some photos of your completed worksheets.
(...)

Figure 12.2 Excerpt from a request for informed consent - my translation (Florença, 2017: 36)

introduced the idea of using a code-name. This appealed to the children's imagination and the feedback from STs was very positive. Batista (2017) wrote:

> All students were favourably surprised when asked for a written and signed acceptance. (...) and their subsequent enthusiasm regarding the choice of nicknames was quite vocal. (Batista, 2017: 11)

Many STs opted for letting the children choose their code-names, instead of just assigning numbers or letters. This contributed once again to enabling a form of participation in the study, but was also enjoyable for the children. This was confirmed in several of the reports: 'I explained everything in Portuguese and they then chose a code name which not only made their identity safe, but was a fun part of the study for them' (Santana, 2017: 8). Code names were allocated in different ways, but usually the STs provided children with the opportunity to select a name within a restricted vocabulary area, for example, choosing an animal, a colour or a flower, or an animal that begins with the first letter of their name.

Checking understanding

Ensuring that children had been given every opportunity to understand what was happening was the objective of all STs; however, a variety of ways were used to go about this. These included providing opportunities for questions during the verbal explanation accompanied by an assurance that the ST was available to answer questions at any time. In addition, some STs included a question at the end of the document: 'I understand what [ST's name] has explained to me about the research project', with an option to indicate whether this was true or false. If the child declared it was false, then the ST would explain further to the child.

One particular approach dispensed of replicating the description of the study in writing and instead used a True / False option for a number of statements. In her report, Santana writes,

> I decided to use a True/False questionnaire as children are familiar with this type of exercise. I explained everything in Portuguese and (...) they completed a form to let me know whether they were clear about what I had explained. (Santana, 2017: 8)

Using statements such as 'Xana explained that she is studying to become a better teacher' or 'Xana needs my opinion about how I feel in our English lessons' or 'Xana explained I could stop participating at any moment' (Santana, 2017: 35, my translation), children were encouraged to reflect on what they had been told and whether this was true or not. This appears to be a particularly valid way to show understanding in addition to giving the children an opportunity to voice their opinion and request further information. In private correspondence Santana indicated that children naturally rephrased their understanding or even explained to one another what they had understood from her explanation, as they went through the statements in class together.

Informal and playful approaches

Visuals played a role in the 'informal and playful' mode of some of the requests for consent documents, with several STs using pictures or emoticons in or around the written information. Pictures included groups of children smiling, English flags with logos like 'English is fun!' or 'Speak English!' and 'I love English' images with hearts.

Figure 12.3 is an excerpt from a request for consent (Nobre, 2017), showing how this ST used emoticons and images in the actual text. Nobre

Dear students, **Hello!** ✿

My name is Sofia Nobre and you already know me from your English lessons 🏴.

The news I have to tell you is that this year I am a student just like you! ❤ ▢ *(...)*

Figure 12.3 Using pictures in written descriptions for obtaining informed consent – my translation (Nobre, 2017: Appendix iii)

uses a sun image, an English flag and immediately after declaring 'I am a student just like you!' she places a heart.

In her report, Nobre specifies why she chose to include emoticons and images:

> In the informed consent document prepared for learners I took into consideration the simplicity of language and I used small pictures almost like the style used in rebus but without substitution of words, the point was to call their attention to each paragraph. (Nobre, 2017: 9)

Some descriptions of the study were also decidedly informal. Often appealing to the children by using words like 'fun' : 'We are also going to do lots of activities, lots of games, listen to music, and read stories because I want you all to have LOTS of fun ☺' (Cunha, 2017: 32, my translation).

Inadvertent coercion

Informal wording

Informality, it seems, allowed for more occasions of inadvertent coercion. Informal playful language such as 'Let's go! I can count on you!' could be read as pressuring children to participate, especially when coming from an adult. Of course, this was not the STs' intention; however, upon careful analysis of the request for consent documents, inadvertent coercion was visible in the several ways children were asked to make a decision. The following are examples of possible unintentional coercive language taken from excerpts in different request for consent documents (I have not cited their sources this time):

> 'What do you say? Interested? Can I count on your participation?';
>
> 'I would really like it if you accepted to participate in my study';
>
> 'I would really like it if you helped me get a good mark!';
>
> 'Thank you for being part of my research. Your parents have already agreed to your participation'.

The first three examples suggest that the child should say 'Yes' to please the adult. The fourth example shows an inadvertent assumption that a positive answer would come from the child, as parental acceptance had already been given on their behalf.

Careful attention should be paid to wording, and in all the more formally worded documents I analysed, inadvertent coercion was non-existent. This suggests that remaining formal might be one way to ensure that these kinds of problems do not arise.

Using emoticons and images

In the documents requesting consent, children were required to indicate whether they wanted to participate in the action research study or

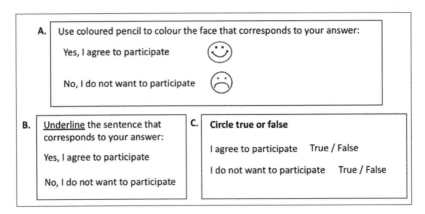

Figure 12.4 Examples of the different ways children were asked to show their willingness to participate in their action research studies, my translation

not. This involved selecting a sentence which indicated whether they agreed to participate or not, for example 'I agree to participate'. Figure 12.4 shows three of the ways this was organized: Example A uses happy and sad emoticons and Example B and C use alternative ways of showing agreement, for example, underlining the correct statement or circling true or false.

After careful analysis of the documents, it occurred to me that using emoticons might also be considered inadvertent coercion. Children might not want to appear sad, so they might select the smiley emoticon. In addition, they might think that the emoticon represented the ST's feelings after their decision, and again, might chose the smiley version so as not to offend. Examples B and C, which require no emotional association, might be more appropriate as options. This would apply for the checking of understanding too, using true and false instead of emoticons. In fact, it might be recommended to avoid emoticons completely, and keep the document clean of faces showing emotion of any kind.

Ongoing consent and presenting findings

The concept of ongoing consent was explained to the STs during the Supervision Seminar; however, I could only find evidence of one ST actually including ongoing consent in their action research activity. Santana (2017) created two sets of consent forms, to be used at specific times during the action research cycles. Her research involved a pre-intervention and post-intervention questionnaire, and she gave the children a consent form before giving the first questionnaire and a slightly adapted one before the second questionnaire.

Cravo (2017) made a very clear point of consistently reminding the children she was teaching that they were part of her study but whether this also gave them an opportunity to opt-out was not clear. In a personal communication in response to a short email questionnaire, Cravo wrote:

> Yes [it is important to ask the children's consent]! Equally important though is to explain how useful their contribution will be for the study and to explain (and remind them regularly) what your study is about. (…) I regularly explained how important each questionnaire and other research tools were for my study. In the end of the study I presented my conclusions to them in a somewhat formal way, as to make them understand how important (even central!) they were.

Cravo, as can be seen, went to great lengths to ensure the children were informed of the results of her study. This again was unique in the two groups of STs. Cravo and I engaged in a long email discussion about how she shared the results of her action research with the children. As she detailed this, it became clear that she wanted the children to understand how her research had had an impact on their learning too. An excerpt from this dialogue follows:

> (…) I told them that only after all my analysis I fully understood how much they had become aware of why they played games and worked in pairs: 'in the beginning you said that we played games mainly to have fun. With time we realized that you played games not only to have fun, but to learn English'. I also pointed out that in the beginning they didn't seem to fully understand why they worked in pairs, but later their answers showed me that they realized that when they are working in pairs they are also learning from each other, not only from the teacher. I pointed out that in the beginning they didn't always understand what 'speaking' meant. I told them that they had told me they had done a speaking activity when they had simply said 'hello', but with time they realized that speaking activity meant participating in a dialogue or making a presentation. Then I asked them what means I used to help them achieve our results, and several students were able to say that I had helped them to reflect upon the work carried out in class. (Cravo, personal communication, 22 November 2017)

Not all STs can go back to the schools to present their results, but as Cravo so nicely states, 'I think that [in] the same way [that] asking the children's consent is a good introduction to our work with the children, sharing the results is a good conclusion of the same work, and the two elements are totally related' (Cravo, personal communication, 22 November 2017). Although Cravo does not refer to the sharing of results as the children's right to know, she implies in her correspondence that she is showing them that the teacher and children have accomplished something together (see also Zandian in this volume).

Student teachers' shared experiences and opinions

During the Supervision Seminar the STs shared their experiences of and opinions about collecting informed consent from the children in their practicum classes. They indicated it took a whole lesson to go through the process of explaining, checking understanding, selecting code-names and signing the consent document. In addition, it was a lesson almost entirely in Portuguese. The school-based practicum runs over a term, around 13 weeks, with two English lessons a week and STs are obliged to teach at least ten lessons, but most teach a full term of resulting in around 24 lessons. However, two STs were only able to teach a total of ten lessons and so giving up one of these to collect informed consent was a dilemma, but needless to say they still did it. All STs agreed it had been hard work and took up valuable time they would have preferred to devote the time to teaching; however, they all recognized the importance of including the children's opinion in such a way.

As mentioned earlier, as part of the data collection for this chapter I also sent an email survey to the 15 STs. It was sent at a time when the first cohort of STs had finished their MA several months before and the second cohort was completing their practicum experience. I received eight responses in total. All but one ST continued to think it was important to ask children for their consent, but still concluded that 'when we [ask for their consent], we make them feel they are playing an important role in the teacher's project. Then, it motivates them to participate' (Inácio, personal communication, 24 November 2017). This was the general opinion of these eight respondents, which highlighted in most cases, that children were highly motivated and also appeared to work harder as they realized their participation was crucial to the learning teaching process. One ST in the second cohort openly admitted to feeling proud of the contribution the children had made to her study,

> I can't feel anything but pride. My class isn't a piece of cake but they have taken a step up just because they felt the responsibility of being committed to something apart from regular schooling. I think they feel special. And they are (...) (Nunes, personal communication, 21 November 2017)

This particular ST also emphasized that she felt the children in her class appreciated the time she took to explain what she was doing, she added, 'Being a part of a research [project] is a huge responsibility and in most cases it even helps classroom management because they feel recognized for the time you are investing in them'.

It might be of interest to the reader how many children did not want to be involved in the STs' action research projects. A total of four out of around 400 children. Those that did not agree to participate completed all the activities, but any data obtained from their participation was not taken into account in the ST's report. One ST under my supervision was rather upset when, in the middle of the practicum, two children decided they no longer wanted to continue participating in the study. Yes, this was a setback, as it would be for any researcher, but it was the children's right to opt out.

Recommendations

The objective of this chapter, and the approach it describes of STs collecting children's informed consent, was to delineate a set of guidelines for future (student)teachers who engage in action research involving children.

First and foremost, I feel that it is essential that informed consent is requested from the children as well as their parents or legal representatives. As such, I would recommend that (student)teachers undertaking action research with primary children ensure the children are informed of the following:

(1) the purpose of the research (e.g. as part of the ST's study programme, to become a better teacher);
(2) what the (student)teacher researcher is trying to find out (e.g. How much L1 the teacher uses and for what purposes; helping children understand learning strategies; how to help children use more English during pair-work activities);
(3) the methods used to collect data (e.g. observation, asking children's opinions etc.);
(4) the intended possible uses of the data collected (e.g. for the STs' final report; to share with other teachers in conferences, to write an article etc.);
(5) what participation in the research entails (e.g. 'completing a survey'; 'giving an opinion'; 'participating in English lessons normally');
(6) what risks or benefits are involved in participating in the research (e.g. understanding how we learn; understanding why pair work is used in English lessons);
(7) that their identities will not be revealed (e.g. the use of code-names);
(8) that they do not have to participate if they don't want to;
(9) that they can withdraw from the research activity at any time;
(10) that they can ask questions about the research at any time.

As children should be treated like any other person involved in the (student)teacher's research, I would also recommend that the children are told as much as possible about the project in their mother tongue. The data I have presented here suggest that the following are important to take into consideration:

(1) A verbal explanation accompanied, if possible, by visuals (e.g. a power point) or analogies which help children make connections.
(2) A set of key true / false statements to check understanding, rather than repeating the oral explanation in writing. This would help children reflect on what they have been told and aid the (student)teacher in eliminating unintended coercion.

(3) An avoidance of smileys and emoticons which might also unconsciously intimidate children into selecting the happy face over the sad one.
(4) A carefully considered revision of all language and terminology.

In addition to the considered language, I would also recommend taking into account the following participation:

- allow children to choose code-names;
- remind children about their voluntary participation often;
- remind children of the aims of the study often;
- share the results with the children if at all possible.

To conclude, I would like to share a diagram suggested by Paula Cravo during our email discussions, and which I have revised slightly. Figure 12.5 shows the diagram, which clearly portrays the process a teacher should follow when engaging in action research which involves children. The figure delineates the relevance of sharing information about the research project by explaining to the children what it is all about. It then highlights respect for the child by asking for their informed consent not just at the beginning but during the research project, in an attempt also to involve them as participants in the project. Finally, the sharing of results, to show children what they, the teacher and the children, have accomplished together. It is fitting that this diagram should come from a ST as she reflected on her practicum experience and the process she went through of requesting informed consent from her primary learners.

Article 12 of UNCRC in child-friendly language implies, 'All children have a right to be able to give their opinion when adults are making a decision that will affect them, and adults should take it seriously' (UNICEF). Adherence to Article 12 is, unfortunately, dependent upon the cooperation of adults and their concerns in enabling this are described as being related to 'scepticism' about children's capacity for meaningful input in

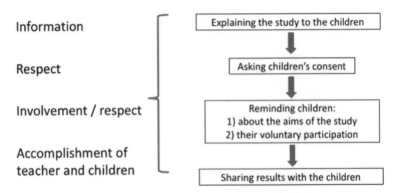

Figure 12.5 The process and implications of asking for children's informed consent during action research projects (with thanks to Paula Cravo)

decision making, unease about 'undermining adult authority' and concern about any additional effort it involves (Lundy, 2007: 929–930). Research in the primary English classroom is becoming increasingly part of teacher education and teacher professional development. Care needs to be taken in ensuring an 'ethical symmetry' so that children and adults should be afforded equal consideration in research – being researchers in the primary English classroom means 'entering a dialogue that recognizes commonality but also honours difference' (Christensen & Prout, 2002: 480). Children should be allowed to give their opinion, be facilitated in doing this and as such, their opinion should be listened to and acted upon.

Acknowledgements

I would like to thank the student teachers at Nova University Lisbon who have contributed enormously to my understanding of what we can do right in the primary English classroom.

CETAPS is funded by FCT, project n° UIDB/04097/2020

References

Alderson, P. (2005) Designing ethical research with children. In A. Farrell (ed.) *Ethical Research with Children* (pp. 27–35). Oxford: Oxford University Press.

Alderson, P. (2008) *Young Children's Rights: Exploring Beliefs, Principles and Practice* (2nd edn). London: Jessica Knightly Publishers.

Alexandre, M.G. (2018) Using pair work to promote students' oral interaction. Master's report, Nova University Lisbon. See https://run.unl.pt/handle/10362/46324 (accessed 19 November 2018).

Batista, D.G.M. (2017) Understanding and improving oral corrective feedback in primary FL classrooms in Portugal. Master's report, Nova University Lisbon. See https://run.unl.pt/bitstream/10362/22121/1/Relat%C3%B3rio_de_Est%C3%A1gio_David_Gaspar.pdf (accessed19 November 2018).

Bogdan, R.C. and Biklen, S.K. (2007) *Qualitative Research for Education: An Introduction to Theory and Methods*. Boston: Pearson.

British Educational Research Association (2018) *Ethical Guidelines for Educational Research* (4th edn). [Online]. See https://www.bera.ac.uk/researchers-resources/publications/ethical-guidelines-for-educational-research-2018 (accessed 19 November 2018).

Burns, A. (2010) *Doing Action Research in English Language Teaching*. Abingdon: Routledge.

Christensen, P. and Prout, A. (2002) Working with ethical symmetry in social research with children. *Childhood* 9 (4), 477–497.

Colaço, M.M. (2017) Raising cultural and diversity awareness in the primary English classroom. Master's report, Nova University Lisbon. See https://run.unl.pt/handle/10362/21596 (accessed 19 November 2018).

Cravo, P.K. (2017) Reflection as a means to develop young learners' metacognition. Master's report, Nova University Lisbon. See https://run.unl.pt/handle/10362/21826 (accessed 19 November 2018).

Cunha, C.S. B. da (2017) Oral communication in the YL classroom: Understanding the use of L1 and maximizing the use of L2. Master's report, Nova University Lisbon. See https://run.unl.pt/handle/10362/21598 (accessed 19 November 2018).

Einarsdóttir, J. (2007) Research with children: Methodological and ethical challenges *European Early Childhood Education Research Journal* 15 (2), 198–211.

Ellis, K. (2000) Perceived teacher confirmation: The development and validation of an instrument and two studies of the relationship to cognitive and affective learning. *Human Communication Research* 26 (2), 264–291.

Fine, G.A. and Sandstrom, K.L. (1988) *Knowing Children: Participant Observation with Minors.* Newbury Park, Calif.: Sage Publications.

Flewitt, R. (2005) Conducting research with young children: Some ethical considerations. *Early Child Development and Care* 175 (6), 553–566.

Florença, E. (2017) The significance of knowing preferred learning styles in primary foreign language learning. Master's report, Nova University Lisbon. See https://run.unl.pt/bitstream/10362/21777/1/Relat%C3%B3rio%20final.pdf (accessed 19 November 2018).

Harcourt, D. and Conroy, H. (2005) Informed assent: Ethics and processes when researching with young children. *Early Child Development and Care* 175 (6), 567–577.

Harcourt, D. and Conroy, H. (2011) Informed consent: Processes and procedures in seeking research partnerships with young children. In In D. Harcourt, B. Perry and T. Waller (eds) *Researching Young Children's Perspectives* (pp 38–51). Abingdon: Routledge.

Jiménez Raya, M., Lamb, T. and Vieira, F. (2017) *Mapping Autonomy in Language Education. A Framework for Learner and Teacher Development.* Frankfurt am Maine: Peter Lang.

Kuchah, K. and Pinter, A. (2012) Was this an interview? Breaking the power barrier in adult-child interviews in an African context. *Issues in Educational Research* 22 (3), 283–297.

Lundy, L. (2007) Voice is not enough: Conceptualising Article 12 of the United Nations Convention on the Rights of the Child. *British Educational Research Journal* 33 (6), 927–942.

Militec, E.A.N. (2017) The role of ludic activities in primary English classrooms – do they really help children to learn? Master's report, Nova University Lisbon. See https://run.unl.pt/bitstream/10362/21868/1/Final_Report_2.pdf (accessed 19 November 2018).

Nobre, A.S.E.C (2017) Listen, sing and learn: The place of songs in primary FL learning in Portugal. Master's report, Nova University Lisbon. See https://run.unl.pt/handle/10362/21575 (accessed 19 November 2018).

Phillips, D.K. and Carr, K. (2010) *Becoming a Teacher Through Action Research* (2nd edn). New York: Routledge.

Pinter, A. (2011) *Children Learning Second Languages.* London: Macmillan.

Santana, C.A.S.N. (2017) Affect: What is teacher confirmation and what effect does it have on learning? Master's report, Nova University Lisbon. See https://run.unl.pt/handle/10362/21949 (accessed 19 November 2018).

Santos, R.S. (2018) Improving young learners' listening skills through storytelling. Master's report, Nova University Lisbon. See https://run.unl.pt/bitstream/10362/47622/1/Final%20report%20-%20Rubina%20Santos%20May%202018%20Vers%C3%A3o%20melhorada.pdf (accessed 19 November 2018).

Shaw, C., Brady, L-M. and Davey, C. (2011) *Guidelines for Research with Children and Young People.* London: National Children's Bureau.

UNICEF, Child friendly resources [Online] See https://www.unicef.org/rightsite/files/rightsforeverychild.pdf (accessed 15 November 2018).

United Nations (1989) *Convention on the Rights of the Child.* UN: New York

Vieira, F. (2017) Formação pós-graduada de professores: Construindo uma pedagogia da experiência, rumo a uma educação mais democrática. *EDUCAR em Revista* 63 (1), 85–102.

13 Revisiting and Expanding Opportunities for Participatory Research with Young Learners in School Contexts

Annamaria Pinter and Kuchah Kuchah

The main aim of this volume was to describe, reflect on and engage with a range of ethical and methodological issues that might arise in language education research involving young learners in school contexts. As we argued in the introductory chapter, the idea of a collection of researcher reflections on ethical issues and methodology in Young Learner research is timely, given the increasing number of children learning foreign languages, particularly the English language, globally (Enever, 2011; Garton *et al.*, 2011), and the growing research in this area represented in the chapters of this book (see also the Special Issue of the *ELTJ*, 2014, dedicated to Young Learners).

To achieve this aim, we have brought together a range of chapters which all offer a rich tapestry of experiences across a variety of geographical contexts internationally, including studies conducted in Japan, Canada, France, Cameroon, the UK, India, Spain, Iran and Portugal. We believe that the strength of the originality of this volume lies in the range of settings covered and the variety of types of studies and tools used for data collection. The volume has opened up some important ethical and related methodological dilemmas in research of all kinds in child foreign/second language education in different school settings.

The chapters are rich in terms of discussing ethics in a variety of types of research, such as large-scale quantitative studies (García Mayo; Murphy), as well as qualitative studies with adult researchers working closely with a small group of children (Ibrahim; Prasad; Zandian; Andrews; Kuchah & Milligan). Some chapters have addressed ethical and methodological issues in different types of classroom research or action research (Mathew & Pinter; Butler; Mourão) and one chapter (Ellis & Ibrahim) has focused on teachers' awareness and understanding about children's roles in research and how these beliefs and understandings have important consequences for their everyday work with children.

Overall, the locus of this volume is in the United Nations Convention on the Rights of the Child (UNCRC, 1989); the different chapters illuminate how the authors attempt to interpret the relevant provisions of this document (see introductory chapter) through the data collection methods they use and how they navigate the ethical dilemmas engendered by these methods.

Ethical considerations constitute a cornerstone of modern research, yet in the field of applied linguistics, this has only recently gained attention. In fact work by Ortega (2005) and Hobbs and Kubanioyova (2008) suggests that research ethics is an area that has been overlooked, or not made specific in research publications, and that researchers seem to lack training and awareness in ethics in research in general (Sterling et al., 2016). The contributors to this book offer honest reflections on their research work with children, openly problematizing issues that are not usually addressed explicitly in journal publications because of lack of space or lack of attention paid to micro-ethical matters. Looking through a sharp ethical lens here has produced a wealth of rich reflections which we hope will help other researchers interested in working with children make informed pre-emptive ethical and methodological decisions when designing child-focused research projects.

All authors report unique concerns that are rooted in their own contexts and they share their stories about how they handled the challenging situations they were faced with. The most important message of this volume is that each and every project will have its own ethical dilemmas and in the absence of clear-cut solutions, every adult researcher must navigate their way through the muddy waters of what is right, fair and feasible, given the constraints of the contexts and the formal and informal ethical guidelines that apply. Giving researchers access to insights about possible dilemmas, how some researchers have navigated these, as we have done in this volume, is a starting point for helping other researchers understand the situated nature of ethical issues.

Despite the unique focus and content of each chapter, some common themes have also emerged, which we discuss briefly below.

The Importance of the UNCRC in Researching with Children

There is a strong emphasis in most chapters on the UNCRC (1989) and its key messages drawn out of Articles 12 and 13 in particular, stating that children have the right to express their opinions and views on issues that matter to them. The UNCRC is in itself a much-debated document and many disagree with the various interpretations of its principles, particularly in relation to what constitutes the best interest of the child, the extent to which children can be relied upon to express their legitimate views and potential for tokenism in the implementation of the provisions of the document. There are also well-recognized contradictions or grey areas in the different United Nations legislation in relation to children which make it difficult to arrive at a homogenous understanding and practice. For example, Article 26 of the UDHR, (1948) entrusts the prior right to choose the kind of education that shall be given to children to adults (i.e. parents) and this adult right thus stands in conflict with Articles 12 and 13. This notwithstanding, the UNCRC offers a useful framework for interrogating and reflecting on our beliefs, philosophical assumptions and episteme in relation to the world of children. It is therefore important that teachers and researchers working with children familiarize themselves with the document and devote time to studying it and working out what the messages mean to them personally and how, if at all, these messages may impact on their ongoing work, teaching or research, with children (see also Ellis & Ibrahim, this volume).

The Challenge of Balancing Macro- and Micro-Ethical Issues in Research with Children

Another theme in the book is related to the conflict between micro-ethical concerns as opposed to ethical guidelines enshrined in institutional codes of practice. In a recent study which investigated the reactions of applied linguists towards scenarios in which the ethicality of action could not be easily identified as right or wrong (Sterling & Gass, 2017) it was found that:

> …participants relied heavily on ethical review board requirements as their guide to making decisions about what is ethical and what is not. Taken together, these data indicate that more discussion in research ethics is needed for the field, especially with elements of academic integrity and ethically grey areas (2017: 50)

While ethical review board requirements are important in developing researchers' awareness of ethical issues that might arise in research, they do not often deal with the ethical complexities that the dynamics of different research projects and contexts might give rise to, especially in relation to young children whose well-being is often the centre of national and international policy and debate. In some cases ethical issues with children can be further exacerbated by differences in local/ cultural norms in different contexts. What is more, the dividing lines between informal enquiry-based practice that resembles research and formal research become blurred in different types of action research, especially if the children take on more active roles as co-researchers. Questions about consent become complicated. For example, if children are invited to participate, irrespective of their level of involvement, their parents' or guardians' consent is needed first of all by law in most contexts, but what happens if the children are co-researchers or indeed act as researchers themselves? How does their active role of actually undertaking some of the research change this situation? What happens if there is a conflict between parents' and children's views regarding participation in research? Dilemmas around consent and the specific details of wording consent forms and information sheets for children and parents runs through as a theme in nearly all chapters. These dilemmas highlight the fact that even where ethical issues might be perceived as universally applicable, approaches to dealing with them is always situated in a local cultural context, requiring researchers to invest in understanding the context before and while they engage with participants. As was mentioned in the opening chapter to this volume, insights from such investment and/or understanding is often lacking in research reports and illuminating some of these, as we have done in this volume, can be a useful way of helping current and future researchers understand and expand their awareness of ethical complexities in research with children.

The Opportunities and Challenges that Arise from Participatory Techniques

The next theme that has emerged from the contributions to this volume is focused on the benefits of various participatory techniques that adult researchers have created to explore how these might help with bringing the children's perspectives to the fore. These participatory techniques can take a range of forms such as using collages and drawings instead of traditional interviews, or inviting the children to reflect on the research process using drama and follow-up activities, and involving children as designers of pedagogical games/tasks. The different participatory techniques illuminated in this volume offer significant opportunities for understanding the cultural and linguistic world of children as well as the interface between research, curriculum, pedagogy and learning from children's perspective; they also offer researchers further insights into the methodological options and ethical complexities of child-focused research in school contexts.

Butler's chapter, for example, situates children as consultants on matters involving curriculum and task design given that, in this context, they are 'digital natives.' Mathew and Pinter's chapter also highlights the pedagogic value, for experienced teachers, of children's involvement as co-researchers in school based action research while Mourão's chapter shows how engaging trainee teachers in classroom-based research with children offers opportunities for reflection on ethical processes that might question and refine trainee teachers' understandings and perspectives about children and childhood more broadly. Chapters by Zandian and Kuchah and

Milligan show how participatory practices in the design of research can help researchers refine their research tools in ways that help them generate rich and authentic data. In both chapters, children are invited to comment on the original research tools and to make suggestions for how the tools might be improved to reflect children's interest and experiences. Ideas from children sometimes challenge adult perspectives giving rise to new understandings. Involving children through the different participatory techniques and for the reasons discussed in these chapters does require an epistemological positioning which recognizes the multiple facets of knowledge construction essential to the development of inclusive research, curricula and pedagogy. Prasad (this volume) confirms this view, arguing that adult researchers working with children need to adopt a disposition of humility in order to reframe children as experts of their world, experiences and practices. The kairos moments she identifies and reflects on all give richer insights into aspects of children's plurilingual practices, which are not directly perceivable by the adult researcher. In fact, it is thanks to insights generated around child-produced artefacts (see also chapters by Ibrahim and Andrews in this volume) that children's voices about their plurilingual experiences are more easily accessed.

The use of participatory techniques in research with children can also be fraught with issues of quality and reliability of the data collected. Participatory research requires rapport building with children and the process might have an impact on what children decide to say or not in research encounters. For example, some researchers might, as part of the rapport building process, try not to look or behave like school teachers (see, for example, Kuchah & Pinter, 2012; Zandian, this volume) in order to be more accepted by the children. Such acceptance, though useful in building positive relationships, which then allow for children to express themselves freely, might influence what children say as they attempt to identify with the researcher (see for example Vignette 3 in Andrews' chapter, this volume). There might also be substantial differences between the adult researcher's agenda and children's expectations: if children think that they will be assessed through participation in research, how might this influence their participation? Another issue arising from participatory research is the conflict between adult facilitation and interference especially in school context that tend to be highly restricting environments. Schools are cultural spaces or venues with a social order of adult control (Barker & Weller, 2003) and, however hard we work to dissipate the power differentials between adult researchers and children, this cannot be fully achieved, nor should it be. It goes without saying therefore that in participatory research practices involving adults and children, attempts by adults to facilitate children's participation might in fact constitute an interference with potential to affect the data generated (see Butler, this volume). At a broader cultural level, questions as to whether there is such a thing as children's authentic voices or whether their voices are socially constructed (see chapters by Butler and Kuchah & Milligan, this volume) or questions about how we can make sense of children's voices when they are so intertwined with adult discourses, point to challenges of interpreting children's views and the need for a framework for conceptualizing adult involvement in participatory research with children.

Overall, participatory techniques cannot always guarantee better quality or more ethical research per se, yet, the collective experience of the authors here illustrates the potential of these techniques for eliciting children's views in a way that can be enjoyable and meaningful from the children's point of view while at the same time challenging adult researchers to continue to critically reflect on their research.

The Importance of Researcher Reflexivity

All chapters emphasize that no research is ever perfect or fully ethical. Questions and dilemmas, often contradictory in nature, have to be resolved by compromise. Authors here reflect on what they could have done differently, how they might have worded their questions, comments or instructions in an alternative way, or how they would have liked to do something but the local restrictions did not allow this. What seems essential is to practise what Warin (2011) calls an 'ethical mindfulness' whereby the adult researcher working with children is engaged in constantly juggling what is fair, right and feasible while challenging his or her own assumptions. The starting point for every adult researcher is to ask the following questions:

- What is my image and conception of the child?
- What is my image of the adult researcher (myself)?
- What is my question and why is my research important?
- What are the different ways (with what roles for whom) of exploring this question?

Having answered these questions the adult researcher can start building up a set of principles that can guide their everyday ethical practice and navigate their path back and forth between codes of ethics and the ever dynamic local concerns and opportunities. Underlying this, is the requirement for a sustained investment in understanding the context in which the research is being conducted. Outsider researchers may not be aware of the invisible features of a school context (Wedell & Malderez, 2013) and might, despite their best intentions, act in ways that have potential to change the equilibrium and/or cause disruption in a school (see Mathew & Pinter, this volume). Where such a sustained investment is not possible, due to the temporary nature of many research projects, some form of institutional support and collaboration from an insider might offer a useful alternative.

Insider/Outsider Adult Researchers

Perhaps the most important benefit that might arise from research which encourages children to play active roles is around the weight researchers as well as end users of research (policymakers, school administrators and teachers) give to children's voices and what the benefits of children knowing that their voices are given weight might be. The practicalities of organizing research in school contexts and the alignment of research activities with pedagogic activities familiar to children in most of the chapters in this volume are the things which make for a successful and efficient study. They also mean that the outsider researcher would be welcomed back, as the study would be perceived as worthwhile to the children and the school. Schools are, after all, places of learning operating within a complex state/national system and it is the researcher who has to adapt, not the school to the researcher. Schools are for children and the teachers who teach them and the challenge for the researcher is how to design a study which can work in that ethos, respecting the legislation and requirements the system imposes and yet managing to implement the research.

In the light of the above, practitioner research seems to offer a more ecologically sensitive opportunity for classroom teachers to engage in research which is less disruptive than research conducted by outsider (academic) researchers. Yet, as chapters by Mathew and Pinter and Mourão reveal, there are a number of issues that might arise too from research conducted by teachers in school contexts. For example, in Mourão's chapter, the issues occur at a micro level and involve student teachers negotiating different ethical dilemmas related to obtaining and retaining informed consent as well as how different levels of (in)formality and the use of multi-modal forms of data collection may engender inadvertent coercion. This chapter confirms the view that not all ethical problems can be solved by adopting 'child-friendly techniques (see Gallagher et al., 2010). Informed consent in research involving children is still fraught with ethical complexities and as García Mayo's chapter in this volume also suggests, while school administrators, teachers and parents might be well informed about the research agenda and potential benefits, it is not always the case that children fully understand why they are agreeing to participate in research especially when decisions about their participation are placed in the hands of parents and caretakers. In fact, in some contexts where there is a dominant language used in education and research, ethnic minority parents rely on teachers to make such decisions on behalf of them (see for example Murphy's chapter in this volume) and it might be difficult for children to even imagine refusing to participate when their teacher has given consent. The extent to which children can make personal decisions and not be influenced by their peers' involvement in research or the desire to please the adult researcher is still not clear and future research might need to develop this aspect of research ethics with child participants.

Mathew and Pinter's chapter shows that the ideal goal of embracing a rights-based approach to research in school contexts, might pose unintended consequences that could potentially be problematic for children, their teachers and the school culture overall. This is particularly the case when the research agenda is initiated by the outsider researcher and where the research process and activities are inconsistent with the existing practices within the school. The ethical issues raised in this chapter equally apply to academic research by outsider researchers in contexts where classrooms are teacher-led and where the prevailing school culture is transmission rather than collaboration (see Kuchah & Milligan, this volume). Researchers working in such contexts would need to exercise due diligence; to thoroughly investigate legislation regarding schools, the national/state curriculum and teaching materials and the rules of the school as well as other visible and invisible features of the context (Wedell & Malderez, 2013) before planning the research. In other words, future research with children in school contexts needs to emphasise and critically examine the place and role of research and the researcher in a school-context ensuring that the values they bring are not such that can upset the day-to-day functioning of the institution. We are guests who have been invited in, and we have to remember this. It needs to be clear that although there are important benefits in participatory research with children in school contexts, such research is challenging to conduct in many contexts and as a result, novice researchers need to be encouraged to develop a reflective approach to child-focused research, which is based on existing ethical review board requirements but driven by a developing understanding of the specific research context.

Another important issue for further exploration would be in relation to children's rights to withdraw from, or opt out of, research conducted in classroom contexts. Whether such a situation arises in research conducted by outsider researchers or in action research conducted by the classroom teacher, withdrawal from research is not always possible especially if a research project involves the whole (Sterling & Gass, 2017: 55) class and work which is perceived by children to count towards assessment. In an ideal situation, the researcher would need the full consent of all students and their parents or stop the project altogether, but these alternatives are not always possible or even useful. Mourão's chapter discusses that student teachers deal with this kind of situation by simply discarding the data collected from participants who withdrew or did not consent to participating in the research. This approach assumes that classrooms are made up of isolated and independent individuals and does not seem to realize that data generated within the classroom are often the result of some form of co-construction and discarding one participant's data does not imply discarding their influence on the data generated from other participants.

What are the Next Steps?

This volume has provided rich insights into local ethical dilemmas relating to working with children in different roles in different projects internationally, and therefore there is, we hope, something here for every researcher to take away when planning their own study. As the different chapters have shown, research with children is central to understanding children's lived experiences and the process of understanding these experiences requires respect for their statutory rights as stipulated in the different UN legislations cited in the introductory chapter to this volume. Child-focused research has become even more pressing given the renewed international focus on inclusive and quality education for all and the promotion of lifelong learning as stipulated in the United Nations Sustainable Development Goal (SDG4, 2015). Respecting the rights of children and creating opportunities for their voices and agency to emerge depends on how adults conceptualize children (see Ellis & Ibrahim in this volume).

At the moment, there is growing work, in young learner research in the field of applied linguistics, about the relative merits of participatory research approaches in eliciting data from children, but there is yet little evidence of how these data are then used to make a difference in the lives of child participants beyond the data collection phase. While some chapters in this volume (e.g. Butler; Prasad) have included children in both the generation and interpretation of some of the data generated, there is still scope for research in our field to include children in data analysis. Besides, finding out about children's lived experiences in relation to particular areas of child language education needs to be accompanied by a responsibility to report back to them about how this has informed how we now view them and how we support their learning. Zandian's chapter reports on the researcher's attempt to report back the findings of her research to her child participants and demonstrates the generative impact of such feedback sessions on children's awareness and understanding of the processes and value of research. Children exposed to these kinds of encounters are more likely to develop interest in inquiry skills and opportunities to explore their own learning.

In effect, the increasing number of children learning English as a second/foreign language around the world, the need for inclusive and quality education (SDG4) as well as the pressing ethical concerns relating to conceptualizing children as 'social actors' (James & Prout, 1997) require research with children in English Language Teaching (ELT) in the future to become more inclusive in terms of the different roles children could take and what the nature of their involvement could be before, during and after a given research project. Indeed, for some, inviting children as active participants or equal partners in research is a political/ ethical calling. However, irrespective of one's political stance, it seems sensible that a critical broader framework of research should encompass *all kinds of research*, including not just research 'on' and 'about' children but also 'with' and 'by' children. Granted that not all children everywhere will be interested in taking more active roles in research, and sometimes it might not be appropriate to involve them actively because of the existing dynamics of their learning context or the nature of the research questions, all adult researchers nonetheless need to be aware of the various possibilities within the broad framework, and have a reflexive approach that allows them to encourage children to shift roles if and when this becomes appropriate and desirable. Learner-centred education cannot be said to be fully achieved without learner involvement; involving learners in decisions about their life and well-being empowers them without disempowering (teacher) researchers; on the contrary, it has potential to build trust between (teacher) researchers and children, a necessary condition for effective education. The chapters in this volume show that children are capable of taking on more important roles in research about their learning if given the opportunity and can be helped along the way to make informed decisions. How and why some children can become interested in taking an active part in research alongside adults in ELT is still an under-researched area and this is where future studies would be extremely useful.

Tsing's (2007) riverbed metaphor (see Prasad's chapter in this volume) is important in understanding how ethical and methodological regulations/procedures may be shaped by the different contexts within which they are applied. Young learner researchers in school contexts are at the interface between academic research norms and classroom cultures, which are in turn shaped by different cultural forces within the communities in which they operate as well as the personal cultures of key actors – students, teachers, administrators, parents or education ministries. It is therefore essential that within our field we keep sharing ethical dilemmas and experiences of working with children in second and foreign language education research of all kinds (large-scale, experimental and exploratory as well as small-scale more qualitatively oriented research), so that all of us can continue sharpening our ethical lens, develop our reflexivity and cultivate 'ethical mindfulness'.

References

Barker, J. and Weller, S. (2003) Geography of methodological issues in research with children. *Qualitative Research* 3 (2), 207–227.

Enever, J. (ed.) (2011) *ELLiE, Early Language Learning in Europe*. London: The British Council.

Gallagher, M., Haywood, S.L., Jones, M.W. and Milne, S. (2010) Negotiating informed consent with children in school-based research: A critical overview. *Children and Society* 24, 471–482.

Garton, S., Copland, F. and Burns, A. (2011) *Investigating Global Practices in Teaching English to Young Learners*. London: British Council.

Hobbs, V. and Kubanyiova, M. (2008) The challenges of researching language teachers: What research manuals don't tell us. *Language Teaching Research* 12, 495–513.

James, A. and Prout, A. (1997) *Constructing and Re-constructing Childhood*. Basingstoke: Falmer Press.

Kuchah, K. and Pinter, A. (2012) Was this an interview? Breaking the power barrier in adult-child interviews in an African context. *Issues in Educational Research* 22 (3), 283–297.

Ortega, L. (2005) For what and for whom is our research? The ethical as transformative lens in instructed SLA. *The Modern Language Journal* 89, 427–443.

SDG4 (2015) https://sdgs.un.org/goals/goal4

Sterling, S. and Gass, S. (2017) Exploring the boundaries of research ethics: Perceptions of ethics and ethical behaviors in applied linguistics research. *System* 70, 50–62.

Sterling, S., Winke, P. and Gass, S. (2016) Training in research ethics among applied linguistics and SLA researchers. In P.I. De Costa (ed.) *Ethics in Applied Linguistics Research: Language Researcher Narratives*. New York: Routledge.

Tsing, A.L. (2005) *Friction: An Ethnography of Global Connection*. Princeton, NJ: Princeton University Press.

United Nations (1989) *United Nations Convention on the Rights of the Child*. New York: United Nations.

Warin, J. (2011) Ethical mindfulness and reflexivity: Managing a research relationship with children and young people in a 14-year qualitative longitudinal research. *Qualitative Inquiry* 17 (9), 805–814.

Wedell, M. and Malderez, A. (2013) *Understanding Language Classroom Contexts: The Starting Point for Change*. London: Bloomsbury.

Index